Slow March
To A Regiment

Alexander M. Ross

Alexander M. Ross

Vanwell Publishing Limited
St. Catharines, Ontario

Canadian Cataloguing in Publication Data

Ross, Alexander M., 1916-
    Slow march to a regiment

(Armchair general series)
Includes bibliographical references.
ISBN 0-920277-81-0

1. Ross, Alexander M., 1916- . 2. Canada
Canadian Army. Field Regiment, 17th - History.
3. Canada. Canadian Army. Field Regiment, 17th -
Biography. 4. Soldiers - Canada - Biography.
5. Ontario, Western - Biography. I. Title.
II. Series

U55.R68A3 1992   355'.0092   C92-094140-0

Vanwell Publishing Limited
1 Northrup Crescent, Box 2131
St. Catharines, Ontario L2M 6P5

Cover: *Infantry* by Alex Colville
Copyright© Canadian War Museum. CN 12170.

Contents

Acknowledgements

Grateful acknowledgements are due to the following for permission to use copyright material:

Chief of Defence Staff for C.P. Stacey: *Arms, Men and Government.*

Elizabeth Whalley for George Whalley: "Canadian Spring" in *No Man an Island.*

Houghton Mifflin Company for Winston Churchill: *Triumph and Tragedy.*

McClelland and Stewart for G.W.L. Nicholson: *The Gunners of Canada.*

National Archives of Canada for the War Diary of the 17th Field Regiment, Royal Canadian Artillery.

The Queen's Printer for G.W.L. Nicholson, *The Canadians in Italy.*

In addition, I must say how grateful I am to Angela Dobler for her generous editorial assistance and to my daughter, Celia, for her help in preparing the typescript for submission to the publisher.

Preface

To write about oneself is to risk condemnation on a broad front. To say nothing and to burn or shred the evidence is widely held to be a matter of much common sense. The past is deceivingly elusive, ever posing new questions about human conduct in the downward spiral of its time frame. To unveil it is hazardous, always tempting us to manipulate and justify.

Letters, diaries, historical facts, and memory hold me to account. This being so, I hope that my experience and its presentation in this memoir is free both from illusion and contrivance and fair to those I've known so well and to whom I owe so much. Where I fail, the responsibility is entirely mine.

It is a hard and nice subject for a Man to write of himself. It grates his own Heart to say any thing of Disparagement, and the Reader's Ears to hear any thing of Praise from him.

Abraham Cowley

Chapter 1

A Backward Look

To begin at once and at the beginning. I was born on January 5, 1916, in Edinburgh Castle, a name my little mother with the long dark hair had given in derision to the big, rambling, old house my father had rented the year before in Embro in the heart of the Zorras. My birth was both prolonged and painful, but, with me finally beside her, my mother accepted her new status trying to forget other circumstances, nearly all of which were worrisome including the bitterly cold winter wind and frost that searched out every crack and cranny of the Castle's inadequate mortar.

With us at the time of my arrival was my father's querulous and aged mother. Having brought five children into the world and having done with little throughout her life for their sake, she had deep misgivings about my emergence at a time when her own numerous ailments demanded much attention. My father, William Alexander, known familiarly as Rab, was the man of the house. As such he watched over my mother and me, his little Sandy, with much solicitude and the assurance that, with any luck at all, he expected to find work by spring.

He needed an interval, he announced, to recover his composure and regroup his resources after having tried his hand in a shoe business with another gentleman, who it turned out knew even less about selling shoes than my father did. For six months their shop's signboard had creaked its message to

Embro's well-shod citizenry and then creaked no more. Shoes were available for local people in greater variety and lower prices through the medium of Timothy Eaton's sale catalogues.

Meanwhile, my father's bank account dwindled while grocery and fuel bills mounted, and local merchants murmured. He then, rather reluctantly, remembered his farm which he had rented out so that he could escape its drudgery for the rewards of life as a shopkeeper. Motivated by the necessity to find food and warmth for his family, he decided to give husbandry another try and returned to the land he had inherited six miles north of Embro, just east of the village of Harrington. Here, on the farm's gravelly acres, he set out again to make a living.

Our farm's greatest drawback was its glacial origin which, instead of good soil, had left us a tremendous inheritance of sand and gravel. We were at the tail end of an esker. At the highest point of the farm stood the frame house and the bank barn, shielded from the sweep of winds out of the west and north by a stand of sugar maples that curved round the buildings in the summer like a great green velvet tippet.

Perhaps it was the panorama the farm offered of West Zorra countryside that enticed my great-grandfather, Alexander, to ignore its stony surface so many years ago. He looked so favourably upon this site that he parted with the sum of five hundred and twenty dollars so that he could have and hold one hundred acres of this crown land.

His wife and children, who had accompanied him from the croft on Balvraid by Skelbo in Scotland, soon outgrew the log house he had built below the crest of the hill to the west. Some time in the late 1850s he moved his family uphill where he had built a frame house. Here, as the sun warmed his fields, he worked out his span of days until, well worn by the exercise, he died leaving behind him an inheritance many times the worth of the stony, wet croft by Skelbo Burn.

The inheritance came free of debt, stones, and trees—save for the woods at the back—to his son, my grandfather, Sullivan, a sturdily built man, clever with tools and talented as a musician who could play both the bagpipes and the violin. If not distinguished in his bearing, he was an engaging person when marching up and down in kilts beneath his drones playing "The Dornoch Lassies." Unlike his neighbours, he regarded farming only as an economic necessity from which he withdrew as often as he could to the charms of his bagpipes and fiddle. To the end of his life he was more fluent in Gaelic than in English.

Well before he took over the farm, he had brought a pretty bride home to share his bed. The marriage took place on October 16, 1857 at a prayer meeting held by the Reverend Donald McKenzie on the second line of West Zorra. Fifteen years later, the Church Session in Harrington, having been assembled and "constituted with prayer," the elders called Sullivan to appear and, after he had been heard "respecting his faith in the Lord Jesus Christ and his obedience to His Commands," the Session agreed to grant his request that the last of his five children be baptized before the congregation on either "the seventeenth or twenty-fourth instant." It was on one of these "instants" that my father appeared for the first time in public.

But five children did nothing to make my grandfather a prosperous farmer. Regardless of the season, or the state of his crops, or the demands of his family, he saw to it that his pipes and fiddle were seldom out of tune. Had he paid less attention to music, he might have spared his wife—whom he always referred to as "she"—the rounded shoulders and stiffened body she got from bending long hours over the loom in the shed at the back of the house where she made woollen blankets both for her own family and for sale to her neighbours.

By 1875, Sullivan's affairs, as revealed in his halfhearted attempts to keep farming accounts, were not particularly flourishing. Throughout August and September, the entries in his ledger book indicated only that he had bought thirty-three pounds of codfish at six cents a pound and that he had paid one dollar for a bottle of brandy, and seventy-five cents for a pound of tea.

But while his crops and the accompanying weeds ripened in his fields, and the loom cracked on wearily, and his children trudged off to the stone school house on the west side of Harrington, Sullivan—remembering what an old pipe-major of the Black Watch had taught him on the brae below the ruins of Skelbo Castle about piping—put in days of painstaking effort committing hundreds of pipe tunes to manuscript and then binding them in book form. Whatever my grandfather hoped to gain by this I do not know. Possibly, as he resigned himself to his acres, the tunes in his head may have eased his mind as he turned furrows, or tossed hay, or tried to shut out the monotonous crack of the loom's shuttle.

Sometimes, when it was necessary to try out a tune on his pipes during the day, his neighbours, straightening their bodies from hoes or cradles and hearing the doubling of an intricate *cruan luach* would chide: "Ay, Sullivan's at it again; anything whatever but the man's proper business!" If he heard the complaint from gossips, he paid no attention. On May 19, 1870, his farm accounts included this item: "Got my new bagpipe as a present. Price $50.00." If his neighbours failed to appreciate his pibrochs, it was obvious that someone else did!

Sullivan's days were long on the land that Alexander had given him. And although his reputation as a farmer was negligible, if not downright censurable, his proficiency on the bagpipes won for him medals, ribbons, and newspaper notices as he played in competition, or served as a judge, or piped for highland dancing at Caledonian games. Always a nice balance in favour of music offset the drudgery of farm life. Friends who dropped in for a "crack" with him could hear "Highland Rory" for the asking. Even his harvest workers could cajole him into a "chune or two" on the pipes over a noon-hour that ended in mid-afternoon with the sheaves still to be bound and stooked and the evening milking much nearer on the clock than it should have been.

As I think of these ancestors of mine, I often wonder about the female side and why the wives that Alexander and Sullivan brought to the farm remain so dim and remote from me. All I have are vague rural eulogies: "Och aye, Sandy, I mind her well, a guid mither to all her bairns"; or "Ech! it's Margaret, Sullivan's wife you mean—indeed I knew the puir soul; I have one of her blankets, it will never wear out, she was always at

her loom—and a wonderful maker of crowdy she was, too."
Even my own mother had little to say about these two women
and that not at all to the family credit for, according to her, my
great grandmother, a Leith from Creich in Sutherland, was far
too fond of brandy. This my mother gleaned from my grandmother in Embro when I was but a baby. At the same time my
grandmother did not escape censure for having cherished and
kept hidden an old clay pipe into which she put ragged twists
of McDonald's plug tobacco which she slyly and contentedly
smoked screened by the old lilac tree at the back of the loom
shed.

But this was the same grandmother who did manage to find
a place in the annals of the Presbyterian Church. On September
30, 1876, she was brought before the Kirk Session for a "misde-
meanour" relating to another lady of the Harrington congregation where

> these parties having confessed the sin of falling
> out by the way and their grief because of the
> scandal brought on the cause of Christ thereby,
> and having expressed their willingness to forget
> and forgive the past with the promise of good be-
> haviour in the time to come were dismissed with
> a justifiable rebuke and exhortation from the Ses-
> sion.

Aside from such indecorum and the accolades of local
crones, the daily lives of these two women in the rural isolation
of West Zorra remain very much a blank— save, I should add,
for the entries in the family Bible that denominate dates of marriage and the births of children. It's a scant record without
epitaph. But that's all I know about my grandmothers, whose
early beauty must have faded quickly on the hill east of Harrington.

But, doing with little and often without seems not to have
shortened the lives of these women or of their menfolk. Sullivan lived on into his eightieth year, giving up finally in 1904
on a warm July night, when my father placed the old piper's
name in the family Bible where the Gaelic of the Old Testament

ended and that of the Tiommadh Nuadh began. The farm which my father inherited came to him bearing a mortgage of $1600 and the need to provide a home for Margaret, the widow, whose aged frame could still be seen in the loom shed sending her shuttle on its clacking course.

Twelve years later, however, she, too, took to her bed for the last time. There, beneath the wool blankets her twisted hands had loomed, she remembered the forty-seven years she had spent ministering to her children and her husband. She remembered how music with its charms had impoverished them and left her alone many a day to mind the children, bake bread, and milk cows while her kilted husband blew his way through Highland games to ribbons and whisky. Such memories of her married life elicited one final request. Calling Rab, her favoured son, in a hoarse whisper to her bedside, she made him promise, as she held his calloused hands, that he would never take up the pipes. My father promised.

And then, as her life's poor stream dribbled to an end, she put all deception behind her by asking her son to prop her up on her goose feather pillows and bring to her the clay pipe and the bit of McDonald's plug tucked away behind the loom. Rab cut off some tobacco, rolled it loose and fine in his hand, filled the darkened bowl, and lit it for her while her shrunken lips around the short stem sucked in the pungent smoke. That night was my grandmother's last resort to what my mother always denounced as "that dirty old pipe." She died the next day.

Chapter 2

Family Fortunes

My mother, Ellen, married my father on March 24, 1913. He was her senior by fourteen years, distinguished locally for having in 1909 published a history of Zorra and Embro for which today's rare book trade demands forty times its original price. My mother was of Catholic origin, a mixture of Irish and Highland Scot, which may help explain a certain natural gaiety which did much to sustain her throughout the many trials which her marriage to Rab brought upon her. Like my father she loved music, especially music she could dance to, and, like him too, she preferred what was past and what was to come to the ever worrying present. Her past linked her to a happy childhood on the shores of the St. Lawrence below Prescott, her future to what she thought she would like to have, but the present was, she found out early, the hapless Rab and his consistent inability to make ends meet.

While I was still a baby, my parents brought my brother, Iain, into the world to share our steadily declining fortunes. It was not an event that I welcomed, and sibling jealousy rather than tender love marked our early years together until the simple requirements of law and order brought me round to a more charitable attitude.

I can remember little of what happened before I was six years of age. In 1919, when I was not quite four years old and my brother but two and one-half, my parents sold the ancestral home and bought a fifty-acre farm at Lakeside, some eight miles away from Harrington. Sometimes I think I can remember this move, but my memory is probably my mother's account of it: she driving the horse and buggy with us two children on either side of her. Ahead of her was Rab with the team and wagon with its hayrack on which were piled high our household effects and behind which he was pulling our democrat. Half way to Lakeside, they stopped for lunch at the bottom of a valley where there was a stream and let the horses rest. While I played about, wondering at the curious appearance of chairs and tables, their legs all pointing the wrong way, Rab took out his fiddle and played for us as my mother set out the sandwiches and cold tea. I can remember later my mother saying how happy my father was as he faced the future brightened by the few hundred dollars by which the sale of the Harrington property exceeded his debts and the cost of the Lakeside one.

At Lakeside my early years were a constant round of "glad animal movements," except for those times when ailments like whooping cough, chicken pox, mumps, and measles kept Iain and me indoors. And curiously, with the exception of expeditions "down the crick" in the spring fishing for suckers, it is what we did in the winter that comes most readily to mind.

Across the lower fields to the west and beyond on a neighbour's land was the only hill in our area suitable for sledding. There we made endless ascents, dragging our sleighs behind us, so that we could exult in the few seconds of speeding to the bottom of the hill. Our concentration was such that frozen ears or noses were by no means rare, until we learned to help each other by watching for the tell-tale whiteness and by keeping toques well pulled down. On milder days our pant legs and mittens would get wet through and by late afternoon, as the temperature fell, we would walk home, our trouser legs rattling like mother's frozen laundry in the wind on the clothesline that ran from the back door to the old butternut tree near the wooden pump from which we got pails of water for the household.

Once we were in, mother removed our wet things, placed

our mittens on newspaper under the great black McLary range with its silver trim, and hung the trousers on a cord that was rigged up on the wall behind the stove. Supper over in the evening and the barn chores done, we added wood to the McLary's fire box and settled in for the evening.

My father, smelling of animals and the barn, would light his pipe, draw a chair to the table and sit where he had enough light from the coal-oil lamp to read *The Globe*; mother, nearer the stove, took up the endless task of mending socks and clothing. For us boys, this was the magic hour as we played in the shadows of the kitchen which the yellow light from the lamp did little to disperse. Into our play we inevitably brought our aged Newfoundland dog, Nipper, who was seldom as enthusiastic at being a third person as we thought he should be.

All this suggests the usual Ontario farm childhood. But I don't think any of the neighborhood boys had music as my brother and I did. My father needed no coaxing to bring out the fiddle. From much repetition I could name all the tunes he liked to play: "The March of the Cameron Men," "The Bard of Armagh," "The Keel Row," "Ye Banks and Braes," "Bonnie Lass o' Bon Accord," "The Barren Rocks of Aden," and perhaps a dozen more. Whenever I wanted such music, all I had to do was ask, and it was given. Mother, too, acquiesced and often sang the old songs to the fiddle music and showed us dance steps as well. That the musical flavour was Scottish or Irish seemed to us as it should be, for we heard nothing else.

Able to play by ear and note, Rab was a fiddler much in demand for country dances where my mother would often accompany him on the piano. I can still remember as a child being taken over snowy roads in winter by horse and cutter to large brick houses near Harrington where the MacKays, or the Ridleys, or the Sutherlands were having parties. Once we arrived, and once the layers of outer clothing had been stowed away, the men would clear the furniture from either the dining room or the kitchen, roll up the rug or linoleum, and set chairs for Rab and a second fiddler by the piano in the parlour, where mother was already sounding the A note and adjusting the height of the stool. As the caller-off summoned the guests to take their partners and the musicians broke into the "Arkansas Traveller," the evening was underway. Sometimes I managed to stay awake but more often, with other children, I went to sleep on upstair beds.

For Rab such evenings were a complete success only when he and seven others could dance an eightsome reel; if numbers were lacking, he would accept a foursome danced to "Mrs. McLeod of Raasay." By midnight a copious lunch restored the merrymakers for the trip home. Fathers brought horses from warm stables, mothers roused children from sleep, and then, under buffalo robes, we set out in the cutter down the lane to the concession road. The party was over.

My parents were particularly fond of storytelling. From Ellen we knew of the Johnstown flood of 1889, which she had heard about when a servant girl working for an Anglican clergyman in the Catskill Mountains in New York State. As well, and with even greater detail, she'd describe family by family and farm by farm the area from Cardinal to Prescott along the St. Lawrence, which had always been home to her as a child. I can still move with considerable geographic success whenever I return to her origins, and I can still attach names to the farms: Scott, Adams, Murdock, Curry, Countryman, Fraser, Huton, and others. It was my great-grandfather on my mother's side who had, on November 16, 1838, heard the sounds of artillery fire in the "Battle of the Windmill," two miles west of his farm, where the so-called Polish patriot Schultz surrendered to Colonel Dundas. That I thought was one of the best of Ellen's stories.

From Rab we had endless tales of pioneer days in the Zorras: of the old log church on the seventh concession, the building bees, and the Fenian raid so manfully opposed by the fifty-five privates, officers, and N.C.O.s of Embro's Highland Rifle Company. And always we heard of that glorious brawny event in Embro when five Zorra men after thirty-five minutes of Herculean effort—with Sullivan blowing them on—won the tug-of-war against the Highland Association team from Chicago. Four thousand people, abetted by the Honourable Sir Oliver Mowat, witnessed this exhibition, which was repeated in

1893 in Chicago when the Zorra men won the championship of America.

One of my father's fascinating qualities was his remarkable ability to embellish his tales, not outrageously, but still with a fine disdain for historical accuracy. About Sullivan he created a charming family legend, perhaps intended to match the international scope of the tug-of-war event. According to Rab, his father at a great Caledonia Society Meet in Lucknow, Ontario, in 1876 won the piping championship of America and, for his achievement on the pasture land of that village, brought back to Zorra a gold medal and clasp. That he was a year out in his date mattered very little, although the 1875 Meet in which his father took part was the first such meet ever staged by the Lucknow Caledonia Society. The fifteen pipers who represented America came from as far away as Hamilton, Ontario. So far as I am aware, however, no other member of our family has ever come so close to gaining international acclaim.

From Lucknow in Ontario, Rab's story telling slipped easily off to Scotland where he could be surprisingly convincing. "I can remember, as clearly as if it were yesterday," he'd say as he settled himself in the rocker which he had drawn up to face the McLary's oven door, "my father telling me that he could remember his father describing a visitor he had one night at his croft in Balvraid: it was my grandfather's brother, Donald, in the dress of the Sutherland Regiment—the 93rd, I think it was—with his bride, a wee Irish girl."

From this point on, my father, happily ignorant of the real history of the 93rd, made my brother and me vividly aware of Donald's gallantry at Waterloo, when with other Highlanders they had formed the squares on which Buonaparte's cavalry broke in vain. Then, caressing the bald spot on his head and drawing vigorously on his pipe, he spoke of the pipers at Waterloo, of how they played on the Highland Brigade in that famous action. "It was there," he declared, "that the chanter on my father's bagpipe was shot away."

Another tale which led me eventually to the Waterloo Rolls in the British War Office was Rab's belief that his great uncle George had served as a sergeant with the Black Watch at Waterloo. "He would have been," Rab asserted with unusual historical accuracy, "with Picton's Division when d'Erlon's Corps attacked. That was when the Gordons followed by the 42nd charged with the Greys. What a sight it must have been!"

It was well for my boyish enthusiasm that twenty-five years separated me from the truth in the War Office files. Sergeant George Ross on the day that d'Erlon's Corps was repulsed, was serving as a recruiting officer for the 42nd Royal Highlanders in the peaceful granite city of Aberdeen. *Sic transit gloria.*

Rab's tales eschewed his ancestor's toilsome, poverty-stricken existence. That existence could not hold a candle to the romance that Rab had unconsciously absorbed from the pages of Sir Walter Scott whom he revered. And, as I remember, it was this romantic yarning which did so much to enliven our long winter evenings in the kitchen at Lakeside. Those evenings inevitably had a chill sequel in the morning when we peered out from under the blankets at our cold bedroom, the windows of which were laced with frosty patterns, and realized that another school day was upon us. Once Rab had the McLary burning well and the kitchen beginning to warm, mother would descend from her own chill bedroom to prepare breakfast. Then, for Iain and me, it was off to school, a good mile away on a road that offered little shelter from wind and snow. With the collars of our mackinaws turned up, carrying a small sack of books and a five-pound honey pail filled with lunch, we trudged due west over the culvert below our farm, up the hill to the jog, then over a half mile of level upland before going down to a corner village where we stomped into a building labelled S.S.#13.

Within our white brick, one-room school—with the pervasive smell of oiled hardwood floors, and the heat that poured from the silver-bright round register at the back—we were prisoners for the day. Brief paroles were granted only for use of the toilets, smelly two-holers well out in the snow at the back where most of the boys, having fished out slippery short penises from within fleece-lined underwear and denim outer pants, hunched and peed in the snow rather than go inside, where misjudgments over the winter built up a treacherous approach and a most uninviting rest for anyone who had to do what was euphemistically described as "number two." I do not remember anyone in winter taking undue advantage of the "Please may I leave the room" request.

Within the school, the routine of lessons was made interesting for me because of the variety. One teacher taught all the grades. What went on in other grades above your level was usually more interesting than your own work. But it was in the stores cupboard at the back of the schoolroom that I found more lasting pleasure. It was a small library of perhaps forty books—a collection which owed its origin to Egerton Ryerson, whose views on education went well beyond those known to our local trustees. Here were books which, if I did not always understand, I often found fascinating.

I've forgotten many of the titles, although I still remember *The Vicar of Wakefield* with its charming woodcuts and its tale that kept me out of much mischief. I was greatly taken by characters winning through adversity to good fortune because I was by then aware—thanks to certain doomful pronouncements from my mother—that our own family fortunes were little more secure than those of the Primrose family when Moses dealt off the colt for a "gross of green spectacles, with silver rims and shagreen cases." And Goldsmith's adventurous piety captivated me, too, being much more satisfactory, I thought, than the long-winded prayers and exhortations which our family heard on Sundays from the pulpit in Lakeside.

One of the school texts that held my attention was *The Ontario Reader, Third Book*, authorized by the Minister of Education. It was a dandy repository of war stories. I still see its title page and opposite it a full-page Union Jack streaming in the wind, and under it the imperial theme: One Flag, One Fleet, One Throne. So displayed it was hard to miss the message. The sentiment was given further support on the title page by the name of the publisher, The T. Eaton Co. Limited, whose catalogue and sales service meant so much to us country people.

And there in my very own book—for in those far-off days students paid for their text books—I found out much about patriotism, courage, sacrifice, and even the glory of battle. I rejoiced in my book's presentation of martial happenings made possible by heroic men fighting for King and Country. How often I imagined Sir John Moore's burial at the end of that terrible march over the Cantabrian Mountains. I still remember C. Wolfe's jingling rhythms:

> We buried him darkly at dead of night
> The sods with our bayonets turning;
> By the struggling moon-beam's misty light
> And the lantern dimly burning.

At age ten or eleven this was for me great stuff, and I am sure I never questioned Sir John being left "alone with his glory."

Better than poet Wolfe's effusion was the "Letter from an Officer's Wife" which feelingly described the relief of Lucknow in 1858 and the effect upon the beleaguered British as they heard "the blast of the Scottish bagpipes, now shrill and harsh, as threatening vengeance on the foe." My father supplied further details, especially Sir Colin Campbell's command: "Bring on the Tartan!" when the 93rd Highlanders from our ancestral shire breached Sikanderbagh and, with the Sikhs, shot or bayoneted two thousand of the murdering mutineers.

And then on page seventy-one of my *Reader* beneath a picture of the Victoria Cross, I found Sir Edwin Arnold quoting Queen Victoria:

> Thus saith the Queen: 'For him who gave
> His life as nothing in the fight,—
> So he from Russian wrong might save
> My crown, my people, and my right,—
> Let there be made a cross of bronze
> And grave thereon my queenly crest,
> Write VALOUR on its haughty scroll,
> And hang it on his breast.'

Whatever influence such verse and prose had upon me, it was one which I accepted almost as my birthright. Even the *Public School Composition and Grammar*, also authorized by the Minister of Education and so highly approved that by the time I bought it for my classes it had been reprinted five times, had its patriotic appeal. My favourite picture in this text was the one heading Chapter 3 with the caption "Faithful unto Death." It was a scene of utter devastation: the sky filled with bursting shells and below a moonscape of splintered trees. In the foreground, a lone gunner standing among wounded or dying members of his gun crew, awaited fire orders. The gun was of a naval siege type, the only one in the ravaged scene which was meant perhaps as a tribute to Canada's heroic fighting men who were, by the time I entered public school, fighting an economic battle at home which was much less publicized.

My first memory of these heroes, who marched away to defend the Empire in World War I, belongs to our kitchen in mid-winter when a hired man from an adjoining farm would visit for an evening with my father and mother. He came from London, Ontario, where he had been unable to find work on his return from the war. For food, and a bed, and fifty cents a day he had hired out with our neighbour. I was not, of course, nearly so interested in his move to the country as I was in his tales of the trenches: of shell holes where men rotted, of barbed wire entanglements in No Man's Land, of tanks and airplanes, of charges through the murderous crossfire of machine guns, and the horror of bayonet work.

All this I absorbed goggle-eyed from my place at the kitchen table where my homework lay undone. It mattered not to me that my hero was still a victim of circumstance, one of a quarter million other heroes who were unemployed unless they accepted farm work for half the wage they had received as members of His Majesty's forces in Flanders fields. But this knowledge was to be mine soon enough when my father, having managed his affairs as badly at Lakeside as he had at Harrington, also found himself by 1928 reduced to the rank of a hired man, having had to surrender his fifty acres, his barn and house to a neighbour who held an eighteen hundred dollar mortgage on the property.

From now on, all was downhill. As monotonously as the bell on the Inchcape Rock, my mother had warned my father of what would happen if he did not alter his course. But this he seemed incapable of doing. Sales took place, heirlooms were sold, money borrowed was never repaid, and the farm that the mortgagee claimed fell behind lamentably. Long periods of sullen unhappiness punctured the balloon of my father's feckless optimism.

Gradually both my mother and father realized the consequences of the loss of the farm just one year before the Great Depression gripped the whole country. Rab had chosen a bad moment in time, as Ellen put it, to let the farm slip through his fingers and become just another unemployment statistic.

Once off his farm, Rab found that getting food for his family was far from easy when you had no money. Zurbrigg the baker made quite clear to us from his old, cut-down Model T Ford, that a loaf of bread required a ten cent piece before it became ours. No money, no bread. Ellen was alarmed; Rab depressed.

But what hurt my parents more perhaps than the lack of money for essentials was the rural declassification they had to face. People who owned their farms in our part of Ontario were set apart from the landless ones or even from those who worked in town for an hourly wage. On the farms, class was most noticeable in the farmer's attitude toward his hired man who, even if he ate with his boss at the kitchen table, was far from being his equal. It mattered not that the owner's pioneer beginnings had been desperately difficult and that his origins abroad were equally as squalid as those of the hired man. What really counted was ownership signalled by the well-anchored mailbox bearing the name of the man who lived at the end of the tree-lined lane.

My parents felt their loss of status keenly. Adversity troubled them severely, my mother more so than my father. To keep up some appearance of well being in the face of failure was more necessary for her than for Rab who could easily, like Micawber, adjust his thinking to incorporate the most insubstantial of dreams. When he was short of cash, which happened frequently, his imagination came to his help as he recalled what an unexpected inheritance had done for other people whom he had known. It was always possible for him to envisage life on easy street. At first he tried out as a Raleigh products man, then as a Fuller brush salesman, and later as a representative of a leading nursery stock company.

But his luck with these undertakings proved elusive. It was understandable. Times, he said, were too hard; people did not have the cash. The truth, however, was that Rab had no ability whatever as a salesman.

There being no other alternative for him to try his hand at, and no friends left who were willing to lend him money, he became a hired man himself and one who was often sought for by farmers needing help. Had he ever worked as hard for himself as he did for these farmers, he would never have had to part with his own fields. So long as his boss was willing to humour him and give him instruction rather than orders, Rab performed well, even willingly in the knowledge that no work meant hunger and shame at home. Neither he nor Ellen was prepared at any time to take relief, which in their eyes was almost as bad as being reduced to beggary. Even so, Rab never stayed longer than a year with any farmer. By that time both men had acquired too intimate a knowledge of each other.

And so we knew, from September 1928 on, several houses that we called home and several one-room public schools. If we were lucky, the school was within a mile of us; unlucky, we might have at least a two-mile walk from our house. Of one thing I was never in doubt, a school would always be found whenever we moved.

From frequent practice our moves became well organized. Riley, the Mover from Woodstock, became one of our most relied upon tradesmen. For ten or twelve dollars he took all our belongings in his large van to the next house, where once the McLary stove was in place and the stovepipes up, Ellen prepared a meal while the rest of us put up beds and fitted the furniture into the new home. Further unpacking was routine as Ellen knew the contents of each zinc washtub, the one square, the other round; of each wooden chest that Sullivan had made; and of the assortment of boxes and cartons carefully kept for the inevitable move.

It was at one our new places, when attempting to get apples left high up on one of the trees near the house, that I shuddered into puberty. It must have been a particularly curvaceous limb pressed upon my body that triggered my sex mechanism and wet my overalls in a very embarrassing way. Happily for me then, I was quite unaware of the long-term consequences of my maturation, of how "treed" I would be for the next twenty years of my life.

Though all boys must learn to cope with such changes, I am sure that torment is not too strong a word to describe some of my emotions. Religious and social taboos made masturbation a kind of sin. The numerous examples which Ellen cited of young people who failed to act decently had, alas, too firm a foundation to be ignored. Rural innuendo, which passed for wit among the men, alerted me to the danger of making myself part of their humour. And then there was a kind of blunt advice handed out by some older farmers among whom I found employment during the summer holidays. Some of this advice lingers with me still, especially old Simon Munro's words: "Boys, if you want to stay out of trouble, the place for your pecker is in your pants." Having fathered five children, Simon, I assumed, spoke with authority.

I think it was in June 1930 that I walked three miles into Woodstock to sit for my Entrance Examinations, which freed me forever from the Public School system and prepared me for the Woodstock Collegiate in September. During July and August I hired for the first time with Simon Munro for ten dollars a month and two meals a day. Self-control was easily effected at Simon's for he kept me much too busy from dawn to dusk to give me time to nourish carnality.

Throughout the 1930s the Great Depression shaped us mercilessly. As it deepened, my mother, who had trained for a short time in her youth to be a nurse, went out to work and found fairly steady employment. As she became known, one family would recommend her to another so that, before long, her income outstripped my father's as a hired man. Her absence, however, added to our burden of household chores, so that the Devil in any form must have found real difficulty getting at either my brother or me.

Even Saturday was filled with work, for then the week's

laundry had to be done by hand: copper boiler heated on the McLary, clothes scrubbed on the washboard in a tub, rinsed in another and, if white things, "blued" in another before being hung out to dry. Ironing was a consequence. Little wonder that my mother's homecomings were greeted warmly. My father, of course, was home only on Sundays so that his contributions to the housekeeping were little noticed.

At this time I was aware of some embarrassment, of a sense of being ashamed of my parents, especially my father, in his patched overalls, his pea jacket, and his cap with its ear lugs— all smelling astringently of what the cows and horses left behind. At the end of the week, unshaven and in need of a haircut, he was not the sort of person I would have liked him to be. And I wished that my mother, too, with her oversized nose, were slender and pretty rather than short and round—plump was the word she used. Unlike his wife, Rab was lean—and rather handsome when he was cleaned up and in his good clothes. As it was, I accepted my parents' appearances and their lack of money meanly and grudgingly as something I had to put up with. Mother, I knew from past bitter judgments, blamed only my father for our fallen circumstances.

Even now it's tempting but unfair to blame my parents for uncertainties that assailed me as a boy throughout the Depression years and easy to overlook advantages which our poverty promoted: the necessity to make and abide by choices once made; the strength to forego present pleasure for future reward; a driving will to succeed; and the recognition that hard work and happiness are somehow related. I accepted these conventional virtues. But what occurred to me almost daily was the sense of doing without. It was this awareness that troubled me most for it defied subterfuge. Its consequences were far reaching, and I took my uncertainty, my diffidence, my lack of social standing with me to high school.

Chapter 3

Lean Years

A three-mile walk each school morning took me in September
to the classrooms and austere halls of the Woodstock Collegiate
Institute. It was presided over by a precise, chalk-chewing man
whose signature, E. P. Hodgins, was as near as anyone ever
came to discovering his given names. Behind his back, we students referred to him only as "Hodge." We respected him rather
than loved him, for we saw him as a man who ruled his Institute with Old Testament efficiency. No mischief-bent boy
ever risked a second visit to the office where, if Hodge's tongue
failed to impress, his second line of defense, a sleek black strap,
invariably improved the miscreant's classroom performance. I
soon recognized the school's regime and adjusted to it and the
hours of homework required.

At the end of my first year in Collegiate, my parents found
it necessary to move to Woodstock so that my mother could
find nursing jobs easily and we could be near school and
church. So began a series of moves from 1931 to 1936 into a
variety of rented houses and apartments along Dundas Street.
My father soon found, however, that Woodstock had nothing
but relief projects to offer him, and these he refused to take,
preferring to walk off to the country to work for farmers for
twenty dollars a month and his board. In town mother found
more than enough patients who were terminally ill and happy
to give her ten dollars a week for her services. And so we met

our rent, paid for our groceries, procured enough clothing to keep up appearances at school and church, and even contrived to buy a second-hand washing machine.

What we feared most of all was illness which might necessitate a doctor's fee and the possibility of hospitalization. We had good reason, for during the winter of 1933 I came down with double pneumonia. For a time my recovery was doubtful. I have little memory of those feverish nights, except to this day I loathe the smell of mustard plasters which, were to pneumonia then what antibiotics are today. But the crisis came, and I survived to become aware of much kindness and concern. My mother was untiring in her nursing efforts. Rab came home to run errands and to ensure the house was well heated. Neighbours, whom we had known but a short time, brought food and good wishes. For a time, of course, our money ran very low, but as soon as I was on the mend both parents returned to work and eventually paid the doctor's bills. Easter came and then the end of June when my brother and I sought work for July and August.

I returned to Simon Munro's for the usual ten dollars each month but with full board and lodging, an item I very much approved of as Mrs. Munro was a good cook. My day at Simon's began at half past five in the morning with Simon lighting the fire in the kitchen range, rousing his household, and then, with two men and me in tow, stumping off to the barns to feed and water animals and clean stables. By seven we were sitting at the breakfast table listening to the news coming over the battery radio with a cheery greeting from Jim Hunter and the music of "Country Gardens." A half hour later we were on our way back to the barns and the day's work.

Simon's farming was essentially a man-and-horse operation. His hay was bundled from the loader onto sixteen-foot racks, hauled by his Percherons to the barns, then unloaded with a hayfork, and spread by two men in the mows. His oats, wheat, and barley were cut, stooked, and later pitched on to wagons and taken to the barns, where the sheaves were once more pitched from the wagon into the throat of a threshing machine that sent the straw in a torrent of wind and dust into the mow or out on a stack, while it dispatched the grain through a round shiny pipe to the granary bins.

From being the boy who perched on the rack at the front of the wagon, driving the horses, I graduated after 1932 to heavier chores, working alongside "the Englishman," the regular hired man. He was the most interesting person at Simon's farm: a young Cockney with no known relatives, an immigrant sponsored by Dr. Thomas John Barnardo. Set apart from the rest of us by his speech and an unquenchable pride in being English, he was less likely than I to be favoured— and favours were few at Simon's.

Hired men were minor figures within the township order. The blue bloods, along the gravelled roads of East Zorra, were those like Simon who had cut and ploughed their way to cleared acres, bank barns, fat cattle, and financial independence. Although all our origins abroad smelled of poverty whether along the Helmsdale River, or in Balvraid, or within the sound of the bells of St. Mary-le-Bow, here on Simon's land we were all aware of the rural pecking order. To be noticed at all in the township, one had to be a "good man," which meant that the emphasis was decidedly upon manual labour cheerfully rendered.

And yet it may have been our common background which made man and master strangely sympathetic to each other. Simon's own modesty was such that he sometimes admitted it was to a hired man's credit if he stayed with him year after year for twenty-three dollars a month, his room over the kitchen, and three meals a day. Such conduct warmed Simon's heart and, on occasion, even drew praise especially when the Barnardo boy performed his tasks cheerfully from dawn to dark six days a week and helped with the necessary chores on Sunday. On Saturday, after he had had a bath and changed his clothes, the man was usually free after supper—if he felt like it—to walk the three miles to town to a show or just to stand on Woodstock's street corners and look at his unemployed brothers and sisters.

From house to barn, Simon's was a remarkably self-contained, independent industry. Like my grandfather, Simon was a skilled carpenter, making his wagon boxes, racks, whiffletrees, wagon tongues, and doing all the repairs to his stables. For him, the outside world had little meaning. World War I meant high prices for wheat. Dollars and cents—so vital a part of his life—never slipped off into economic abstraction. Nor did it ever occur to him that he had denied himself anything, and he saw only good sense in his home having neither hydro, nor telephone, nor a bathroom.

Rab, in contrast, had a vivid sense that obeisance to the squat god Work was contrary to man's natural motion; it was a sense, of course, that left him in the end a hireling, a man carrying regrets to his life's end. But with these he carried also the comfort of the past which he absorbed from books which were meaningless to Simon whose life resided in his fields, his livestock, and his bank account. For my father, living meant leisure, a fiddle tune, a warm fire, friends, and talk of what had been or might be. It was a way of life that brought both misery and happiness to his family.

It was, in retrospect, a curious shadowlike existence that I led at Simon's during my summer vacations. Here I learned to work hard, even to rejoice in it as I tried to please the "boss" and keep up with the Englishman in all the work we shared. For two months I never read a book, saw a show, talked to anyone about ideas, or spoke to a girl of my own age.

Summer after summer throughout high school I served Simon because I thought he treated me fairly and paid me as much as any other farmer would and fed me better. I suppose I absorbed unconsciously some of his relentless energy so that I was always welcome whenever I appeared at his farm. Even the Easter holidays found me at the farm usually splitting and piling wood for the next winter.

Holidays over, it was back to Woodstock where in spring the high school always began to put its cadet corps in motion and to issue the wool tunic, breeches, wedge cap, and puttees—the whole smelling strongly of seasons in mothballs. With the uniform came a leather belt with its curious brass snake that served as a buckle. We took the issue home, shone the buttons and the snake, pressed the tunic and breeches, and began learning how to roll puttees neatly around our thin legs, an art that demanded much attention.

Teaching us how to form four ranks from two, to march and wheel in platoon formation, and to stand properly to attention while a visiting military figure inspected us in Victoria Park was the sole responsibility of the physical education teacher. He was, I think, a good man for this work, having been trained himself, people said, in the German army. For me and Iain, it was a good experience in dress, discipline, and coordination; for me, especially, it was a corrective to my sloping farm gait, set off by overalls, pea jacket, and heavy boots. Our inspection each June always drew a crowd of Woodstock's citizenry.

High school was, as I think of it now, made unnecessarily difficult by my determination to do well. Because successful rote performance was not only necessary but also well rewarded, I spent more time memorizing French irregular verbs, geometry theorems, and history dates than I did thinking about what I was doing or even why I was doing it. The niceties of Latin grammar overshadowed the sad loneliness of Horace's Eheu fugaces, Postume, Postume/Labuntur anni[1].

My teachers accepted me as I turned out: the same shirt worn to class each week and renewed in the spring when my mother turned the collar round, the same trouser seat shiny or mended, the walk and manners of a country boy. How straitened my teachers themselves were financially in those days I do not know. But the Woodstock *Sentinel Review* of May 26, 1932 had a column headed "Teaching Staff Salaries Cut for New Term." The Board of Education had notified the teachers that they were to have a new contract at the end of the school year "providing for reductions of 5 per cent on salaries of less than $2000.00 per annum and 7 per cent on all other salaries." No talk of strike! It was not the best of times.

During the summer and autumn, following my graduation in 1935 from the Collegiate, I worked again at Simon Munro's. My father was with another farmer, my mother on nursing assignments, and Iain with a farmer, too, for the summer. This

---

1.   "Ah me, Postumus, Postumus, the fleeting years are slipping by."

employment freed us from immediate worry and even gave us a certain status in the community. We were not to be counted among those on "relief."

But the future, if not the present, was worrisome. Rab was sixty-three years of age, with little hope of ever earning enough money to support his family. Although she was reasonably well, Ellen's varicose veins and occasional sick spells made us mindful that her years in service to others were limited. Serving as hired men for local farmers could not possibly provide either my brother or me with savings necessary for future education. Attendance at a university seemed as remote as the moon over Simon's fields. I had, however, taken one step that was to set me in the right direction. Shortly after leaving high school, I had written two sets of Civil Service examinations, one of which was for employment in the post office. Nothing at the time came my way except notice that I had passed.

As I think of it now, my life in 1935 seems curiously shuttered, intense enough perhaps at home, but feebly indifferent to alarming events farther afield: the Regina Riot, the poor showing of the C.C.F. in the 1935 General Election, the anti-Jewish riots in Berlin, Mussolini's invasion of Ethiopia, Mackenzie King's worries about a "war crisis," or even Mrs. Telford's execution by hanging on December 17 in the Woodstock gaol. My indifference, especially to politics during this year, may have been owing in part to the demands of Grade XIII, or it may have been just part of the Canadian stance. At Simon Munro's, where interminable rows of mangolds and turnips awaited me at the end of June, I was well insulated from current events.

The farm offered me a comfortable, if mindless existence. Once hoeing was over, the seasonal turn brought haying and harvest. That behind us, we turned to fall ploughing. By November, we had winter needs in mind. The details of one chore in mid-November still stick in my mind. Simon had decided to kill one of his pigs for meat for his household and had chosen me as his assistant executioner, so that I ended astride the pig's belly holding on to its front feet as it squealed its objection to Simon making a short incision on its neck before he went deep for the jugular. What I remember more than the actual sticking was the sight of the doomed animal getting to its feet and wandering drunkenly off by the straw stack, streaming blood, until, too weak to stand, it fell on its front legs, making suffocating noises until it died. Then followed the scalding, when the body was sluiced up and down in a barrel filled with boiling water so that the bristles could be easily scraped from its hide. Next came a long incision on its underside to remove the warm guts. The smell stays with me, as does the odour of the scalding. And I am sure I had some sympathy for this beast that I had so often fed and cleaned and now had helped kill to satisfy our own appetites.

November was a slack month at Simon's so that on weekends, when I returned to town, I began searching for another job and managed in the still grey light of dawn to enter my name for employment at the Dominion Rubber Company. Nothing happened immediately, and I stayed on at Simon's on a part-time basis. The news of an opening in the Company came to me at the end of a cold, wet November day, when we were trying to round up the last of a pen of little pigs to castrate the males. Two of our intended victims had escaped into an outer enclosure where it took much ingenuity and sliding about in mud and manure to round them up and deprive them of what rightly belonged to them. To leave the mud and blood of the pig pen to go off to work in town seemed to me that night an escape to a better life.

When I reported for work the next night at the factory, I discovered I was the one who fed the boot jack during the graveyard shift which lasted, I think, from nine at night until three or four in the morning. If it wasn't difficult or heavy work, it could be trying enough at times when the lasts coming up on the truck from the curing room had not been piled in the proper order. The turning of night into day, too, was at first a trial, but gradually my body or mind accepted the change as night followed night. My pay cheque was little enough, just $19.20 for two weeks' work. If I were to deduct the cost of my board and lodging, I was making less than I had at Simon's.

Furthermore, I preferred the work at Simon's, as hard as it might be, because the Munros were always kind to me. A mistake at Simon's was never a cause for a stinging remark. But any error on my part as I unloaded the metal boot forms from the truck at the head of the boot jack immediately drew scathing comment from any of the fifteen men affected by my mistake. Perhaps it was because the work was so mindless that tempers flared whenever the jolting passage of the belt suffered delay. And it required constant vigilance on my part to detect a missing or misplaced form. Constant repetition, however, bred moments of carelessness when I would be startled by: "Wrong last!" And then in pitying tones, "Jesus Christ, kid, what else did you learn in school? Tell me about it; I'd like to know!"

It was in the summer of 1935 that, acting on the advice of my former Latin teacher, J. H. Stewart, I enrolled in the Extension Programme sponsored by Queen's University. For nearly two years I devoted my spare energies to this mail-order education process. When lay-offs occurred at the Dominion Rubber, I returned to Simon's where I arranged to work four days of each week so as to have time to do my reading and prepare the assignments. They demanded much and were usually rewarded by C+s and B-s. During this time we kept the home together, my father working for farmers, my mother nursing, and I at first alternating between Simon's and the Dominion Rubber.

Some assistance came to us when my brother, on graduating from high school, apprenticed to a local druggist, where his pay for three hard years rose from five to seven to ten dollars a week. We were beginning to win our way forward. We had no debts, and each Sunday Ellen was able to find a dollar bill for the collection plate in Knox Church.

What the Church meant to us is not easy to put into words. It was, on Sundays, a sort of community centre which brought a very independent cross-section of people together where, for a least an hour each week, we had to listen to a carefully elaborated sermon, a very long prayer, and some indifferent music and singing. Arrayed in our Sunday best in the large semi-circular pews that distinguished Knox Church, we were very conscious of good order, of the neatness of our dress and of others, and above all of having our place in the scheme of things earthly and heavenly. Respectability was the password.

But Knox Church was much more than mere appearance. Our north-of-Ireland minister saw to that. And when it was my turn and then Iain's to teach Sunday School, help organize Young People's events, and even take part in special Church services, I think we could distinguish between show and substance. And we had, too, the advantage of hearing speakers whose own religion was not the "faith of our fathers" about which we sang so lustily. On one occasion we heard Rabbi Eisendrath from Toronto speak from our pulpit on the question: "Will We Have War?" We were charmed by his delivery and alarmed by his subject even though the fate of millions of Jews in Europe lay obscure in the years just ahead. On the question of war, however, our Church never wavered. We would fight for the Empire as we had done but twenty years earlier.

When it came time for Iain and me to face up to our Christian tenets and decide for Christ, we vacillated and then reneged. And I think we did so because we had the good sense to realize how far our ideals were from those of true wayfaring Christians. What we lacked was conviction and fervour. We were not prepared to deny the self and risk the possibility of having to move from one uncomfortable church manse to another on a minimal stipend for the rest of our lives. For such Christian commitment, we had too nice a perception of what was required of us.

Meantime we continued with our local church activities for within these we found friends of our own age. It was in the Young People's that I met Hugh McWilliam with whom I spent many hours on Sunday evenings caught up usually in current events, not religion. Our talk ranged widely: the return to power in 1935 of Mackenzie King, the work camps in Northern Ontario for single, unemployed men, the stir which Mitchell Hepburn was making among provincial civil servants and, far away from us, the Civil War in Spain. Hughie had a sceptical bent which I found both disturbing and fascinating. He questioned what I merely accepted as *status in quo*. It was a trait which he inherited or acquired from his parents, the mother a plain-spoken Yorkshire lady and the father a Border Scot whose soft burring speech concealed a mind that was shrewd and practical. ~~His~~ The father had been an infantryman in France. He had succeeded well in Canada, even becoming a homeowner during the Depression years.

Sometime in early spring, 1936, the graveyard shift at the Dominion Rubber was reinstated, and I left Simon's once more, tempted, I think, by a small increase in hourly pay and the need to have more time for my books. So, again, I stood by the jack belt. On the night of May 26, 1936, I stuck 1364 metal forms on the belt for making such wear as 75 pairs of "Men's Short Boot J.F., Scab, No. 180 M Export Bulk"; 78 pairs of "Women's Ockley Black No. 156 W Export Pack Bulk"; and 42 pairs of "Child's Leys Brown, No. 1760 Export Pack Bulk." As boot form after boot form jerked its way along the belt, the fifteen men, their hands deft and calloused, added particular pieces of rubber and canvas to the boot being constructed.

I can cite these details for two reasons: one, I kept the work order because I put it by accident in a letter which I had brought to work with me that night; and, two, I kept the letter because I thought it rather special, having come from my cousin, Mabel, who was then in London, England, as an exchange teacher. Her letter placed me that night an ocean away from the boots circling under the glare of the lights. Like my father, I saw my job that night as an unwanted necessity. Across the Atlantic, a king's death and a prince's coronation took my mind off the production of Export Boots, a risky proceeding if I made any mistake. But that night the curing room people must have loaded their trucks without error, and I do not recall any vilification that disturbed my imaginings. Mabel's news was of war.

"Rumour has it," she announced, "that Hitler and Mussolini are joining forces for a big drive." Later, she described "a demonstration of response to an air raid alarm which was well done by searchlights, guns, and miniature planes at the Royal Tournament at Olympia." She gave no indication of how desperately inadequate British defences really were.

But of such things I knew nothing either, so that her brief description of the Royal Tournament appealed tremendously to me, and I was proud to hear of England's preparedness in the face of German expansionism. For the remainder of the night by the belt, I thought of little else but the war that threatened Europe. And I am sure I was jealous of Mabel in the midst of such drama whilst I was a mere adjunct of a revolving mechanical belt in what seemed to me the dullest workplace in the western world.

Hughie and I, of course, had often talked about war but never as something that might disrupt our futures. Hitler's occupation of the Rhineland in March 1936 or German bombers over Guernica a year later meant little to us. Like Mackenzie King and thousands of other Canadians, we questioned the need for Canada to rearm for a second Great War. If that kind of money was available, much better we apply it to provide food, clothing, and jobs for almost 2,000,000 Canadians, who could be described as public dependants, than to purchase weapons and munitions for another war.

On this issue, we never thought of questioning Ottawa's responsibility toward the unemployed or of declaring our political structure and its economic vision inadequate or even reprehensible. And we were never prepared to admit the sensible socialistic proposals of the new C.C.F. party. Nor did we salute J. C. Woodsworth when, alone in the House of Commons on September 8, 1939, he opposed the declaration of war. We were uncompromisingly Canadian.

During those last years of the Depression, my own sense of justice, either at the international or national level, may have been dulled by the rise in our family's fortune. We were all employed. Iain was making seven dollars a week by 1937, and I sometimes made as much as $9.25 in one week. My father usually earned six dollars a week and my mother perhaps ten. It was enough to feed, clothe, and house us. Our very busyness served to keep us together as a unit, even gave us aspirations for a better life which continued, however, to elude us.

But mere busyness did not serve to obscure what was immediate and frustrating. Factory employment was a dead end. My eight pay cheques from January 25 to April 30, 1936 had totalled only $134.75. When I deducted whatever I spent on room, board, and clothing, I needed no convincing that full-time study at university was very far-off indeed as a prospect. My response to this conviction was both prompt and illogical. On Friday, April 29, I told my boss on the jack belt that I was quitting to go north to seek work in the mines, where I could earn at least $.58 an hour—a fact I had from a school friend who had been chucked out of Queen's after one year in Mining Engineering. It was a hare-brained decision for I very well knew that, just a year before, the government had closed down the relief camps in northern Ontario, turning hundreds of unemployed men onto a desolate marketplace. Some of these men I could see any day passing through Woodstock on the top of C.P. or C.N. trains.

The reaction of the jack belt personnel to my plan was predictable. They, with some perspicacity, regarded my announcement as proof of how my education had failed me. Their scorn was wonderfully blunt and, as usual, suitably embarrassing: "For Christ's sake, kid, why the hell do you want to go North? What makes you think anybody wants you underground? You know what, kid? You know what I think? You're figgerin' on a good lay with an old squaw! Aren't you?"

And there was more of the same throughout my last shift until late in the afternoon, when I was summoned to the office to take a telephone call which, in itself, was unusual enough to silence my critics. Their astonishment was as great as their silence when they learned that I was to report for work the next morning at 6:15 at the Woodstock Post Office to assume the duties of a temporary letter carrier. So ended, in a most satisfactory and unexpected way, my work with the Dominion Rubber and my plan to go North.

For all their bantering, the men on the jack belt were in the end rather kindly to me and interested in what I was going to do. They meant well in the face of my own oddity. It would have been asking too much of them to accept my churchy habits and my years of book learning. We belonged to separate societies. What they did was lay bare my private life, my work at home as a char and cook, my uneasy respectability, my beleaguered sensuality, my fear of "being found out." In vulgar honesty they reciprocated by sending their private and public lives night after night around the belt with the Men's Short Boots, the Women's Ockley Black, and the Boy's Tuffley toward Henri, the French-Canadian inspector, who was even more interested in the flaws of a human being than he was in those of a rubber boot. If it hurt me, the experience probably did me less harm than I thought at the time. It was good for me to be exposed to plain speaking that disturbed my cover-up, for my mask was never as secure as I thought it was.

In the post office I found a more congenial work force despite the fact that the posties had much the same level of education as the rubber workers. For both, the work was manual and strenuous; both belonged to the city and could speak plainly and bluntly. The difference lay in the posties' kindly humanity which set them apart from the men on the belt. How much this quality owed to their nearly all being veterans of the Great War, I do not know. Whatever the reason, none of them displayed the prejudices, and the love of gross, bawdy humour and stinging profanity that enlivened the boot jack.

From 6:30 a.m. until 8:00 a.m., we stood before our sorting desks and arranged the morning's mail for delivery. What we could not put in our sacks, we made into tightly-bound bundles which were sent on ahead for us to pick up later. The only sound was the whisk of letters being sorted or the odd questions asked about someone who had moved and left no forwarding address.

Some time after eight, we buckled and shouldered our bags and set out, each with five or six miles of city streets to cover. I soon found out how painful blistered heels and toes could be in a new pair of boots and also with what fury a housewife could set upon you when you inadvertently left a letter addressed to her at the house next door. Two qualifications for this job were essential: good feet in good shoes and an unerring knowledge of the names of all those who lurked behind the letter boxes on your route.

My success in gaining temporary work in the post office may have been what encouraged my mother to rent one half of a duplex and give up nursing for keeping roomers and boarders so that she could be at home. As admirable as she thought this scheme was, she soon found it had disadvantages. It was especially annoying to her to find that the six dollars a week which she received from her residents—and also from Iain and me—left her no profit whatever. The rent of thirty dollars a month, the cost of the food that met her standards, and the expenses of heating a three-storey building in the winter took every penny she made, including Rab's monthly wage. As his health was becoming increasingly uncertain, that wage could not be relied upon. So long as I was earning eighty-five dollars a month at the post office, I was by far the best paid member of the family. But even here was another worry, for I was already trying to save money to go to university, a plan which had my mother's full backing—for whatever else a university degree represented—it was for her a passport to a very necessary prosperity.

When the postman I was replacing returned to work after his illness, I was again able to find a job. This time on a highway survey crew as a rod-and-chainman. My two months as postman had hardened me physically for this work which, however, had its own peculiar requirements enforced by a conscientious, irascible Queen's civil engineer of giant proportions who soon made me aware of the importance of precise measurements. As well, he took for granted much knowledge which I did not have and when I failed him—as I did often—his wrath was such that I more than once had to duck to avoid a clout on the head from his broad hand.

Gradually I became useful. Armed with an axe, a bundle of stakes, a hundred-foot steel chain, and a blue marking pencil, I served my exacting taskmaster as he ran centre line, took shots on culverts, cross-sectioned borrow pits, or established points for spiral curves. Of one thing, however, I was eventually certain: I had no real talent for civil engineering despite its obvious usefulness to mankind. My mind was and still is such that it resents application to exact mathematical procedures.

I cannot now be sure of how I was paid for my highway work except that it was on an hourly basis and that between July 12 and September 20 I received cheques totalling $189.00, which compared favourably with the $190.56 I had earned as a postman from May 1 to June 26. Altogether my income from January 1, 1937 came to $514.13, of which I gave my mother $200.00 for board and lodging. As well I earned extras by moonlighting in town or at Simon's on long weekends. By the end of September I had $325.00, with which I proposed to spend a year at Queen's. Hughie had decided to join me. As he did not have to pay room and board at home, he had been able to save $425.00. Once we deducted $125.00 for fees and made allowances for necessary texts, it was plain to us, before we set off by thumb from Woodstock in late September, that survival at Queen's would require the greatest financial care.

Chapter 4

Queen's And One Pip

In Kingston, Hugh and I found a much used, grease-spotted room on Earl Street, where a kindly, garrulous landlady of Irish origin rented us a room with a double bed. She agreed that we could have light housekeeping privileges which included the use of a refrigerator, the bathroom as a source of hot water, and a one-burner hotplate. The rent was $3.25 a week which we shared. Three engineering students occupied three other rooms in the house and accepted our ménage with both wonder and amusement.

Fortunately our campus society was then free of today's sexual obsessions. We defined "gay" as "disposed to mirth" or "showy" and read A. E. Housman happily ignorant of that poet's homosexual propensities. That Hugh and I shared the same bed witnessed only to our need each night for as much sleep as we could get and invited no scurrilous labelling.

Within our crowded quarters, cooking called for much ingenuity, even though it seldom extended beyond the simplicities of oatmeal porridge, fat bacon, boiled potatoes, bread, butter, corn syrup, and jam. A five-pound tin of Benson's corn syrup lasted us barely two weeks. This plain, unbalanced diet was supplemented whenever one of our families sent us a parcel. Dispatched in Woodstock before 5:00 p.m., it would be delivered to us by noon the next day. Best of all food arrangements, however, was dinner at the Union whenever our bank accounts seemed to support such a culinary event. I managed it very seldom.

Although neither of us was military-minded and would never have considered at any time joining the Oxford Rifles in Woodstock, we did, in October, 1937, join the Queen's Canadian Officers' Training Corps. The main reason for this warlike move was, I am sure, the pay, which was little enough for the two hours we gave up on Wednesday night and on Saturday as well. Later, we justified our action on the grounds that military preparedness was necessary, and, if the worst came, we could win through to a commission. And so, into our crowded bedroom, we stuffed two issues of C.O.T.C. great coats, long trousers, tunics, wide web belts, forage caps with white bands, ties, shirts, and bayonets. No rifles were issued.

In the course of the year the C.O.T.C. connection proved its worth. For one thing we widened our acquaintance with other students and met really memorable instructors like Lt. Col. L. J. "Blimey" Austin (who three years later removed my appendix). As well, the parades got us away from our books and desks to remind us of the practical world outside, whose penchant for international disaster was once more drawing young men and women into its fearful current.

Two years of lectures every Wednesday night and of parades on Saturday morning had to pass before I qualified as a lieutenant, infantry (rifle). The highlights of the training were the annual inspections and the annual mess dinners, the latter of which we enjoyed very much for food, cigars, and port wine were plentiful, and guest speakers like Dr. Austin delighted us. His stories, for gentlemen only, circulated long after the year ended.

It is easier now for me to recall this C.O.T.C. work than it is to remember the details of the years of academic course work, where lectures in various subjects blur into one another, and where my memory is only of Christmas, and final examinations, and the anxiety to maintain Honours standing. What does come back to mind, however, from this first year at Queen's—in the midst of glowing autumn colours—are the geology trips which Professor Rose arranged for us. He was, in the classroom and outside, a remarkably good teacher who knew how to make practice illuminate theory.

At the end of the first term and for three years thereafter, Hugh and I both served as helpers at the Woodstock Post Office where we usually reported four or five days before Christmas and worked through until Boxing Day. It was fourteen hours of punishing footwork each day including Christmas Day. I even recall going in for three hours on a Sunday to make our work on Boxing Day more manageable. Such postal service—devoted or blind—no longer belongs to Woodstock. But it made timely employment for Hughie and me, and we accepted our pay— never more than twenty-five dollars each—very happily.

After that first Christmas rush of mail, my parents provided a delayed Christmas dinner on December 27 followed by music and dancing. Rab told his usual stories, especially the one about Sullivan being well schooled on the bagpipes in Scotland by the old pipe-major who had a croft on Skelbo's east side. "And it was many a time," my father asserted, "that the two of them took their pipes over the muir to the old castle by Loch Fleet and there played for their own amusement, for their only audience would be the startled sea birds and the seals that basked on the sand spits of the Loch—and maybe the ghosts of those Jacobites who had sheltered in the castle in the '15 and the '45." And so family story and legend became—if one was a good listener and a bit naïve—family history and fact. Even Ellen accepted the embroidery of Rab's genealogical ramble into our past history. It was, I must admit now, not bad tale-telling and served to draw us together as a family. We had a past. And I really preferred this tale to those of Harrington, especially the oft-told story of the Murray who was the seventh son of the seventh son and to whom my father was sent as a small boy to beseech him to save the life of one of Sullivan's colts that was in danger of bleeding to death. The Murray went off by himself, returning later to my father saying that all was now well with the colt. When my father returned home, the bleeding had, of course, stopped.

Holidays over, Hugh and I returned to Queen's to receive the results of our term examination. They were a shock, and I realized at once that some drastic change had to be made in my study habits. What had sufficed amply at the Woodstock Collegiate would not do at Queen's. During the second term my work pattern became one of long hours spent during the day and night in the Douglas Library.

Just as I never questioned the platform or functioning of the Liberal Party of Canada, so, too, I never conscientiously examined my C.O.T.C. connection—nor did Hughie. My Presbyterian catechism offered advice which I ignored; the sixth commandment, so categorical about killing, was replaced by current shibboleths. Both Church and State underpinned my position. I accepted the "old Commandments" and Rudyard Kipling's verse in the *Shorter Poems*:

> There is but one task for all—
> One life for each to give.
> Who stands if Freedom fall?
> Who dies if England live?

I was, despite the Statute of Westminster, a proud British subject whose overriding duty was to the Empire and to England, a country I'd never seen.

Most of my professors at Queen's had British connections and strengthened my imperial stance. Few of them were better at stirring my mind than James Roy in English, as he fought back tears over the conquest of Czechoslovakia and the loss of great nationalists like Mazaryk whom he had known personally, or than A. E. Prince in History as he recalled his experience of "standing to" at dawn on the fire steps of the trenches at Gallipoli. What the rest of each man's lecture was on such days my memory has ignored. Neither man glorified war but saw it as a necessity. Roy, in particular, had a Scottish bent toward the macabre which came through as he described the long lines of dead from the Ypres Salient which he had observed one evening while a lone piper sent the wailing notes of "The Flowers of the Forest" over the broken landscape.

Queen's professors, of course, touched our sensibilities in other ways and sometimes beyond the confines of the classrooms. Perhaps remembering their own undergraduate experiences in Oxford, or Cambridge, or Harvard some entertained us in their homes. It was a distinct surprise to me to find that an evening with Dr. Gregory Vlastos of Philosophy was both informal and very stimulating. His living room with students in it was quite unlike anything I'd experienced in Woodstock's sedate parlours. Lacking enough chairs to seat all of us, Mrs. Vlastos simply sat on the floor with others of us, while her husband in the course of the evening jarred our political sensibilities by announcing that Canada could, in a few years' time, become a socialist country which might, he thought, be of some consequence for teachers in Western Canada earning $350.00 a year. A generous supply of tea, sandwiches, and small cakes brought the evening to a close.

Other professors entertained us more formally but not any more agreeably than Gregory and his wife. I was, however, very sensitive to the old-world charm with which Professor Prince or Professor Alexander in English served afternoon tea, and with the more precise but just as friendly way in which Colonel Jemmett of Engineering performed the same ritual when he entertained members of the C.O.T.C. in his fine old home that looked out on Lake Ontario. Such old world ceremony and kindness linger on brightly in my mind, and I am still grateful.

By the autumn of 1938 I managed happily to better my living accommodation. It happened because Hugh and I both decided to live separately. We could not face another year on Earl Street even if the rent was just $1.62 a week for each of us. My first alternative led me into bed bugs, and I was forced once more to take to the streets and the round of Kingston landladies. My next choice was one of the best I've ever made: a room and a kitchenette, comfortably furnished, and a charming, kind landlady. Here I spent the year as impecuniously as on Earl Street but alone and much more comfortably.

My earnings for the summer of 1938, again from the Post Office, amounted to $308.47, which, after deductions for room and board, left me with $198.00 for the year at Queen's, obviously not enough. By December I was in sad financial shape. Lacking collection for Sunday service at Knox Presbyterian Church, I stopped going. The Christmas holiday brought the usual employment. But the winter term of 1939 brightened considerably for me when my mother's father died leaving a small legacy to my mother. On the strength of this inheritance, I received more help than usual from home and so survived the term much better than I had anticipated.

It may have been the knowledge, however, that our family fortunes had improved that encouraged me to risk dating one of the co-eds who sat near me in our lectures. Until now I thought I had to be content with just looking at Elizabeth. And even just looking had its merits not the least of which was the interest contributed to some of the weary detail of lectures.

From my present vantage point of white hair and common sense, I do not suppose Elizabeth was much different from many other trim young ladies on the campus: hair upswept, then waved back to where it was either gathered with a bow or left to fall to shoulder length; below was the collar of a plain blouse covered by a sweater that was demurely spacious. Unlike the sweater, the tartan skirt was cut to reveal the curve of firm hips and just long enough to leave a bit of bare leg above the roll of knee socks. The skirt itself shifted ever so enticingly as the girls walked to classes in their low-heeled saddle shoes.

But my choice seemed to me astonishingly right, and, since I was the one doing the choosing, it never occurred to me that I might have done otherwise or that she might have other ideas about me and my intentions. What really mattered was that she agreed to go to a movie with me and seemed grateful. Some time later I was emboldened to try something much more daring.

It all began because of the kindness which an old family friend, Mrs. McRuer, had shown me. In order to make some return for her having so often invited me to her home for dinner, I decided, having made the acquaintance of a livery stable man, to take her for a cutter ride. This I did, with such success, that I devised the same entertainment for Elizabeth, who gave me to understand she'd love such an outing.

She agreed to wait for me at her boarding house where I'd arrive with my outfit just after eight in the evening. Attired with my Queen's tam and scarf, I took the reins and set off, this time with a more spirited horse than the one I had for Mrs. McRuer's outing. To avoid Division Street traffic, I decided to follow Barrie south to the University area. About one block away from Princess Street a small band of Kingston street urchins saw my approach and lent destruction to my evening by throwing snowballs at my driver, which reared and bolted. With the bit firmly in his teeth, my horse took off for the lights at the intersection of Barrie and Princess Streets where, with fine disdain for the headlights of a huge transport careering down upon us, he galloped through the red lights to the open-mouthed wonder of local pedestrians. Two blocks farther on, by getting one runner up on the snow piled at the edge of the street, my Bucephalus dumped me and my Queen's regalia on the street and then galloped onward to the corner of Earl Street where, for irrational equine reasons, he surrendered to alarmed citizens who blocked his path.

It was, of course, too good a story not to attract the attention of the *Whig Standard* and far too delicious an item not to rouse the ribald appetite of students, who knew me from now on as "Gilpin." They inquired very seriously regarding the purpose of my mad ride.

"Were you hurrying to enlist? How much money did you get from the *Whig* for the article about you? Were you carrying classified information? Did you have police approval for running red lights?" And much more of the same.

For a week my embarrassment was much more painful than my bruises. My young lady said little—for very good reasons—but my landlady, on my return so soon from my outing, was very sympathetic and brought me hot cocoa and some aspirins. Since that night I have eschewed horses attached to cutters, in fact that was the last time I ever travelled in a sleigh of any sort.

For the remainder of the term I led a much more secluded existence, with the C.O.T.C. taking up most of my spare time. In November, 1938, I had become Corporal Ross, a distinction I coveted not so much for the two stripes as for the additional twenty dollars it meant to my pay. Throughout 1938-39 I gave up seven hours a week for military lectures, drill on vintage weapons from the Great War, and manoeuvres directed by a bull-chested regimental sergeant major on the floor of the Armouries. I learned as leading corporal to bellow out, "At the halt on the right, form line!" and to offer instruction to my classmates on the parts of the old Ross rifle and those of the Lewis machine gun. Then it was my turn to be instructed on the Boys Anti-Tank Rifle, which was an excellent illustration of how antiquated our national preparedness for modern war was. In Germany, meanwhile, Hitler was even now finding pretexts for armed intervention and, in early November, for anti-Jewish terror in Berlin as a result of the shooting of Ernest von Rath in Paris. But what went on in the Armouries, under the direction of men who had served in World War I, was connected only abstractly in my mind with events in Europe. I do not remember thinking that our drill was in any way to be associated with the plight of Jewish people in Germany, a plight headlined and editorialized in *The Globe and Mail* on November 12, 1938. Perhaps "appeasement" numbed any sense of outrage. Meanwhile the autumn moved quickly to the term's end with essays to be completed, examinations to be written, and mail bags to be carried in Woodstock. Christmas and New Year's over, Hugh and I returned to Kingston by thumb, where we turned once more to the books.

By spring I was preparing for the examination of what was known as the Certificate A in Infantry which, if I passed, would make me eligible for a commission in Canada's Active Militia. These examinations I tried in March, 1939. I have few details of them except that they were far from easy and included practical sand-table exercises. One of these called upon me as the leader of a rearguard action to decide when to open fire upon an enemy patrol approaching in single file along a roadway that offered considerable cover. I gained the approval of my examining officer when I opted to hold the fire of my men until the enemy were within twenty-five yards of our position. The reasoning I advanced for my decision was that we were, by such derring-do, more likely to kill or wound all the enemy and, therefore, not give them a chance to send word back to their main body about our position.

In the end, for the many hours of work I had devoted to things military, I received a splendid scroll by command of His Excellency, the Governor-General. It read in part:

> GEORGE the SIXTH, by the Grace of God, of Great Britain, Ireland and the British Dominions beyond the Seas. King, Defender of the Faith, Emperor of India, etc. To Our Trusty and well beloved Alexander Murdock Ross Greetings. We, reposing especial Trust and Confidence in your Loyalty, Courage and Good Conduct, do by these Presents Constitute and Appoint you to be an Officer in our Active Militia of our Dominion of Canada from the First day of October 1939. You are therefore carefully and diligently to discharge your Duty as such in the Rank of 2nd Lieutenant.

More of the same followed with appropriate capitals, enjoining me to "exercise and well discipline in Arms, both the inferior Officers and Men" serving under me "according to the Rules and Discipline of War."

The C.O.T.C. year ended with the usual Mess Dinner with its port wine, cigars, and "Blimey" Austin's incomparable stories. After this event came the final examinations for our five academic courses and the last opportunity to arrange a date with a co-ed. I had neglected the object of my ill-fated sleigh ride rather badly; to restore the relationship, I took her to the British American for dinner and afterwards to see Ginger Rogers and Fred Astaire in *The Castles*. It was a good choice and, to my delight, Elizabeth coaxed to sit through the second show. After a sedate promenade along the lakeshore, I said goodbye to her at midnight, returned to my room for my bag, and then—penniless but happy—hitchhiked home.

I spent May doing odd jobs and looking for regular employment. Having free time on Monday, May 22, Hughie and I hitchhiked to Toronto to see our Queen Elizabeth at the ceremony of trooping the colours at the Provincial Parliament Building. We caught a glimpse of her afterwards chatting to officers of the Toronto Scottish and later saw her as she turned her head in the royal car to wave at the crowd in front of the Ontario Museum. I thought her a very beautiful lady. About 7:30 that evening we saw both the Queen and the King as they inspected a guard of honour of the Queen's Own Rifles drawn up in front of Union Station. Despite the crowd we had a good view, especially of His Majesty, George VI. As a show, it was prelude to fearful years. But, on that May day, Hugh and I were impressed, proud to be loyal subjects of the House of Windsor.

When I finally found work in June, it was as a beam trucker in the Woodstock Firestone plant. To set up and tie seven sets of these eight hundred pound spools of thread to the frames was a good night's work for which I was paid thirty-five cents an hour, not enough to provide for my last year at Queen's.

Sometime that summer my brother decided he was not interested in becoming a druggist, even were he ever able to own his own store. If he enrolled in university, it would be to seek a degree in Chemistry. As he had very limited savings, his decision further complicated our lives. The future was fortunately a bit brighter than in the past because, when my grandfather's estate was settled up, my mother found she had inherited $1,800.00, a larger sum than she had ever known as her own. Rab was ecstatic as he contemplated the uses to which this small fortune could be put, one of which was to free him from his servitude to local farmers. Ellen had other ideas.

Her boarding house, she had discovered, was not a money-making proposition. For all her hard work she had little more than the gratitude of those whom she sheltered and fed. Her own health was uneven, and her husband's earnings increasingly uncertain as he took ever longer breaks from his farming to enjoy, as he put it, "a few days' rest at home and some good meals."

It may have been Rab's doing in the end that led to Ellen's decision to close the boarding house at the end of September, store the furniture, and accompany her two sons to Kingston, leaving her husband to fend for himself. It seems to me now a hard decision. I should have enlisted then and declared my parents dependants. Rab was, after all, sixty-six years of age, and neither as strong or healthy as he once was. But deep down I suspect he was as much in favour of furthering our education as his wife was. For both of them, education for their sons held out the promise of security for their old age. As he thought of the unknown labour market in Kingston, Rab may well have preferred staying behind. Better the farmers he knew than those he didn't.

The parting, when it came, and the surrender of the house on September 20, 1939, was celebrated the night before by a party: three violins, piano, square dancing, and even a schottische to the 4/4 time of "Moniemusk." I enjoyed the night especially as I had Marion, one of my mother's pretty maiden boarders, for my partner. The next day brought the mover. The three of us then said goodbye to Rab and set off for Kingston, where we found a small furnished flat on O'Kill Street and settled in. Ellen was happy, happier than she'd ever been, Iain was content, and I was liberated from my basics of porridge, potatoes, onions, bread, and corn syrup. Life was much better.

War was now a certainty. It was early on the morning of Friday, September 1, 1939, that I had been awakened by the novelty of a newsboy hawking *The Globe and Mail* on our street and bawling out: "Extra, Extra, Germany declares war!" Then, as the German Panzers lanced into Poland, a small British expeditionary force moved into France. The stage was set for tragedy. On September 19 the Canadian government announced its intention to organize and train a division for service overseas. The alarm over, we quieted down into what Churchill called "The Twilight War" which lasted throughout the fall and winter as our studies proceeded.

By October I was spending as much as ten hours a week on C.O.T.C. work. In November I removed my corporal's stripes and became, with a fine disregard for the intervening N.C.O. ranks, 2/Lt. Alexander Ross or, in later Army parlance, "a one-pip wonder." This promotion brought more pay and more work as I undertook, without much grounding, to "exercise and well discipline in Arms," Queen's students less knowledgeable than I in matters military.

Talk of war now even crept into the austerest performance

of our most scholarly professors. Some were, of course, more willing than others to make passing reference to the horrors headlined by the newspapers. News of conditions in Britain came first-hand to us when Professor Roy, fresh from his beloved Edinburgh, appeared before us brimful of air raids, of sand-bagged cities blacked out at night, of balloon barrages, and of the treatment Germany was meting out to its aliens and Jews, and especially to Czechoslovakia. He never got to the subject of the Romantics on that first day. But the novelty of such overseas news wore off as we slipped into the familiar routine of lectures and essay writing.

During this last year, I paid more attention to Elizabeth than I had in the past, when my efforts could only be described as rare and cautious. Early in the autumn, after a football game, I brought her to O'Kill Street to meet my mother who thought her a very sensible girl. By December 9, I was reckless enough of money and her reaction to invite her to the Arts Formal where, for the first time, in a borrowed tuxedo, I kissed her someplace just below the left eye. We danced until morning. I felt almost cosmopolitan as I handed her out of a taxi at 4:30 a.m. as the milkman was delivering his supplies at her boarding house. The Formal was a great event for me, and its memory remains fresh in the Queen's *Tricolour*, where I can see her black evening dress and the tumble of her dark curls that I knew so well from my vantage point in our lectures.

Final examinations and my family obligations dampened down any danger of an emotional entanglement. Later, I remember walking with her to see *The Beachcomber*, then playing at the Capitol. For any other young couple, the omens in the sky that night would have brought them to a fine emotional pitch, as the northern lights arced over Kingston and sent streamers of blue and green quivering across the sky to where a quarter moon hung shyly between the towers of St. Mary's Cathedral. But we escaped from this magnetic glory into the smell of popcorn and the illusion of flickering action in black and white upon beaded glass to forget ourselves and our worries about summer employment. Afterwards we had coffee and sandwiches in the Kent Tea Room before walking quickly back over creaking frosty snow to Elizabeth's boarding house.

And so my last year at Queen's moved to its close. I had worked hard and loved prudently. It was a year made pleasant and possible by my mother's effort and money, for though I had been awarded a small bursary, had returned at Christmas to work in the Post Office, had larger C.O.T.C. pay cheques, I could not on my own have financed the year or have been so well cared for without my mother's assistance. Her money was, of course, slipping away quickly, but she had no regrets. She had enjoyed her year and moved her sons nearer to the goal she had in mind.

Although I had told Elizabeth that my obligations to my family were such that I could make no commitment to her, I thought I was "consumedly in love with her." Whether this was really so is hard, after so many years, to sort out. Her reaction to my putting my family's needs first and hers second, was a sort of sad resignation that left me puzzled and in much misery for several days.

One outcome of my stunted approach to her was a decision to correspond with her throughout the summer. It was a device which appealed to me because I thought our hesitant attachment might be maintained and could even simmer away until my circumstances might risk the heat required for a formal engagement. This was entirely my idea, and a bad one, as love rarely thrives on as low a temperature as I was willing to apply. But both of us agreed and then turned to our books and the final examinations. What I thereby missed, I think I lost forever.

The final examinations were a surprise for I wrote them from a bed in the Kingston General Hospital where, in late April, Dr. Austin had removed my appendix. Discharged on May 5, I was in time to watch my mother packing up for a move to Johnstown, where she had rented a cottage for my convalescence. With tape across my abdomen and feeling depressed at being deprived of all the attention I had been given at the K.G.H., I did not welcome the transition to Johnstown as much as Ellen did, for she would be back again on the St. Lawrence which she had known so well as a girl. The cost of my operation, eighty-eight dollars, and the knowledge that Ellen had spent over one thousand dollars during the past year did little to cheer me.

Chapter 5

A Pedagogue

Four days after our arrival in Johnstown, while General von Bock was sending twenty-five divisions across the Meuse towards Holland and Belgium, my diary relates that I visited the Scotts, my cousins, where I painted the bottom of a boat, milked two cows by hand, and afterwards drove the herd to the river for water. Two days later, while the nine divisions of the British Expeditionary Force held along the River Dyle, I spent the morning turning a fanning mill and the afternoon improving my fieldcraft by hunting groundhogs with a .22 rifle at the back of my cousin's farm. The news that the Dutch High Command had given up came to us on May 15.

Convocation at Queen's took place on May 17, the day that the Germans entered Brussels. My parents came to Kingston to see me go forward in Grant Hall to receive my B.A. degree in English and History. Afterwards we all returned to Johnstown. Rab was in a festive mood as he contemplated my future as a high school teacher and his own freedom from farm work. Ellen was much less joyful as she took time to make the future, as she saw it, clear to her husband. That future depended entirely upon getting both sons through the process of higher education: Iain to Queen's for his second year and me to the Ontario College of Education. As her own money was running out, it was essential that Rab continue working for farmers, that she find work as a practical nurse, and that the war not spoil the investment she was making for her future in her sons' education.

On May 22, as ten Panzer Divisions roared west and north toward Boulogne and Calais to threaten the rear of the B.E.F., Rab packed his things in his grip and returned to a farm near Woodstock. My diary entry was brief: "I wonder if I'm wise in listening to mother. My enlistment could release us all from the financial corner we are in."

May was a wet, dismal month. With my strength returning, I looked for work. It was easy enough to find so long as I did not expect payment from the local farmers for mending fences, ferrying cattle to Drummond Island, splitting potatoes for seed, or helping load elm logs for the sawmill in Spencerville. Even so, I enjoyed the work, often delayed when my cousin took me fishing on the St. Lawrence.

On June 4, the day the British took the last of 338,226 men off the beaches of Dunkirk, I did, however, earn two dollars for helping plant potato splits. From then on, thinking I was strong enough, I sought regular employment: the Kingston Airport, the Johnstown Elevator, the Queen's Employment Office, the Kingston Shipbuilding Yard, and even a railway extra-gang; they had nothing for me. No one seemed to want my 135 pounds of willingness or the imprint of a year's intensive study. At the Gananoque Airport construction site, I was told that I needed "pull" to get a job there. That evening I met Mrs. McRuer's son Allan in Kingston where, after coffee downtown, we saw a large crowd following a hundred or so troops marching along Princess Street. To show its displeasure of Mussolini's declaration of war on Britain and France earlier in the day, the crowd was intent on smashing shop windows belonging to Italians. At one point a man heaved a rock through the plate glass window of Zakos' fruit store. Greek or Italian, I said in my diary that night, made no difference to him.

For the next few weeks in Johnstown the shadow of the war gave me many uneasy hours. Even Allan McRuer, now back in Kingston, managed to contribute his share. On June 18, the day before Churchill's "finest hour" speech, I received a letter from Allan which concluded thus:

Frankly, my boy, I feel England is doomed although she may hold out many months. But she
can't stand gas and civilian slaughter indefinite-
ly—no country can! If I were the British, I'd blast
hell out of the French fleet right now just in case
it falls into German hands. I see where Franco
wants Gibraltar and a share in the spoils of
France. Wouldn't it be rich if the thieves began
to quarrel among themselves over the loot? And
for God's sake, Sandy, stay out of the army.
Don't be swept away by propaganda. Try your
best to get to O.C.E. this fall.

What I did next seems to me now very contrary and difficult to explain in view of some of the advice I was getting. Perhaps it was the knowledge that His Majesty George VI had
appointed me to be an officer in Canada's active militia that
sent me off on June 10 to the C.O.T.C. Orderly Office in
Kingston to volunteer my services as a 2nd Lieutenant, Infantry.
As a consequence, I was told to keep myself in readiness as
there were fewer than five names ahead of mine. That evening I
dated Jeanie, a nurse I grew to like during my stay at the
Kingston General. I found her open and agreeably engaging.
Early next morning a transport driver dropped me off in
Johnstown.

I have no record of what Ellen thought of my volunteering
for active service: probably sad resignation and the hope that I
would not be called up on the grounds of the greater contribu-
tion I could make to Canadian society by being a teacher rather
than a soldier. We must have had several silent meals.

I awaited my call-up by helping excavate a cellar by day
and, by night, paying more attention to a pretty Catholic servant girl than Ellen thought prudent. Felicity worked for our
landlady. Pie socials, square dances, and canoeing by moonlight on the St. Lawrence had caused me to mention her rather
too warmly to mother. "Catholics," she pointed out bluntly to
me, "are always on the alert for a good catch, and you ought to
remember Elizabeth." My mother's deep distrust of all Catho-

lics had been fostered by some sixty years of exposure to protestantism. No matter that she herself had been baptized a Catholic. Felicity was one of the R.C.s and well outside our tribe. But I liked her. She had laughing eyes, a lithe body, and full cotton frocks smelling of the wind and sun from the drying line.

Unlike Elizabeth, who had not yet written to me, Felicity was near at hand and, whenever free of her duties, very attentive to my suggestions. Evening soon became as blissful as the day was worrying while I waited for the mail and a letter from the Orderly Office. Not hearing for two weeks, I went to Kingston to inquire and was told my name was next on the draft list. Back in Johnstown, another two weeks passed and still no reaction to my having volunteered. I had good reason to think I was being passed over.

Without money and unwilling to use my mother's limited resources, I was increasingly unhappy. It was also an embarrassment to meet local people who knew I was well enough to work but had to rely upon my mother for room and board. Disillusioned with the response to my having volunteered, I altered course suddenly by throwing in my lot with Frontier College. It was, I found out, a very different institution from any I had known. The Toronto faculty and staff consisted of four people only: Dr. E. W. Bradwin, the Principal; old Mr. Longmore, a general factotum, whom the Principal was wont to describe as "all wool and a yard wide"; Miss Jessie Lucas, a devoted secretary; and a representative whom I never met. The purpose of the College in Dr. Bradwin's words was "to bring men in isolated places some opportunities to improve their education." The instructors were third-year undergraduates and graduates of Canadian universities; they served as manual labourers on work gangs where they were expected to hold classes five nights a week. In addition to their pay as labourers, they received from Frontier College an honorarium for a four months' season of one hundred dollars.

On July 17 I became a member of Frontier College's band of labourer-teachers on my way to an extra-gang whose bunk cars were on a siding alongside the Welland Canal near Port Colborne. In a letter to Ellen I said that I

> narrowly missed having to sleep on the bunk car
> floor on my arrival but was able to rig up a bed
> by placing two old green coach cushions end to
> end. 'Cookie' gave me two wool blankets so I
> was warm. As there are no screens on the cars,
> we have to fight off flights of mosquitoes all
> night long. I do what the other men do—put
> socks on my hands and sleep with a towel over
> my head. It's going to take me some time before
> I can sleep right through the night as freight
> trains roar through on the adjacent track about
> six feet away from my head in the dark.

At first with no accommodation for a classroom, my teaching was negligible, but by using the end of a car, or the dining room when "Cookie" was absent, or, later on, a corner of the station at Onondaga, I was able gradually to put together a class: some Ukrainians, three Poles, two Hungarians, an Italian, and an Indian from the nearby reserve. For a time attendance was up and down, but eventually it steadied, and I could count on having about fifteen men every night. The curriculum was elementary: reading, writing, and arithmetic. Most of the men could neither read nor write in English, and their spoken English was uncertain.

Perhaps the most popular learning tool at my disposal was *The Globe and Mail* which the College sent to me. Night after night toil-worn men puzzled out the headlines and asked questions about the progress of the war. I, too, read it eagerly and still remember the drama of one thousand enemy planes over England challenged by R.A.F. Spitfires and Hurricanes.

And I do not now know what I did or did not do about the offer of my services a month before to the Canadian army. Certainly no letter ever came to me from the Orderly Office, where someone must have deleted my name. Meantime, tamping stone and trimming track were poles apart from exercising and disciplining in arms members of His Majesty's forces. That's not to say that the army was absent from my mind. Even my brother, Iain, now working as a drug clerk in Toronto for $27.00 a week, saw the army as a sort of escape route: "If only," he wrote, "we can scrape through this coming academic year, we could in the spring enlist and at least get rid of this spectral wolf that slinks about our doorway."

Ellen's summer was darkened by the eroding away of her inheritance and by her worry about Rab who had had weak spells and had to give up his work in the midst of haying. "He will soon," she wrote, "be sixty-nine, and, although the doctor says there's nothing wrong with his heart, he has advised him to have a rest." My father accepted the doctor's advice cheerfully and at once by giving up his job and taking it easy with old friends at Harrington.

As well as worrying about her husband, Ellen continued to resist the suggestion that her sons should join the army. "Should you enlist," she told me in late August, "I hate to think of what you may go through. It hurts me more than you can know even to think about it. The training of a military man, I suspect, has about it a certain grasping fascination for young men, but in later years they must bear its scars."

Fortunately for me, I was so busy during the summer that my mother's warnings or our family worries were seldom foremost in my mind. I did, however, look forward very much to letters when I came off the handcar in the evening for supper—letters which I read in my bunk when the class was over. Writing to Rab in August, I described my employment:

> We work [I told him] ten hours a day six days a week for thirty cents an hour. From my pay six dollars a week is deducted for board.
>
> I don't mind the work on the tracks now for I can tamp, trim, line, and shovel all day as well as most of the men. Lately I have been on the jack. That's hard work especially with a six-inch lift and loads of gravel on the ties. As yet I have not used the spike hammer, and I doubt if I'll have a chance as several of the lads like spiking and are very good at it.

The only serious complaint I have is with the dining car and Crawley McCracken's food. Even though it's plentiful, I dislike eating when the car is full of house flies. Can you imagine no screens on the dining car and open latrines about seventy-five feet away? Why we do not have some sort of epidemic is beyond me. Fortunately, however, illness is nearly unknown among us.

From time to time, I had a letter from Hugh who was also with Frontier College on an extra-gang one thousand miles away at Niddrie, north of Dryden. He told me he belonged to "a motley gang of ninety men of many nationalities in which Ukrainians predominate. As well we have a few Poles, some Canadians, Russians, Germans, Roumanians, Czechoslovakians, one Italian, a Dane, and one Indian." His gang was even more polyglot than mine. Hugh liked the work, and Bradwin's summation of my Queen's roommate indicated that he approved of him: "Age 24, height 6', weight 165 lbs.; final year student, Queen's University, member of the Officers' Training Corps; active, strong, observant, gave whole-heartedly to the men."

July and August passed very quickly. On my last day as a Frontier College man, I told my brother that I had put on anchors all day getting wet through in the afternoon when it rained heavily. You must, I said, nearly drown before you stop work on an extra-gang for no work means no pay. At my class that evening, I was greatly surprised when my students gave me a going-away present of nine dollars. It was a most generous gift from those with little to give.

From the bunk cars at Cainsville, I used a rail pass to Woodstock to visit Rab who was on a farm north of the city. He, in his usual optimistic way, promised to send me cash throughout the winter, to help out as he put it, while I was at the Ontario College of Education. "I don't make much from these close-fisted farmers," he said, "but whatever I have, Sandy, will be yours if you need it."

In Toronto I talked to Dr. Bradwin who expressed his satisfaction at my going to O.C.E. Later, in Johnstown, I saw Ellen who told me that she didn't care if it took the last cent she had to help me this winter for she'd much rather I had a good school than that I was in the army. And so honouring my parents and setting aside my country's need for infantrymen, I enrolled at the Ontario College of Education on Bloor Street in the heart of Toronto.

My year at O.C.E. was on the whole a cheerless time. I had a third-floor attic room above a millinery establishment on Avenue Road. My rent, nine dollars a month, covered the cost of a gas plate for cooking. My landlady—a fashionable, managerial type—directed the work of three or four women during the day. On Saturday nights they often enlivened the premises with a good deal of convivial merrymaking at which men were never present. The clinking of glasses and cigarette smoke drifted up the stairway to my desk where I hunched over my books.

I missed the friends I'd made at Queen's. Pedagogy, as prac- tised at O.C.E., was very demanding of time and energy. Money was scarce. Iain at Queen's was as much in need of it as I. Ellen was still in Johnstown earning little more than her board and room. Rab was working for farmers; in the autumn he earned as much as thirty-seven dollars a month; in the winter much less. By Christmas my summer earnings and Iain's were nearly exhausted.

The one extracurricular activity I had was command of an oversize platoon of sixty-nine pharmacy men at the old Ar- mouries on University Avenue. I especially liked the authority that my rank conferred upon me and the protocol which the C.O.T.C. personnel emphasized on the Armoury floor. I told Ellen about it in one of my letters:

> My corporals and my sergeant who is in
> medicine are very keen on propriety and
> surprise me by their reverential 'Sirs.' Their for-
> mality also holds at higher levels. On parade, for
> instance, if I am drilling the platoon and the Cap-
> tain is some distance away and wants me, he
> sends a sergeant to me, who steps up smartly,

salutes and says: 'Captain Llewellyn's compliments, Sir. The Captain would like a few words with you, Sir.' I then reply, 'Thank you, Sergeant,' while returning the salute. He steps back a pace, salutes again, and retires. I then march to the Captain, salute, and remain at attention while he delivers his sentiments. I suppose you think this is a curious artificial rigmarole, but here it's the fashion.

For four hours each week such social conventions distanced me from high-school textbooks and the odour of cooking on the two-burner gas plate in my attic hall. For those four hours I was a temporary gentleman, a role I innocently fancied. Back at the college, I was only a student in large classes where rather tedious ex-schoolmasters schemed to make a new batch of schoolmasters. Their pedagogy demanded much. Twenty written examinations covered a wide range of subject matter: from educational psychology to school management, from English literature to British history. In addition, the practice teaching sessions required a fairly comprehensive knowledge of Latin verbs, the geography of darkest Africa, French grammar, and the ability to teach English composition and literature from the first to the fifth forms. A minor in School Librarianship further added to my mix of subjects. I was much busier than I had ever been at Queen's.

Sometime in early November Rab took a weekend off from farming and came to see me. I arranged bunkhouse accommodation by having him sleep on my mattress on the floor while I—having covered the springs of my daybed with a week's issue of *The Globe and Mail*—slept on top of it. The next day I took my father to see the Ontario Art Gallery and showed him about Hart House and the University Library. With the exception of his taking me to lunch downtown, we had the rest of our meals in my room. This somewhat sly economy on my part meant that Rab was able on his departure to give me seventeen dollars. It was a welcome gift, part of which went to pay for a new Sam Browne belt which I very much coveted to complement my appearance as a 2nd Lieutenant.

Early on a Monday morning Rab said goodbye to me and returned to his farm work. As always, within his means, he had been generous, and I hoped I had made his visit a happy interlude away from bush work and barn chores. Nonetheless his departure left me uneasy for I was more aware than ever that his days as a hired man were numbered. He was more stooped than usual, and he complained about rheumatism in his hands. Indeed I needed no more than a glance at his swollen finger joints to verify how painful manual work must have been for him at times.

Over Christmas, when I stayed with Hughie's family and worked at the Woodstock Post Office, I saw my father but once, he having come to town with his employer who was doing his Christmas shopping. Rab was not his usual blithe self for his shoulders as well as his hands were hurting him. By the end of our visit, it came to me clearly that I could not much longer postpone the need to end Rab's working for the local farmers and somehow provide a home for him and Ellen.

To enlist was, of course, an immediate solution to this problem. As a way out, it was especially attractive late at night as I laboured over the dull material of my texts. Interestingly, it was on the first day of February, 1941, that my future artillery regiment, the 17th Field, was officially formed in Petawawa. Three and one-half years were to go by, however, before I wore the shoulder flashes of this regiment. Mine was to be a slow march up to the guns. All this was, of course, veiled from me in my garret on Avenue Road where I was resigned to accepting O.C.E.'s prescriptions, Rab's few dollars, and Ellen's determination to get me safely installed in a classroom in Canada.

For Ellen in Johnstown, the winter passed slowly. It was bitterly cold, the river froze from shore to shore, and flu beset the local people. Ellen got it and was no sooner on the mend than she had a badly infected hand, the result of being bitten by a neighbour's dog. Over the winter, all her letters emphasized how much she wanted a home of her own—not in Johnstown—but back in Woodstock where she was sure she was better able to make a living.

These details remain with me in letters and in the intermittent entries I put in my diary, one of which noted that on April 5, in the midst of my Easter examinations, Ellen came to see me.

> Great rejoicing and much talk all afternoon. In the evening we went to the Embassy to see George Formby in *It's in the Air*, at which I laughed more perhaps than the show deserved. We ended our evening out having hot chocolate in Diana's. Some time after midnight we returned to my attic: this time I slept on the floor, having made the daybed as comfortable as I could for Ellen.

The next day she told me that she had decided to set up house and make a home for us. A few hours later she set off by train for Woodstock. As soon as my examinations ended, I joined her, and together we searched in vain for a house she could afford. On Sunday we went to church where, to my surprise, I found Hughie with his parents. My surprise was even greater after the service, when I found out he had enlisted and was off to an officers' training course in Brockville in a week's time. Queen's had given him his final examinations. His enlistment made me envious and discontented.

Unable to get a house, Ellen took a job as a practical nurse in Woodstock for ten dollars a week. For the remainder of my holidays, I went out to Simon's where I was put ploughing at a dollar a day and my board. The activity did much to take my mind off househunting—and Hugh.

Once back at O.C.E., my time was very much taken up with practice teaching. Joe Gill, a critic teacher, was quick to spot one of my weaknesses: "You know, Ross," he said to me at the end of one of my sessions, "I haven't seen you smile once. You're too serious. You must try to loosen up." It was fair criticism of what poverty and perhaps Calvinism had made of me.

The very next day, however, my spirits rallied when I received a ten dollar bill from Rab which improved noticeably the holdings of my larder. Then, on May 3, I received $42.50 C.O.T.C. pay, nearly twice what I expected. Out of this I paid

$22.50 for a khaki drill tunic and two pairs of slacks which I needed for the camp I attended at Niagara-on-the-Lake from June 8 to June 22.

Here with good food, good weather, and good companions I enjoyed living. The significance of my one-pip status came home to me on the first day when I returned an elderly sergeant's salute only to find that the sergeant was Professor B.C. Diltz of O.C.E. As a one-pipper I was, of course, entitled to the amenities of the officers' mess where, before dinner, smartly attired waiters brought gin Collinses to us in the shade of near-by elm trees. I liked both the attention and the drink. During this splendid sunlit holiday, the army made a very favourable impression on 2nd Lt. Ross.

Camp brought another paycheque for $43.59 which I sent on to Ellen who had succeeded in renting for twenty-five dollars a month a small red-brick bungalow in Woodstock's east end. Her bank balance of $69.00 meant that from now on she was my dependant and needed the money I had borrowed from her during the past two years.

My affairs now took a turn for the better. By the end of May I had been hired as a teacher by the Timmins Board of Education at what seemed to me the very handsome salary of $1,800.00 a year. Ellen was delighted. In addition, I had accepted summer's work as a Field Supervisor for Frontier College which meant much travel by train to such distant places as Levack, Heron Bay, Kakabeka Falls, Ferland, Nakina, Negogami, and Sioux Lookout. In each of these I visited Frontier College men to assist them, when necessary, with teaching suggestions and to write reports of their work for Dr. Bradwin whose letters awaited me from time to time on my tour. One of them I still have; it's typical of this humane man, of his interest in me and in each of the men whom I visited.

> Now what I want you to do is to consult your timetable and see what connections there are between Nakina and Hearst; then inquire if it is possible to drop off the train at Negogami. If no stop is made there, find out what would be the

closest station where you could get off. You might then get a freight or 'hoof it' to Negogami.

The young man located at Negogami is Coatsworth; he is the grandson of Judge Coatsworth and quite a promising boy. He is, however, barely twenty-one and the work is a regular rough-and-tumble job. But from his reports I think he is measuring up well. There is, of course, the old trouble of shifting men, changing plans, reducing camp—as well as the impact of new arrivals. But then—that is camp life, that is why Frontier College is there. Our field is the migratory worker.

If you go to Hearst, I would suggest you stop at Anderson's boarding house—if it's still there— it is a Swedish stopping place—clean as a pin.

When you are in Hearst, I want you to feel, Ross, you are at an old rendezvous of Frontier College. . . The little river you cross before you get into the place, I crossed with a pack on my back by 'cooning' a pole which lay across it. It was dark and at flood time in the month of May. The river that night seemed to me a regular Niagara. . . That was, I would say, about 1910.

I have given you a big task for you have to carry Frontier College on your shoulders wherever you go. And I want you to be proud of your work.

p.s. If you find the agent at Nakina obliging, be sure to slip him a good ten-cent smoke.

Negogami remains in my mind still as a very bad location. On July 31 in a letter to Iain I described my visit to Coatsworth:

I walked in 9 1/4 miles over a corduroy trail to the camp on the TransCanada Highway. It was the most forsaken place I've ever been in—a real sump of muskeg and stunted jackpine. The drinking water rates Grade E, government

70

tested. They dope it themselves with chlorine and chloride of lime. Imagine! They simply pour a quart solution of chloride of lime down the shallow well and then treat the water afterwards with chlorine before drinking it. It's most un-palatable. While I was there several men booked off sick—sore throat and cramps. The Frontier College man is sticking it well. I got a ride out on a 'cat' which is the only machine that can travel the road. The black flies are bad, and I have swol-len lymph glands on my neck.

Altogether, this was a fascinating summer that passed too soon into the routine and tensions of the classroom. Rommel's successes in North Africa and the crushing speed of the German advance into Russia's heartland hardly troubled me as I seldom saw a newspaper. But even so the war did creep into my correspondence. Hughie in Petawawa spoke of a demonstration shoot of twenty-nine rounds he had seen fired by a troop of 18-pdrs. "During the first fifteen rounds we were at the O.P., and the guns were some 3500 yards away. It was thrilling to hear 'SHOT ONE' over the telephone and ten seconds later hear a whistle overhead, then see a puff of smoke a few hundred yards ahead where the shell had burst." Later in his letter he said he had been one of the numbers on a special 25-pdr. gun. Although I had no way then of knowing that the 25-pdr. was to be one of the great artillery pieces of World War II, the knowledge that Hugh was training on such a weapon and that his everyday life was so filled with stirring action made me very aware of something I was missing and grudged him. Fortunately for me, I was soon much too busy to allow envy a place in my affections.

By autumn, I had once more placed a divider between myself and Canada's active army. Instead of observing shoots at Petawawa with live ammunition, as Hughie was, I was teach-ing five second forms in Canadian history, two first forms in British history, and two others in English. Timmins, I soon found out, however, was not a kind of educational oasis in the north woods.

Newspapers and radios kept this gold-mining community just as aware and sensitive to the outside world as Toronto was. The war, for example, intruded into nearly all aspects of the school's life. My own classroom was no exception where the class's purchase of War Savings Stamps was entered daily at the back of the room on a large painted thermometer which bore the caption, "Way Hey Up She Rises!" The rest of the bulletin board at the back was given over to maps and pictures of the war as it raced over Europe and North Africa.

The surrender of the Winnipeg Grenadiers and the Royal Rifles of Canada after the fall of Hong Kong on Christmas Day, 1941, brought the war menacingly close to all Canadians. Other events before Christmas were much more serious: the Japanese assault on Pearl Harbour; the loss of the *Prince of Wales* and the *Repulse* off Kwantan; and, on December 11, the declaration of war on the United States by Germany and Japan.

The war made its mark, too, on my paycheques which showed a deduction of $12.60 a month under the heading "War Defense Tax," $4.00 for War Savings Certificates, and, in the new year, deductions for Income Tax. By the time I had sent money to Ellen and occasionally to Iain, I was often left with a bank balance barely enough to cover board and room. Even so, I told Ellen I intended to come home for Christmas.

Ellen's reply to this letter made clear that she, too, had her own financial worries. She was not going to make a Christmas cake or send out Christmas cards. Coal, at $16.00 a ton was expensive enough to cause her to sift all the ashes. But her greatest worry was Rab's health. He had been home for three weeks complaining about indigestion and shortness of breath. "If it's his heart," she wrote, "he may not be here another Christmas. Seems as if there's always something to take the joy out of life."

With papers to mark and four long, hard days carrying mail at the Post Office, the holiday time passed very quickly. I did, however, have a date with a nurse named Eileen who was altogether too warmly interested in my career but was really good fun—much livelier than Elizabeth. I had not heard from her for over six months.

I returned to Timmins on January 5, my birthday, and settled to the classroom round, writing regularly to Ellen who had gone back to nursing an elderly lady. Late in January both she and Rab had flu. She recovered quickly, but he became steadily worse and could not sleep for severe pains in his head. When these left, his head broke out in a mass of sores. Ellen gave up a nursing job she'd just accepted, this time to care for Rab. By February 17, Rab was in bed all the time, and Ellen was entirely dependent upon my help. On March 14 she wrote to me saying that she thought my father was not going to get better; "he is very thin and can no longer get out of bed by himself or even stoop to put on his slippers."

But despite his condition, Rab did begin to recover slowly as March moved to its close. Perhaps it was his reviving health which encouraged them to think of moving away from Woodstock. A visit from an old friend in West Zorra seems to have offered the necessary encouragement. This time the move was to an abandoned manse and glebe a mile east of the village of Harrington, where they thought they could succeed much better than in town. The rent for the huge red brick house was just $8.00 a month, and as the glebe of four acres had a small coach house on it, Ellen immediately decided to raise poultry while Rab promoted the idea that they should have a cow to produce their own butter and milk—and, he was sure, milk cheques every month.

At Harrington, Rab's health slowly improved as did his mental outlook. He was back home again where his life had begun just above the manse and inside the guarding ring of maples on the outer edge of the esker. It was his grandfather who had given the land where the manse stood to the church some eighty-six years previously.

Although the manse was at least twice too large for their requirements, Ellen's ability, both to collect belongings and to keep them, meant that she had furniture for most of it and was able to make it homelike. The old coach house was close to derelict status—even the rats had left it—but, with Iain's help in the spring, Rab made it reasonably comfortable for a Jersey cow and for the chickens, ducks, and turkeys which Ellen hatched from settings of eggs. They planted a large garden, and Ellen looked forward to their being self-sufficient.

Meantime my teaching was eventful enough. I was determined to keep good order among my restless forms for the O.C.E. word was that a poor disciplinarian was a person who soon got noticed and was likely not to last long in the profession. Of the nine forms I taught during the week, the most trying was my home form of thirty-six boys of whom twelve were repeaters. To maintain discipline was a challenge which I did not always rise to humanely and creditably. But I survived, and 1G seemed none the worse for the experience, although I still regret having slapped one of the repeaters for being insolent.

And so, throughout the winter, my apprenticeship in front of large classes ran its course. Each of them left me at the end of thirty-five minutes to be replaced by another throughout the day whenever the bells sounded. Once a week I had a spare period. My nights were given over to lesson preparation and the unending drudgery of marking assignments. It wasn't easy to simulate enthusiasm the day after in the classroom, although some days went well and even brought surprises as when one of the boys in 1G brought me a bound edition of newspapers dated 1792-94. It was a treasure. I read the account to the class from one of them of the execution of Louis XVI which impressed them much more than the one they had in their history text. Another student, a second-form girl, brought along a set of pictorial magazines of the Riel Rebellion containing maps dated 1885. Teaching at such times, I wrote, could be fun.

By the end of the spring term, I was tired and the rewards of teaching hardly discernible as I continued to keep order and stuff facts into heads that refused rightly to be so stuffed. I could not then and never did give sufficient recognition to one of B.C. Diltz's off-the-cuff remarks; "So what the sweet hell, Ross, does it matter!"

For me at that time everything did matter. Even my Sundays were committed to busyness as I noted in my diary:

I went to the Presbyterian service last Sunday
after I had taught my Sunday School class at the
United Church. I was astonished to find I am a
distant relative of the Presbyterian minister,
scions of the same crofter stock. I was invited to
his apartment after the service and found both
him and his wife friendly and warm-hearted.

From now on I appeared regularly at both the United and
Presbyterian churches. I've forgotten now why I began attending the nearby United Church when I was a Presbyterian. My
pious activities, however, had consequences. What I heard one
evening from the Presbyterian pulpit at the end of a lengthy
prayer quite unsettled me. Straying to current events and his
country's need, my relative in a burst of fervour concluded
with these words: "Lord, if it be Thy will, place us all in the
firing line." The next week, after my Sunday School lesson, my
diary entry was both cryptic and prophetic: "Good God! What a
hypocrite I am becoming."

If my church connections were troubling me, my civilian
status was of even more concern. Despite the need for me as a
teacher and the security offered, I thought there was a far
greater need and a more honourable role for me on Active Service. I could not accept the possibility of being labelled a draft
dodger. My unrest came to crisis on April 5, 1942 when I
handed in my resignation to Principal Murray. Twelve days
later I had a letter from the Timmins Board of Education grant-
ing my request for "leave of absence for the duration."

In the classroom my spirits flagged. "Teaching," I complained to Iain, "has stultifying requirements."

Of these the most annoying are the five sets of
reports I have to prepare for the nine courses I
teach throughout the school year. For my 225 students these add up to 2025 entries, each of which
is the result of averages derived from marking
hundreds of assignments and grading tests and
term examinations. It is a soul-destroying operation and one which daunts me as I think how

often it must still be performed before I am superannuated about A.D. 1977.

The last day of classes was June 6, 1942. On that day, nearly six thousand miles away, General Rommel had outfought General Ritchie's Eighth Army and forced its retreat towards Egypt. Two weeks later Tobruk fell and with its fall 33,000 men of all ranks passed into German captivity. In Britain on June 11, Churchill decided that the ill-fated Dieppe raid should take place. At sea, between January and May of 1942, the British lost about 282 ships, for the most part in the west Atlantic.

The war was, of course, like mention of the weather, all about us, especially in the great black headlines of the newspapers and in the despatches from war correspondents. Of my close friends from Queen's days, both McRuer and Jenkyn had enlisted, the former in the Air Force and the latter in the army by way of the Officers' Training Corps in Brockville. Jenkyn took delight in addressing me as "dear draft dodger" and in warning me how gruelling the course was. He alarmed me, too, by pointing out that the demand for officer material was slackening off because more and more N.C.Os from Overseas were being sent back to Canada to be trained for commissioned ranks.

Because of the bruising demands I made for myself in the classroom, I remember my year in Timmins with little warmth. The friends I made did their best to loosen me up with invitations to dinner, bridge games, and bowling. The male teachers included me in one or two of the beer sessions which they staged in the winter behind closed drapes in their homes. In the spring, they took me on fishing expeditions up the Mattagami River or out to Frederick House Lake. But such social activities—kindly meant as they were—I often resisted as inroads on my work time. For this reason, too, I made no advances to young ladies and worried little that my correspondence with Elizabeth had withered away. What I more and more looked forward to was my release from the classroom.

The last day of classes, however, presented a surprise which I recorded with just a little pride in my diary:

I said goodbye to my classes and twice was roundly cheered—whether out of relief that I was leaving, or from patriotism, or affection I cannot say.

The finest compliment, however, was from my home form 1G, who with impressive volume and much discord, sang 'For He's a Jolly Good Fellow.' Such display of emotion made me wince and regret that I had so often tyrannized over them for the sake of discipline, but there they were—all smiles and pushing a spokesman forward who presented me with a fine Buxton wallet—something I needed.

I am, as I think of this boisterous lot, just a bit proud of my home form which surpassed all the classes in the school in their purchasing of War Savings Stamps. I wonder, too, if I've given teaching a fair trial period.

A few days later, while I was in the midst of supervising examinations, for which I was paid six dollars a day, I was again surprised when the whole of one of my second forms trooped into my room before nine o'clock. From their midst I reported:

Pretty Betty Simpson, with some poise and charm, came forward to present me with a sterling silver disc and bracelet engraved "A. M. Ross from 2D." As well, she gave me a lovely farewell card on which all of them had put their names. I hope my stumbling words of thanks were adequate, for I was very touched. And now that I look at the bracelet I am anxious to wear it. It's just possible that had I been more civil—even affectionate—in my classroom control of such groups as 2D I might have enjoyed this year much more than I have.

That night I was invited to a farewell dinner with my landlady and her husband. It was a delicious meal with a blackberry cordial. The dinner remains in my mind for the reproof I received from my hostess; "Sandy, you are a fool to enlist!"

Chapter 6

Brockville And Petawawa

I left Timmins gladly on a Monday evening after having received a telegram from Major Miller of Toronto's C.O.T.C. telling me to report on Tuesday, June 16, at the Stanley Barracks for the preliminaries leading to Brockville. He said he could recommend me there as an Infantry Officer. It was a long night in the Northland coach marking Canadian history papers, a task which I completed the next day between interviews and a medical. The results and the papers were dispatched late Tuesday to John Bowden who had agreed to enter the marks for me at the school office. So ended my obligations to the Timmins Board of Education.

On Thursday I completed another interview which followed an intelligence test given by Captain Kitchin at the Horse Exhibition Grounds. "God knows," my diary reads, "how I managed to make a credible showing on the "M" Test, but the results were such that I was recommended for either Signals or Artillery." With Hughie in mind, I chose the guns.

Pleased with my military progress, I gave way to a capricious humour to see the long-silent Elizabeth. I found her telephone number in the Hart House Directory. She recognized my voice and warmly invited me to the flat she shared with her sister and, when I appeared, just as warmly walked into my arms and a kiss. I thought her every action charming. We dined at the Honey Dew and afterwards saw Jean Gabin in a movie at the Imperial. I left her much later wondering why our acquaintance had to be so intermittent and determined not to let it lapse again. The next day I was in Stratford where I met Harold Wilson, an old family friend, who drove me to Harrington. My parents had few words when I told them what I had done in Toronto.

As it was a month before I had to report again at the Stanley Barracks, I worked at home in the interval painting two rooms, and the long verandah with its endless spindles, and cutting brush along the fence lines. As well I helped Rab with his chores for he still had very little strength in his arms. Toward the end of my free time, I made a trip for Dr. Bradwin to De Cew Falls to see a light-headed theological student who had come to the conclusion that his position in life conflicted with that of the workers on the extra gang.

On Sunday, July 12, attired in the battle dress I had bought in the Stratford Armouries for twelve dollars, I was back in the Stanley Barracks, very content with myself. That night my diary entry was succinct: "It's the greatest relief ever experienced—to be finally in khaki." I made no effort to explain.

Was it a comfort to be free of responsibility for my parents? To be free of the carking troubles and cares of the classroom? To be able to delay giving an answer to Principal Bradwin who, at lunch on July 11, pressed me to consider taking a doctorate after the war so that I might be his successor at Frontier College? Was it a solace to feel no need in the future to tote mailbags on Christmas Day? To be forever beyond the whisper of "draft dodger"? Or was it, as William Empson put it, merely "the best thing to be up and go"? Whatever it was, I was satisfied; I had at last pitched my tent in a sunny field.

Late that evening I wrote to Ellen telling her of the financial arrangements I had made for her and Rab:

> Most of the enlistment details have been attended to. I've even made my will and arranged an allowance for you—nine days' pay a month, total of $38.25. Because Dad is unable to work, I expect your total allowance and assigned pay

will amount to $63.25 a month.

I told the people here that in the last six months I had contributed $360.00 directly to your support; in addition, I paid $150.00 in medical bills for you. This latter figure is high, but the former may be low. Please remember these figures as a government pension man will in all probability visit you.

I must sign off now for I can hear the pipes leading a battalion off to Church parade. They are playing "The Barren Rocks of Aden." Dad would love to see and hear them.

Ellen replied to this letter the same day she received it. As usual she sent some clouds across my sunny landscape:

Yours received today and was surprised at your being in Toronto and so not even one holiday for you.

I have read and re-read your letter and have resolved if that Pension man comes and tries bantering to give him what's coming. I shall tell him you did not enlist because of higher pay. Do you realize you will make $350.00 less this year than if you had been teaching? I shall tell him you did not enlist because you couldn't get a job and also I will tell him your education was partly to help support us in our old days—something we looked forward to.

I smiled at the nature of your will. I mean—I hope you will never leave Canada—and come back safely. This winter will take quite a bit... I have figured thus: $20 fuel per month, $8 rent, $3 electricity, $16 provisions, then feed for the hens, then clothing. How much would we have left out of sixty dollars? Besides there is the upkeep of the manse.

There was no mention of Iain. Since mid-May he had been out for Frontier College at the McKenzie Red Lake Gold Mine where he spent his days underground tramming ore from the ore pass to the cage. The food, he said, was excellent but cost $1.40 a day; wages were low, $4.75 a day, seven days a week and two holidays a year, July 1 and Christmas. Many of the miners were Manitoba farmers who usually stayed on the job for four months and then returned to their farms for seeding and harvest. Because of camp amenities, Iain was having trouble attracting men to his classes after work.

Not until August 4 did I find time to resume my diary. Brockville left little time for idle writing, but I tried to give some impressions of the life I was now leading:

> On our arrival we were greeted by a group of of-
> ficers in training inside the compound who set
> up a hellish din of 'on the double, you guys!', an
> order impossible to obey because of the duffle
> bags and stacks of pamphlets which encum-
> bered us. Since then, we have been treated very
> much as if we were privates in the poor bloody
> infantry.
>
> You say 'Sir' respectfully to 'one-pippers'
> and to the C.S.M. Fatigue and shorts are the
> dress including putties, which I can now put on
> tolerably well. Reveille is 6:00 a.m.; P.T. 6:15;
> breakfast 7:00-7:30; and markers are called at
> 7:40. The parade square is a kind of *Sacra Via*
> where we put ourselves on display before a
> variety of tyrants whose scrutiny and frequent
> damnation ranges from the tilt of your pith hel-
> met to the neatness of your shoe laces.
>
> We drill or manoeuvre in both rain and
> shine. Have had one night route march in which
> we got lost somewhere beyond Tin Cap. By 1:00
> a.m. we were safely back in camp tired as dogs
> out of harness.

The Common-to-Arms Training proceeded very quickly. Two days were spent back in the sand hills firing infantry weapons, the nights sleeping on the ground. It was decidedly chilly but "the next time," I said, "I shall know how to roll my blankets." Back in camp, parade square drill, theory in class-room, and tests kept us constantly busy. My tent mate was a Rhodes Scholar just returned from England with an Oxford First in Mathematics and Economics. I wondered if the army could not do better than make him an infantry officer. Six of the men in my platoon were N.C.O.s back from Overseas.

Our course ended with a twelve-day scheme held some twenty miles north of Brockville. The instructors tried to make it as realistic as possible, even to blowing a man's finger off when a thunder flash was carelessly thrown. We had very little sleep. As we had been told that we'd have a long weekend before beginning our Special-to-Arms training, I had written to Ellen to find out if I could bring Elizabeth home with me for that time. As well, I had an interview with Colonel Gregg, V.C. who accepted my transfer into Artillery. Ellen's acquiescence made the prospect of this weekend altogether very cheerful.

At the last moment, as I hastened to remove the grime of the twelve days in the open, when it had rained much of the time, I made the necessary travel arrangements. The camp barber scalped me because I fell asleep while I was in his care. "I must," I told Iain, "have looked like a raw recruit." But wearing my new wedge cap, gleaming Dack boots, my summer drill, put-tees neatly rolled, and with my swagger stick horizontal to the good earth, I regained my aplomb and entrained for Toronto. All went well until Elizabeth and I left Stratford about 9:00 p.m. on the bus to St. Mary's. I told Iain what happened:

> I was dreadfully tired for I had had little sleep
> for forty-eight hours. Elizabeth was demurely
> quiet and left matters very much in my hands—
> which, I suppose, was quite proper—if most un-
> wise. I told the driver to put us down at the
> Halfway House where Dad and Harold would
> be waiting for us in Harold's car.
>
> What happened was that I fell asleep. The
> bus driver forgot my instructions and when I
> awoke we were in St. Mary's, five miles beyond

the Halfway House. I protested, but I might better have held my breath.

But for once St. Christopher was with me, even at 10:30 p.m., when the last bus for Stratford was due to leave St. Mary's. We took it, and I shall never forget the relief I felt when I saw Harold's car in the headlights of the bus. He had guessed that we had missed the stop and had waited. I must say Elizabeth seemed much less worried than I, but then she was innocent of the six miles of lonely country roads that wound away from the Halfway to Harrington, of parents who did not have a telephone, and of a boyfriend with less than five dollars in his wallet.

The visit home, however, went off very well despite the cistern being dry and I having to carry water from the well for the bathroom and toilet tank. Ellen had the manse spotless and served delicious meals from her favourite recipes. Elizabeth and I made the acquaintance of Rab's cow and pig and Ellen's poultry, visited the village, and walked about the glebe in moonlight. Elizabeth pleased both parents and surprised Ellen by sending her a four-pound box of Laura Secord's from Toronto and a letter thanking her for her hospitality. It was, Ellen said, the largest box of chocolates she had ever received. My own fear that Elizabeth might find us meanly straitened proved groundless either because she was too polite and tactful to betray any concern or because Ellen's efforts had created a fairly attractive facade that screened our shortcomings. On our last night we had neighbours in for dinner after which Harold and Rab got out their fiddles and played for an hour. The evening ended when Ellen served coffee and large slices of her white layer cake with its rich lemon cream filling and icing. The next day Harold took Elizabeth and me to Stratford.

Back in Brockville, I began the month's Special-to-Arms Training in Artillery. It proved much more difficult than I imagined, both theory and practice. The latter was particularly confusing because we trained both on 18- and 25-pdrs., the drill for each of which was sufficiently different to confuse me. The technique was, of course, child's play for the gunner N.C.O.s just back from field regiments in Britain. Meantime I struggled on, just passing tests and consoling myself by saying, if the worst happened, I could always transfer to infantry.

On August 22 Ellen was informed by the Dependants' Allowance Board of the Department of National Defence that in addition to my assigned pay, Dependants' Allowance in their favour had been granted at the rate of $25.00 a month effective July 10, 1942. For the first time in her life she now had a regular income. Already she was putting this allowance in the bank while depending upon her farm produce to meet their cash needs despite fatalities: "Since I last wrote to you, the smallest of my turkeys has passed on, one of the ducks was killed on the road, and one of my grey chickens hung itself on the cotton netting in the stable."

From now on Ellen's existence was tied to the minutiae of the house, the barn, the bank, news of her neighbours, and letters to me. Iain's letters, she complained, were too brief and infrequent. As always, Rab remained in the background, a kind of liability, a marital blunder which she was too proud to proclaim but which her letters to me made obvious. On October 7 she told of Rab's having forgotten to arrange to have a cheque cashed. As a result she had to go herself to to the bank in Embro. Going, she got a ride with a neighbour driving to Woodstock. Returning, she found no one to offer her a ride. The consequence was that she walked six miles back home; the weather was cold and threatening rain. "Never, never," she avowed, "will I ever depend upon your father to do any business for me again."

That same day I wrote to her saying that 25 percent of my class had failed the Special-to-Arms Artillery qualification— and that I was one of the failures and had to repeat the course, which I told Ellen was better than being turfed out into the Infantry. All my leaves were cancelled for the next month, and I could not graduate until November 11. I did feel discouraged, I said, because I had never driven myself so hard to achieve something I wanted.

Ellen's reply to this letter was prompt:

> Sorry you feel so badly over your failure, but as
> 25 percent of your class failed, I do not see why
> you should worry. For my part, if they had sent
> you skylarking home, I would have been tickled
> pink.
>
> But perhaps ere now you will have some
> idea of how I loathed seeing you go into the
> army—not because of selfishness (as you probab-
> ly thought), but because I knew what army life is
> like, its hardships and the seclusion it imposes
> from civilian company and comforts. And above
> all, I know your strength is not enough to cope
> with that sort of life. Coming directly from high
> school teaching into the military was too much
> for you. That's why your nerves are so bad. Any
> time you feel like getting sick and coming home,
> you will have a warm welcome here!

Other letters arrived, too, at this time. McRuer wrote, spending much of his ink bewailing troubles that he was having with
his girlfriend with whom he had been fighting bitterly and
whom he thought he'd never marry now. Toward the end of his
letter his tone was lighter as he described his latest adventure:

> Spent a night feeling the breasts and legs of an
> Air Force girl on the train; her grammar was
> homicidal but her breasts untrammelled by a
> brassiere were comely and full, her legs round
> and soft. Were I not haunted by ghosts—ghosts
> that track the very cobblestones of the soul—I
> could have fallen in love with the lass.

Elizabeth, too, wrote. She had nearly completed the requirements for an M.A. at the University of Toronto and was now at
the Ontario College of Education which she was enjoying much
more than I had. Her letter was a cool and measured statement
giving no indication that I was at all essential to her happiness.

In Brockville meantime, I told Iain, I was learning much:

No marks lower than 90! And we had the
advantage of travelling last Saturday and
Sunday to Petawawa where we took four of our
25-pdrs. for a live shoot. The training area there
is sandy with much scrub bush, just open
enough for guns to deploy easily.

Once there we drew 150 rounds of high explosive and several rounds of smoke. The
repeaters manned the guns with the instructors
helping. We had our own field kitchens and
spent the night sleeping out on the ground. The
exercise has given me much confidence, and my
nerves have steadied—no more getting rattled.

On our return, the repeaters were unexpectedly given a
forty-eight-hour leave presumably because of the hardships
which we endured while at Petawawa but more likely because
the instructors wanted some time off. I ended up at a Convocation dance in Grant Hall in Kingston because I had failed to
find Iain. Fortunately I did find Jeanie, the nurse I had had for
my appendectomy. What I said in my diary entry was that we
danced until midnight and then, at her insistence, spent an hour
walking in a warm rain along the lake shore. It was during this
walk, as we stopped to watch the dim lights off the islands, that
Jeanie impulsively threw her arms about my neck and on tiptoe
kissed me as I'd never been kissed before. Then, as impulsively,
she withdrew and said, "That's the last one for you—no more,
ever. Guess why?" As I couldn't imagine what had caused this
emotional spasm, she explained that in one week's time she'd
be engaged and wearing a diamond. The rest of our walk filled
in details. If I returned to my brother's quarters better informed,
I was at the same time not a little saddened.

The next evening in Toronto I took Elizabeth to dinner and
to a show of her choosing. In my diary I complained that she
seemed more reserved than usual, somewhat uncertain and unable to relax with me—quite unlike Jeanie. Maybe, I wrote, it's
just that Kingston is more suited for lovers' moods. Toronto
crowds and traffic dampen your vital spirits. But, whatever the

reason, I left Elizabeth, as I had Jeanie, somewhat melancholy, and spent the rest of my leave quietly at home.

My Officer's Record of Service Book shows that I was attached to A-2, Canadian Army Training Centre, Petawawa from 14 November 1942 until 17 June 1943. A week after my arrival, I noted the occurrence of snow on the ground, P.T. outside at 0640 in the moonlight, and a new roommate, Fred Cooper, a graduate of the Ontario Agricultural College.

As at Brockville, I was given on my arrival a horde of pamphlets and told I'd have to work hard for the next eight weeks if I were to graduate and get my second pip. But by December 6 I had decided that the course was not nearly so trying as Brockville's and that I very much approved of the conscientious batman who had been assigned to Fred and me for shining our shoes and buttons, scrubbing our floor, and making our beds.

A letter at this time from one of my former 1G pupils in Timmins must have pleased me; in part it read: "I congratulate you in obtaining a commission. If you succeed as well against the enemy as you did against the more troublesome pupils of our class, you shall soon, I am sure, be appointed a Field Marshall! We all miss you very much and wish you were here to teach us history which is a sore subject with the majority of our class."

On the last day of the year, I wrote home to thank my parents for the good Christmas I had had. Dinner was memorable for the twenty-one pound turkey and the mince tarts that Ellen placed on her table. Visitors were frequent, and one evening we had a dance: Rab and Harold with violins and Ellen on the piano. It was fun, and I managed to dance with all the ladies. Afterwards on the way back to camp, I saw Elizabeth for a swift and blissful date until nearly four in the morning. "I am sure," I noted in my diary, "that she cares for me now as I do for her."

Hardly had I returned to Petawawa when I learned I was to be given furlough and embarkation leave from January 23 to February 8. From diary entries it appears I spent the first night of my leave with Iain in Kingston finding it not at all easy to appear manly when it was time for our farewell handshake. In Toronto, on Monday evening, I found Elizabeth who was frantically preparing lessons for her practice teaching at Forest Hill Collegiate. Eventually we set the lessons aside and went to see *Here We Go Again,* a very disappointing show, starring McCarthy and Fibber McGee. On Tuesday we had dinner at the Stoodleigh and then enjoyed *Claudia* at the Royal Alex even though an old lady near us, and the *Saturday Night,* too, said it should have been censored. Elizabeth looked very pretty and wore the brooch I had given her for Christmas.

Then came our goodbyes. I told her I loved her, and she admitted her love for me. Quivering lips sealed the understanding just before midnight. "I suppose," I wrote in my diary, "if I had had any money, that would have been the perfect time to have given her a diamond, but the formal engagement must wait." That decision proved to be perhaps another of my overly cautious approaches to this fascinating woman whom I never really knew.

I left Toronto on the 7:30 a.m. train, got off the bus at the Halfway House only to find six miles of snow-blocked roads ahead of me. In places not even a sleigh track was visible and, when such a track did appear, it was often off the road entirely and in the fields where the snow was less deep.

Sixteen hours of sleep at home put me to rights, and I enjoyed my leave, even managing a side trip to Woodstock to see friends and Hughie's mother and father. Hugh was with a L.A.A. Battery in Labrador. Eileen, I was told, had already enlisted and was Overseas with her hospital unit. When it came, the parting at home was a wrenching experience. It was a relief to be back on the train and enroute to Petawawa, where the month of February was just as cold as January had been. The pace of training, however, never slackened.

We were out nearly every day on deployments and shoots. I remember one night deployment when it was so cold that the firing mechanism on the guns would not work because the grease had congealed. In February, I had one of my bombardiers make me a trunk of fir wood. It was large enough to hold all my gear and even had a cedar tray in it. We couldn't find metal handles in the Pembroke hardware store but finally found them in a local undertaker's establishment. The trunk, in consequence, was dubbed "The Coffin."

Furlough and embarkation leave for me proved a false alarm because shortly after my return, I was chosen along with a former sergeant from Overseas (who was now commissioned) to remain off the draft and serve as instructors in Petawawa. Although both of us were disappointed, I was pleased to think I had so justified my enrollment in artillery. Ellen was delighted and hoped I'd now stay in Canada. Elizabeth, too, seemed pleased.

With the exception of a two-week stay in hospital, I was from early February until late June an officer in charge of a troop in A Battery. The close relationship with N.C.O.s and gunners was very good for me as I supervised progress from basic to advanced training. And I still remember my satisfaction when I presented certificates to several men of my troop who, under my instruction, had qualified as gun layers, a technique I had found so confusing in Brockville.

Always at A-2 we were kept busy: learning to drive wheeled vehicles; taking part in innumerable training sessions on the care and maintenance of the guns; being Camp Orderly Officer; digging and revetting gun pits; taking part in Church Parades; arranging and taking up night positions; and even serving as a junior officer on parades where offenders stood stiffly at attention for their sins of omission or commission before the fearsome, lean visage of Colonel E. B. McPherson. All this and more made my transition to an active regiment much easier than it might have been.

As always, I looked forward to the arrival of my mail. Elizabeth, at first, wrote regularly—on January 4 and 17, on February 7 and 19, then a delay to May 21 and another to July 1 when she told me she had accepted an appointment in a high school near Ottawa. Throughout her correspondence, she remained calm, not at all like one who had given her heart away. "I am so constituted [she told me] that I can't write very frequently. I'd rather save up my news for a really big splurge. But even so I'll do my best to remind you that you have a girlfriend on the bleaker side of the Atlantic." Because she left Toronto in early spring to spend a month with her parents in Sturgeon Falls, I never saw her again. What I expected of Elizabeth and what I deserved, as time went on, were two very different things.

During that spring, I took my duties with the Battery seriously, even selling $2800.00 worth of war bonds to members of A Troop. At the beginning of May, A Troop's relay team came second in the fifty-mile road race, for which act of endurance the team received fifteen dollars worth of War Certificates. Each week had its rigorous training schedule. Through May 11-15, the troop had, for example, two night deployments, an all-day route march (when rain wet all of us) and a shoot with live ammunition. On the shoot I served as the Gun Position Officer and thought that the men I had trained performed well and were steady during firing. That Saturday night I was a member of the Pembroke Patrol designed to help police the town's streets, especially after closing-time.

Because I had measles early in April, I was put in the Isolation Hospital where eventually I gained access to the Nursing Sister circle. Once I had recovered, I decided to take one of the Sisters who had nursed me to dinner at our Mess. It was not as simple an arrangement as I thought it might be because Sisters had to go out in threes. But when the time came I marshalled my three ladies in their "blues," took them to the Mess where the extras were quickly commandeered by other officers for the evening. The diary entry says only, "We had a good time, and I intend to see Louise again."

At the end of May, I was given a long weekend and asked Ellen if I could again bring Elizabeth home with me. This plan foundered when I discovered that Elizabeth had already left Toronto for the visit to her parents in Sturgeon Falls. Consequently, I went home alone to find Ellen and Rab well and the countryside freshly green with lilac coming in flower. Harrington seemed to me much more attractive than Petawawa's sandy scrub to which I unwillingly returned on May 30.

Quite unexpectedly I was given a second embarkation leave on June 11 for six days. Again—to the amazement of the local people—I appeared in Harrington. I could not see Iain in Kingston because he had gone out for Frontier College to work on the Alcan Highway. And I was unable to find Elizabeth in Toronto because she had lengthened her stay at home to be with her mother who was ill. From something I had said in one of my letters about going on to S-, she was expecting to see me in Sturgeon Falls, a reasonable assumption on her part. But my S- was meant for Stratford. The muddle was my fault and not least because I had left Petawawa in a great rush with hardly time to pack my haversack. Had I telephoned her from camp, I could have remedied matters. As it was, I disappointed her.

And just how clear my mind was on the morning I left is a question that still embarrasses me a little. Despite Ellen's warning that I should be wary of those Nursing Sisters, I had been attentive to Louise since late April. At home on June 14, when I had time to bring my diary up to date, I referred to a "real whipper-do" of a party put on to celebrate the opening of a new wing at the Petawawa Military Hospital the night before I went on this embarkation leave. "We danced until 2:00 a.m. Then Louise and I walked beneath the moon and the sky of stars, and I know now how really warming and unrestrained her kisses are." Compared, however, to Elizabeth, Louise had "no mind to speak of." It was a snobbish comment, a mean excuse for my own willingness to be her accomplice in setting amorous brush-fires, the limits of which were somewhat disturbing as I reviewed them the morning after. The embarkation leave offered a cooling respite.

The stay in Harrington was quiet. Ellen and Rab were anxious and uneasy as they knew this was really my final visit. While there I attempted to write a poem. My dissatisfaction with my muse appears in the many changes I made in the first two stanzas. The last one with its echo of other men's lines I left untouched.

Before Embarkation

I turn from the maples to the east,
    Westering down where the furrows fail
To greet the dusty road and feast

On sweeps of bird song from the swale;
And slowly trace the deep black earth,
    Mindful of my crofting stock and birth
        In Zorra
    Zorra, so rich and rarely mine.

Now from the piper comes "the Keel Row,"
    While man and maid take up the glad
Rhythms of the night's wildering flow
    Of schottische, reel, and folded plaid —
Until the morning's chastening theme
    Reminds a lad he may but dream
        Of Zorra
    Zorra, so blithe and rarely mine.

And if I walk not this way again
    Nor see moonlight on the misted stream
Nor hear the elms soughing in the lane
    Above wild roses in silent sleep—
May others sense and love and dream
    Of this good glebe, that I esteem
        In Zorra
    Zorra , so fair and rarely mine.

The return to Petawawa was uneventful. Again in Toronto I
telephoned Elizabeth, but she was still away. In camp all was a
mad rush as we had just the day to get ready for departure. At
last the "Coffin" was labelled and roped. My old trunk I sent
home. In late afternoon my battery major and captain so plied
me with rum and coke that my elevation became all too noticeable and my gait exceedingly uneven. Only by going to sleep in
my room was I able to lower my sights.

Once recovered, I checked to see that my gear had been
loaded and then returned to the Mess for dinner. Afterwards, in
light marching order, I set off for my *inamorata* at the hospital,
who was also under departure orders. Both of us had two
hours left. On the A ranges, on high ground overlooking the
transport, but conveniently screened, we established a tem-

porary bivouac. Inspired or debased by the demon rum, I took the ground sheet from my small pack, spread it on the ground and invited my Sister-in-Arms to recline. She accepted, and we had a good hour of body skirmish and testing of defenses. These held until I had to break off the assault and assemble for roll call and the three tonner that was taking us on the first leg of our Overseas journey.

Louise's departure was delayed at the last moment, and it was another month before her group left the country. That evening I became vividly aware of bruised lips and an embarrassing ache in my nether regions. "It may have been natural," I wrote, "but it hurt" and added that "Elizabeth, of course, would have had more sense than to roll with me on a ground sheet." I then quoted Wyatt's lines which I must have thought a comfort, maybe some justification for my shifty virtue: "Blame not my lute! for he must sound/ Of this and that as liketh me."

Throughout my love tangle with Louise, I had, in the inside pocket of my battle dress blouse, Elizabeth's last letter to me in Canada which I had found in my mail slot in the Mess after I'd slept off that afternoon's rum and coke. The letter's close was terse and affectionate: "Bye, Bye and God bless you. Yours , Elizabeth." For some days, the memory of Elizabeth's farewell and the largesse of Louise's breasts and lips mingled distressingly in my mind.

Gradually, however, my distress lessened as we moved by train to Windsor, Nova Scotia, where we waited for a Halifax convoy. From Windsor I wrote to Ellen asking her to keep all my letters and those of others that I sent home. I also gave her my forwarding address, #1, C.A.R.U., Canadian Army, Overseas.

On July 17, 1943, I finished a letter to my parents which I had begun aboard ship someplace in the western Atlantic.

> Our vessel and the whole convoy are now
> blanketed in fog so thick you cannot see an ob-
> ject two hundred feet away. For hours now we
> have been steering a course by compass alone.
> All about is the hoarse cry of fog horns. Without

them, it would be mere guesswork to say we are but one of a hundred ships being shepherded by the Navy to our destination. And I think the shepherd is magnificent.

So far as my own living accommodation goes, I have never known such luxury as I now have. I'm on a 'Banana Boat' where I have a stateroom to myself in which there is running water, a clothes closet, a full-length mirror, three lights, two port holes, an electric fan, heater, chairs, curtains and rugs on the floor. The colour scheme is light green and cream.

The stewards bring a pitcher of hot water to you in the morning for shaving; they draw your bath, make your bed, and even light your cigarettes for you if the opportunity offers. Last evening for dinner we had roast chicken and plum pudding. I am quite sure that very few of His Majesty's troops have had this treatment.

It all seems so dreamlike until it's your turn to man the Ack-Ack guns, which chore may come any time of the day or night, if you are an artillery officer. Last night my watch was from 1:00 a.m. until 2:00 a.m. on the forward starboard gun, and how cold and lonely it was with the masthead doing its slow evolution about the stars, the wind in the rigging, and the ship making its way through the waste of cold, green seas. And all the time the sounds of the fog horns of our sister ships and the short, shrill yelps of the corvette escorts. I doubt if I really know how perilous this journey is. If anything does happen, I suspect one has little chance of living to tell about it.

I wish, however, I knew more and could tell you about the shipping, especially its appearance on a clear day. Since all the ships in the main convoy travel at the same speed, you have the illusion that they are stationary on the heaving waters. Sometimes in mist or fog it's hard to recognize them as ships. Thank heaven the U-boat menace has eased off. Only once did I see our escorts drop depth charges and only once, as we neared port, did an air raid alarm sound. I doubled to my action station as the Captain gave the order 'Strip the guns!' Fortunately the enemy failed to get through to us —and a good thing, too, as I had decided early on that I was a very vulnerable target behind the Oerlikon. At least a 25-pdr. has an adequate shield.

But really this crossing has been for me pure sensual delight. No hardships. Wonderful service and food. Today I bought two cartons of chocolate bars (48) at five cents apiece. After that, flat on my back in my cabin, I finished reading *Cranford* from the ship's library. Do try to get it if you can. It's a wonderful release from this too, too sad world.

But the world I was about to experience was not a sad one —at least as I saw it at first and wrote about it.

Chapter 7

England

Although Bordon in Hampshire was a large, inhibiting, uninteresting military camp, its immediate environs were fascinating. On my first Sunday I walked beyond the camp to the east along narrow roads with hedgerows arching overhead, creating an inviting green tunnel for traffic and a rather dangerous passage for me. The weeds of the verges, the moss and vines on the trees, the lack of directional signs, the traffic on the wrong side of the road, the fields glimpsed through soft English air, even the sky itself, were new and strange.

About a mile away from Bordon's brick monotony, I found lovely country cottages set in shrubbery with their garden gates and walks edged profusely with roses and dahlias. And I also came upon the Red Lion, my first English pub, where I sat in the early evening with a pint of brown ale in my hand. Around me were local citizens chatting over their glasses or playing darts, Canadian gunners drinking quietly with their English girls, and even grandmothers knitting and sipping their pints on the green outside with their dogs curled up at their feet. It was all so different from a Canadian beer parlour.

Many miles south of Bordon on a shoot, I discovered another landscape: the South Downs and in their midst another English institution, the church. I saw the former for the first time from an artillery Observation Post. Huge, rolling, bare-backed hills with great fleecy clouds sending blotches of shadow racing over them and strong Channel breezes winnowing fields of wheat below in the valley. Huddled away in a fold of the hills just beyond our firing area was an old flint church at one end of a village. The walls of the church were made of flint, the same rock that made digging slit trenches on the Downs so frustrating and hard. The church's tower was rectangular without a steeple. Moving from the litch-gate to the west door and through the nave to the chancel was like walking from the handiwork of this century back to that of the Normans, and then, at the altar, to that of the Victorians. Much of my two hours there in the evening was spent reading the entries on the brasses—a chronicle of parish nomenclature and history from 1080 A.D. to the present.

My sightseeing, of course, suffered much from the demands of artillery training which soon became just one course following another. After a refresher in gunnery, came a week on Motor Transport, where I learned to double clutch and drive field artillery tractors; and then I was given a week on motorcycles on the sandy wastes of a heath not far from Bordon. It was here that, misjudging one of the tracks through the broom and gorse, I drove my Harley-Davidson over the edge of a gravel pit for a vertical descent of at least twelve feet, I flying off one way and the bike another. No harm was done, either to the bike or to me. I was lucky.

My walks about Bordon in the evenings were made much more interesting when, shortly after my arrival, I met a C.W.A.C. private walking in my direction. Barbara was, as I explained a little unwisely to Ellen, attached to the army laundry unit outside the camp. My mother made no comment; her silence was enough.

It was not long, however, before Barbara appeared in my diary as "my petite C.W.A.C." with comments on how she liked long walks and how amusing her constant chatter was. She was, I averred, distinctly pretty with as trim a figure as any I've ever wished to hold in my arms. Once it was dark or nearly so, we could drink together in the pubs, and no one was likely to notice our ranks. I found out much about her by just listening while she complained about her coarse khaki issue underwear, told me about her birth in Wales, a spell as a nurse in training in Canada, and her work in the laundry. It was from her lips that I first heard the song "Roll Me Over in the Clover." The time was right and the location, too, but I took no advantage of the suggestion. So far as I know she was not disappointed.

Later I undertook an adventure with her that could have landed Sandy Ross, officer and gentleman, into real trouble. I took my C.W.A.C. to a dance at the Officers' Mess. It was very much a cloak and dagger affair. I smuggled her into my room after dark, where she removed her tell-tale identity, donned a most becoming evening dress and necklace, and then proceeded to have a very good time with half the unattached subalterns of the Mess. She was a most charming package when arrayed in satin, silk, and slippers. But as successful as this venture was, I decided not to run such risks again, and I did not mention the indiscretion to Ellen.

Fortunately for me Barbara left Bordon at this time for a month's course in Wales so that subaltern gossip cooled, and I had a chance to regroup and to catch up on my letter writing. For some time, too, I had been thinking about Eileen whom I remembered from Woodstock days. That subject blossomed when I heard from her. She thought she'd be free for a party in a week's time and suggested I seek out her hospital unit north of London. As I had had no news of Louise, I thought this a good idea and accordingly made my travel arrangements.

My visit to Eileen was full of the unexpected. The message relayed to her led her to believe that the date had been cancelled so she made other arrangements and went off to London for the weekend. Happily, when I arrived at her hospital, I met an M.O. named Ross who immediately decided that one of his own clan had to be accommodated. He not only found his clansman a bed for the night but, my diary relates, also came up with "a veritable cherub of a Sister who sweetly volunteered" to care for me throughout the evening, providing I could put in an hour by myself until she completed some work that had to be done first. While waiting for the Sister, I fell into the hands of another M.O., a visitor, who decided we should walk about the grounds. Whether it was intentional or not on his part, we ended up in the morgue where an autopsy had just been performed.

The body lay glaringly nude on a white enamel benchlike table under bright lights. A very voluble Staff Sergeant was sewing the corpse up from navel to chest with a coarse needle and heavy thread. My peripatetic doctor wanted to know the details, which Staff was only too willing to provide while I stood uneasily trying not to look as if I wanted to be any place else than where I was. Staff began at the beginning.

The corpse was that of a Canadian soldier who, in life, had been married twice, once in Canada and again illegally in Britain where his search for even fuller sexual satisfaction had given him both syphilis and gonorrhoea. From the ravages of these, he had slowly wasted away. The Staff Sergeant then gave an account of the effects of the diseases upon his vital organs, using medical terms unintelligible to me.

What I could comprehend was the intense starkness of the room and its centrepiece, the dead man, whose body brought back to my mind Simon Munro's scalded pig. Some details went beyond the scene by Simon's straw stack: the dry odour of disinfectant, the human head, the red cord around the penis and the cork in the anus—and just the bare efficiency of the place. Other details paralleled the pig's appearance: the body with its long incision from neck to pelvis, the lips drawn back from the teeth, the sunken eyeballs, the hands and feet so white and pointed, and in the corner the guts gathered together in a large shiny bucket.

Eventually my M.O. had enough medical history from the Staff Sergeant, and we left the morgue—I rather sick and faint but pleased, too, that I had survived unnoticed, especially since I had had nothing to eat since noon. I remember little of what my doctor guide said to me afterwards or even where we went next. But for the rest of the night I saw the corpse sometimes juxtaposed with Simon's pig, always making conversation with my pretty but shy partner difficult, as I thought of how the cadaver underscored Simon's advice about the safest place in which to store your pecker. Finally the party ended, and I tumbled into a bed in the doctor's wing of the hospital.

In my account to Ellen, I omitted my adventure at the morgue telling her of other impressions belonging to my trip, of the big double-decker red buses with the driver up front in a closed cab and the "clippies," usually women in slacks and jackets of rough blue serge with leather cuffs, dispensing tickets which came from a silvery metal box suspended by wide leather straps about the shoulders.

"Once the passengers are all on board at the stop," I wrote, "the clippie sings out 'Hold tight' and the bus lurches away into the traffic. Then she begins cranking out tickets from the metal box with one hand while with the other deftly making change from a large leather pouch that hangs at her side." I still think of these wiry women, in charge of their great swaying buses with the corkscrew stairs linking the decks, as remarkably efficient and cheerful, willing to answer patiently the same questions posed by anxious soldiers day after day.

Then I told my mother about the London Underground which I first encountered at Waterloo Station where I stood like a country bumpkin in the midst of hundreds of rushing people all more certain of what they had to do than I was. When I did realize that the dozens of kiosks, ticket counters, and trains on the surface were not what I needed, I found the entrance to the Underground and began the descent.

Dante, I said, could have used my impressions as I was carried about three hundred feet down on escalators bearing travellers stacked one below the other to a dusty cavern through which snub-nosed trains bore down upon me like things demented and condemned to run forever upon an electrified track. Once aboard, I was whirled in a crescendo of sound through darkness with just a few inches to spare between the car and the walls around it. Lighted openings came up, I said, with names strange yet familiar: Charing Cross, Leicester Square, Camden Town, Highgate. From Waterloo on, I saw many signs of people having slept in these underground tunnels at night to escape air raids: double deck beds, makeshift dividers for some privacy, old suitcases, and the usual debris of discarded newspapers wildly stirring in the windy passage of the trains.

Once off the train, I ascended to the real world where I said I took a "Green Line" bus to Eileen's hospital to attend a dance until midnight. There I was astonished to meet Harry Jeffries, with whom I had worked on the railroad at Onondaga; he was now an Orderly at this hospital. I concluded my letter by saying I had enjoyed my evening very much—hardly the whole truth, but comforting for my reader.

Rather strangely, few references to the conduct of the war appear in my letters home from Britain, although it must have been a lively topic wherever I went. I did say, however, that I had survived my first air raid shortly after my arrival in Bordon. "I was," I told Ellen, "sound asleep when the sirens went off and quite bewildered until I got my bearings, my blanket, my gas-bag and—amid a turmoil of pyjama-clad subalterns—joined the sprint to the slit trenches. The explosions when they came were some miles away; at the all-clear we returned, impressed and shivering to our beds." In another letter, I mentioned seeing a flight of Spitfires scream low over my camp. But that's all. It's possible, of course, that the scarcity of war news in my letters came about because I wanted to spare my parents anxiety or that I was really concerned about the censor's scissors.

In the Officers' Mess I certainly read the English newspapers in which war was the main topic, but I made only one reference to this source in letters home. "Funny," I told Ellen, "how small the papers are here—no advertisements at all. One of the most popular is *The Daily Mirror* because it has a strip cartoon called 'Jane,' which many of us look at before we bother with the news. Jane is endlessly concerned with her undergarments and often appears nearly naked. She's supposed to be good for troop morale."

What I never knew while I was Overseas was how much Rab and Ellen read about what was happening in Sicily, France, and Germany; it was considerable for they listened to the radio and got *The Globe and Mail* regularly from a neighbour. They could not miss the great black headlines on the front pages or the more muted announcements of the dead, wounded, missing, and presumed dead columns to be found inside the paper.

On August 20, 1943, they saw the First Division's casualty list that named 25 officers and 360 other ranks killed. By the end of the Sicilian campaign, those numbers moved up to 40 officers and 522 other ranks.

Ellen wrote to me every week. It was a task which she seems to have guarded jealously as her own. No letter survives from Rab. Sometimes hers are trivial and disjointed as she runs on from subject to subject:

> Have had the oats cut on the glebe. Dad has been off to threshings. Have been studying your letters and think I know where you landed in England. Liverpool?
>
> I saw the metal part of your old baby buggy on the stone pile above the manse. It brought back happy memories of home when you and Iain were small. Helen, the Jersey, has cow pox and kicks when Dad tries to milk her—so I've been milking her lately. Churchill has been fishing in the Laurentians; he will broadcast this afternoon. Hear on the radio that Canadians will be much to the fore in the invasion. Peaches $1.10 for a 6 quart basket.
>
> Well Denmark is getting coralled these days.[2] My cream cheque minus one pound of butter was twenty-one cents this a.m. Dad spilt one mess; the neighbour's cat got in another, and the cow had to be kept in the stable for two days.

From Elizabeth, after a long wait, came a letter to say she had begun teaching on September 7. She rallied me for having morbid thoughts and told me I was kind to suggest she seek out male company occasionally. In view of my own track record, my suggestion probably owed more to an uneasy conscience than it did to magnanimity, and the word "occasionally" damns me dreadfully.

In late September, on only a few hours' notice, I was given a

---

2. August 1943, Germans established martial law in Denmark.

seven-days' leave which, without much thought, I decided to spend in Scotland. Clad in battle dress and trench coat and carrying only a haversack and Newnes' *New Motoring Atlas*, I crossed the border by train about 7:00 a.m. on September 21, 1943. According to my diary entry, the train was unheated, dimly lit, stuffed with kit bags and service men of every stripe, and smelling very much of unwashed bodies, tobacco smoke, and lavatories.

Clearing beaded damp off a window in the train's corridor in the early morning, I saw Scottish scenery for the first time. Through a mass of black cloud in the east, I glimpsed a forbidding coast line and a wind-tossed grey sea. As dawn brightened in the east, it revealed stone fences, herds of beef cattle, flocks of sheep, grain in stooks, and now and then stone houses and stables. Somehow, it was not the Scottish countryside I had imagined. No castles, no frowning hills, no tumbling brown waters—all very matter of fact—like Simon Munro.

After I'd arrived in Edinburgh and when I'd got my accommodation at a Knights of Columbus hostel, I wrote of trying to see as many of the sights as my long legs could possibly carry me to: the Castle, St. Giles', Greyfriars, the Covenanters' Prison, the wynds and closes of the Old Town, and the shops and views from Princess Street. I even took in *Blithe Spirit* at the Lyceum in the evening.

The day after, I was on my way to Stirling where I was given a tour of the Castle by a kilted major with Great War ribbons up who was happy to be of service to a colonial. Leaving his imperial highness on the Castle's ramparts with my thanks and a smart salute, I went on to Glasgow and to Loch Lomond where, at Luss in the Colquhoun Arms, I had tea with a bouncing Nursing Sister from Canada who tried to persuade me to make the ascent of Ben Lomond with her on the following day. As she seemed to me too stout a creature for such a venture, I evaded her invitation by saying I had to be in Edinburgh that night.

Later in the Glasgow train station, I fell in with an Air Gunner. The two of us were comfortably seated in a compartment on the Edinburgh train when we were joined by two girls, one in civvies and the other dressed as a Women's Land Army girl. My Air Gunner acquaintance at once commandeered the W.L.A. girl and moved off to another compartment, and I was left alone with the other who proved to be a Gaelic-speaking Irish girl with a great tide of talk upon her and, so far as I could tell, no inhibitions. In the blacked-out compartment, she settled cheerfully in my arms murmuring her heathen endearments and letting me kiss her while she put my hands on her breasts which swelled below a very thin blouse. Her nipples felt firm like nearly ripe raspberries.

Very near Edinburgh, disappointed perhaps in my slow progress or emboldened by the proximity of the journey's end, my temptress asked me outright what I thought about sex. To conceal the shallow well of my experience and the fatigue that numbed my body, I dodged her question saying magisterially that I thought it was an overrated pastime. Fortunately for me, the cross-examination never got under way for at this moment the train began to slow on its approach to Waverley Station, and we had to untangle and collect our belongings.

Once past the ticket barriers, the four of us met, and the two girls invited us to their room for tea—"rather an unusual beverage," I recorded, "for such a time of night." But the hope of something more rewarding than tea I suspect brought our immediate acceptance. To get to their place, we had to take a street car and make a change. I had no sooner got my colleen on the second car than I realized I'd left my haversack in the first car. A mad dash back to retrieve it—only to see, on my return, that the second car with the girls and the Air Gunner had pulled away into the fog of the Edinburgh night. Having no idea of where the girls lived, I returned to my hostel and slept for eleven hours. "Strange," I wrote, "how circumstances can contribute to virtue."

The next day I shopped in the morning and then crossed the Firth of Forth Bridge to visit Dunfermline Abbey, and Pittencrief Glen where a well-informed custodian took me on a tour. Grateful for the man's interest in me, I tendered him a shilling on parting which the old gentleman, either disdaining so small a coin or offended by being taken for a mere guide, dropped on the ground, walking away without a word.

The following day I took the train to Melrose, where I stayed at the King's Arms. In the afternoon I climbed Mid Hill of the Eildons from the top of which I saw the Cheviots to the south, the Lammermuirs to the north and, near at hand, Galashiels and a stretch of the Tweed below me. That evening I spent an hour amid the ruins of Melrose Abbey because I remembered one of Scott's jingling couplets: "If thou would'st view fair Melrose aright/ Go visit it by the pale moonlight." I told Ellen I was lucky "for the moon did show clearly among ragged clouds and shone palely through the ruined windows and across the grassy nave upon the broken stone. I was alone and in silence save for the bells of a nearby flock of sheep—very romantic, and, I admit, much to my taste."

A day later I tried to get transport to St. Mary's Loch because I wanted to see the waterfall known as the Grey Mare's Tail. But no luck. From Selkirk I marched out to the Duke of Buccleuch's estate where I found a Scottish regiment quartered with a courtyard packed with bicycles. Thinking I could borrow one, I tried the direct approach at their R.H.Q., but they really did not see how regulations would permit their lending me a machine.

Back to shank's mare and a long walk to Newark Castle, where I recorded climbing the winding stair to the top and walking about a narrow ledge a hundred feet above the lovely Yarrow which flows into the Ettrick just above Selkirk. The view was worth the risk. That evening I had small blisters on both feet and a great longing for food, as I had had nothing to eat since breakfast. A hot bath, a very good dinner of roast lamb, and twelve hours of sleep put things to rights again.

The next day I entrained for London where I arrived at 9:32 p.m. The trip back for me was spoiled when, having nothing else to do, I began reckoning the cost of my leave. At the outset in London, I had gone to the Bank of Montreal and withdrawn twelve pounds, which, but for a few pennies, had exhausted my account. On my leave I had spent five pounds on presents, cards, travel booklets etc. and another five on room and board and bus fare, leaving me with two for my return to Bordon.

It was, however, the sudden recognition that I'd overdrawn my bank account by ten shillings five pence that alarmed me. What I'd forgotten was that I'd issued a cheque in Bordon to pay for a pair of coveralls just before I had left to go on leave. That cheque, I was sure, was now at the Bank of Montreal with no funds to meet it . I had been told over and over again at #1 C.A.R.U. that officers who abused their banking privileges could be cashiered and returned to Canada. So instead of going on to Bordon, I spent a long, uncomfortable night in the waiting room at St. Pancras Station, where I slept fitfully among the coming and going of all sorts of people.

With nothing better to do while waiting for my bank to open, I brought my diary up to date:

> I have been very careless. If, as I hope, the che-
> que to the Quartermaster has not been sent to
> the bank, I am safe; if not, I suppose I am in real
> trouble—and all for a pair of bloody coveralls.
> And what an uncomfortable end to so good a
> leave. If I hadn't bungled this last day, I could
> have stopped off for half a day in Farnborough
> and looked up Louise.

As it happened, I found my night of worry in St. Pancras Station was in vain. The Q.M.'s cheque had not arrived at the bank where a pleasant pin-striped clerk assured me that my credit and reputation at that moment were as secure as the bank itself. There followed breakfast and the return to Bordon where, after a week on a Signal's course, I was ordered to report by October 14 to the 5th Field Regiment as an officer on Special Increment.

The intervening days were quiet, and I even managed a Saturday in London where I spent an afternoon in Westminster Abbey which, even in its sandbagged condition, seemed to me the most remarkable pile I'd ever seen: a wonderful medley of memorials, chapels, and architectural styles. At one point I noticed that I was standing on smooth flagstones on which was recorded that below my feet were buried the bodies of twenty-six monks who had died of the Black Plague. I regretted that my knowledge of history was not at all adequate to answer all the questions that arose in my mind as I wandered about this tremendous stone encyclopaedia of England's past history.

That evening I saw Shaw's *Heartbreak House* at the Cambridge Theatre, directed by John Burrall, with Robert Donat playing Captain Shotover. I told Ellen that I enjoyed the play but disagreed with Shaw's anti-romantic ideas. Of the characters, I sympathized most with Ellie Dunn. The air raid at the close was so real that the effect was more than a little chilling. Perhaps troubled by the richness of my existence as compared with that of my parents at Harrington, I concluded my letter by saying: "You must think I'm a curious sort of soldier only seeing shows and larking about Britain, but I'm sure you'll find my travels more interesting than the details of all the courses I have to attend."

Chapter 8

A Regiment And Battle School

For the next two months I was a Special Increment Officer attached to the 73rd Battery of the 5th Field Regiment which had its headquarters in Rottingdean on the south coast. It was a good experience for me in every way, and I was made aware of how much all my past theory and training needed to be rounded off by the activities and spirit that bonded a fine regiment.

My fellow battery officers were billeted very comfortably in a vacated home near the village. It was a newly-built house where each of us had a room to himself. Mine faced the south where, at sunset, I could see the shadows lengthen over the lazy roll of the Downs. The view from the hill that sheltered the house, looking obliquely out to the white cliffs, the Channel, and the sentinel windmill outside the village, was even more impressive.

The village had an old church dating back to Saxon and Norman times with windows in the chancel and tower by William Morris, narrow streets, flint-stone buildings, a convent, and over all the steady Channel wind. I told my mother that I'd like to holiday here when the lurid realities of this war are past.

The lurid realities were made clear on the night of October 18 when Jerry bombers with a fighter escort roared in low over our area toward Lewes. I stood in the dark and watched the Ack-Ack explode like ugly yellow pimples in the night sky. As well, a nearby unit was firing tracer which arced in searing white lines over the Downs. When you were inside the house, the explosions sounded as if someone were walking over your head in the room above wearing very heavy boots.

Outside, I became so interested in the fireworks that a woman warned me to go inside for my "tin hat," as fragments from bursting shells were bouncing off the tiles. The helmeted English stood about and watched almost nonchalantly. One old lady, moving inside with her dog on a leash, ardently wished that the A.A. gunners would get a Jerry so that she could see the "booger" come down in flames.

What was spectacular, I wrote, was the illumination from the "bread baskets" which the Germans dropped over Lewes. Then came the dull crumps of exploding bombs, at which time I felt very much for the poor townspeople on the receiving end. It was my first experience of wartime action.

Later, the 5th Field took part in a Divisional exercise, in which I took the place of a senior Gun Position Officer who was on leave. The scheme was a demanding one in which we had little sleep for over three days. A real plus for me came when, after driving in convoy all night, I saw in the early morning light the city of Canterbury with the barrage balloons hanging like silver sausages over its ancient towers. At the end of the scheme on the way back at night, while my driver was asleep, I drove the "George" vehicle for several miles along roads that I imagined Romans, Normans, and pilgrims must have travelled. Keeping my distance in convoy wasn't easy as I had only the bobbing tail light on the vehicle ahead to help me gauge my distance and, of course, no road signs whatever to indicate where I was if I took a wrong turning.

Back in Rottingdean I found letters had arrived from Ellen, Iain, Elizabeth, and Louise. Ellen had dispatched another parcel weighing just over five pounds on which the postage was $1.20. She said that they were all waiting for the results of Italy's surrender. From Iain came word that he had sent a bottle of Hudson's Bay rum inside a loaf of bread to me.

Despite my complaints to Ellen that Elizabeth seldom wrote, the record is that from August 30 to November 26, 1943,

109

she had written at least seven times and twice at length as she described the pattern of her life in the little town where her school was. And despite my warnings to her about getting too involved in local affiliations, she was now the prisoner of a host of extracurricular activities including the Literary Society and the Anglican Guild. But her teaching was going well, and she was adapting to the amatory gossip of the place which linked her to a variety of possible suitors. The scarf and pin which I had sent her from Edinburgh pleased her. Hers were good letters in which she sent her love to me and even included a lipstick kiss. To Iain, on December 8, I confided that I was sure Elizabeth was my very own.

Once off the scheme, several subalterns from the 5th Field and I were sent on a gunnery course for two weeks at Seaford, which I referred to in a letter to Iain on November 8:

> At first, while the surroundings were new, it was rather novel, but in a few days many of us were browned off, and for my part, I think, with some reason. After all, I've been on courses for twelve of the seventeen months I've been in the army, and it does grow tiresome when you endure much repetition.
>
> The one exception to the boredom happened half way through this course when three of us beetled off to 'Smokey Town.' I broke away from the group in London and saw *Arsenic and Old Lace* rather than get drunk and go wenching. The play was not in the same league as *Heartbreak House*, but I enjoyed it pretty much as I do all stage productions. I had a seat in the pit five rows from the front for only 13/6, and this will impress you—I had the usheress bring me tea and cake at the end of the first act. Whatever would Simon Munro think of that extravagance!
>
> During the show an air raid alert went, and the guns opened up, but since no one in the audience seemed to pay the least attention, I hid

my concern and tried not to let ideas of bombs and death mar the frivolity before me on the stage.

We returned to the Regiment in time to go on an anti-tank shoot farther along the coast at Lydd. No hop fields as around Canterbury, just a flat gravelly landscape dotted with stunted shrubs for mile after mile where the sea once had been. Farther inland the fields had a speckled look because of the granite and quartz in the soil. The shoot went off very well as we potted away at silhouettes of tanks moving in and out of screens of shrubs and down and up from sandy hollows along the shoreline.

Back in Rottingdean, I found a letter from Ellen written on December 13 in which she said that they had

> sold thirty ducks and just think we had to pick them all. What a job! They averaged about six pounds apiece, so that at twenty-seven cents a pound we made almost fifty dollars. We will be butchering the pig in a week or two, but it is so mild that unless we put all of it in the locker, it won't keep without salt. Tomorrow I may try to make a Christmas cake. Cannot get nuts, dates, figs, or coconut so must make do with raisins, currants, and peel. Got three grapefruit for nineteen cents in town.

Ellen was very pleased that the 73rd Battery officers had enjoyed a jar of honey which she had sent and which they had on toast with their tea at night. It was too bad, she said, that two of the apples she sent in the parcel had spoiled. "Perhaps," she added, "russets would keep better than spies."

I was sorry when my tour with the 5th Field came to an end, and I had to return to Bordon. Regimental life was much more satisfying than the rather aimless existence at the holding unit. Back at #1 C.A.R.U., I was again—and a little reluctantly—within easy range of Louise, who had made plans for me to spend Christmas Day with her. At the time Elizabeth, too, was much in my thoughts as I worried over what I should send her for a Christmas present; I settled eventually for a satin evening bag.

That worry out of the way, I gave my somewhat divided attention to Louise whom I hadn't seen for a month. The Christmas celebration was wonderfully inexpensive, just 11/6d for train fare to Horley and my bottle of issue Scotch. My bed in the doctor's wing of Louise's hospital cost nothing.

Christmas dinner was turkey, plum pudding with brandy sauce, and a good wine—all served in an eighteenth-century pub. It was all very dignified, and Louise was both attentive and charming. In the afternoon we walked for a long time down a misty English lane. No snow, about 65°F, perfect for walking and stealing kisses. In the evening we attended a buffet supper and dance in the Mess. "But," I confided in my diary, "it's always the same with Louise: I lead her down the garden path—or think I do—and then complain that she chases me. It's scrubby behaviour. I shudder to think how Elizabeth would view my actions. But she's not here, and the slopes are so slippery."

But, if she were not there, Elizabeth had written to me just after the New Year to thank me for the lovely evening bag I had sent her. By now she was not at all certain that she liked the town she was in. "I've decided that small towns are picturesque only in story books; in real life they are indescribably dreary. I should not mind preparing lessons five nights a week if the weekends promised some real diversion. But a game of bridge or a gossip over teacups is not my idea of fun. And there are *no* persons here exactly my age."

Six weeks later she wrote again to say that the school play she had directed had been surprisingly successful: "I even found myself sitting open-mouthed through the whole performance!" After the play there was a dance in the gym when Elizabeth dared to doll up by donning an evening gown, gold sandals, and gold earrings and piling her hair in a curled pompadour. As well, she told me she had carried the evening bag I had given her.

In Ellen's next letter, I had her account of Christmas as they had celebrated it in the manse; Iain was home with them. Much of her letter, however, was taken up with the allied bombing of Berlin. "My," she exclaimed, "what terrible destruction, so many poor souls homeless and so many killed—and all in such bitter weather! I wonder how necessary it all is."

Meanwhile, my existence was lively enough as I chronicled it for Iain:

> I am now about due for seven days' leave when I hope to spend a few days in and about Cambridge, as well as seeing Ely. After that, I am to report back to Louise. As Popeye would say, ' 'at's a goofy dame, she loves me'.
>
> And, oh yes, did I tell you that my little Welsh washerwoman has reappeared in the nearby brambles and bracken of Bordon. Her boyfriend just now is far, far away so that we meet often even though it is a bit chilly after hours. She's another good sport who demands nothing from you but the semblance of attention as she rattles on. Even in khaki she is downright pretty, more so by far than Louise.
>
> By the way, what are the duties of a best man? I am to perform as such at Freddy's wedding. You remember he was the chap from O.A.C. who roomed with me at A2. We have been much together at Bordon, and it was perhaps my insistence for taking in all the ENSA shows that came to camp, that resulted in his meeting a little English girl who worked at the box office. As a consequence I have not seen much of him lately. I wish he were not marrying, but then I may be either jealous or envious.

In another letter to Iain, who had wanted to know how I'd spent New Year's Eve, I described the party which my petite C.W.A.C. had invited me to. It was held in one of their Nissen huts which was gaily lit and decorated throughout with holly, the red berries making splashes of colour on the walls. I'm not at all certain now why it was that rank was no barrier. But I had, according to my letter, a bang-up time. Barbara, I said, "is full of music, dances like a sylph, and sings all the lyrics as the orchestra plays. I did not miss a dance, and, cold sober at midnight, I even kissed the matron. After this ceremony, all of us attended to a delicious buffet lunch." To show our appreciation, two other officers and I took our girls to dinner the following week at one of the old hotels near Bordon.

It was about this time that my hopes for a leave and an extended visit to Louise were dashed when I was sent on yet another gunnery course. This time it was on the south coast where I had a chance one weekend to walk the field on which the Battle of Hastings was fought. I couldn't help wondering how events would have been changed for us, had the Germans like the Normans so long ago, succeeded in their invasion plans for 1940. How much difference would it have made over the next one thousand years? "Where William and Harold faced off in 1066," I reported, "is now peaceful meadowland containing beautiful old trees. The Abbey itself is an uncared-for ruin. I climbed one of its towers for a view for miles over the Downs."

Once the gunnery course ended, I returned to Bordon where I hoped I might have a seven-day leave. In an effort to find out when it was scheduled, I was paraded to see the Major in charge of such details. Iain was told about it.

> He was a purple-hued, old maltworm whose self-importance was writ large. I was, however, polite and told him that some idea of the date on which I could expect my leave would help me in planning my travels. But at my request he took offence and began lecturing me as if I were a new recruit. 'Didn't I know that leaves were a privilege? Didn't I realize that he could not make separate deals for every junior subaltern in the camp?' And he added, with some relish, 'Didn't I realize that, if the Army wished, I could be sent to Canadian Training School, No. 5, Battle Wing?'
>
> All this old-soldier arrogance made me a little angry, and, I suppose, reckless so that I simp-

ly thanked him for his information and told him bluntly that I did not care where I was sent, but it would be helpful if I knew a bit in advance. I was certainly not going to whimper about Battle School, which is an advanced training unit for infantry officers and somewhat feared by the few Artillery personnel who have been sent there.

Well, the result of my pronouncement to this old walrus could have been foretold by any half-witted Cassandra. I have been detailed to attend Battle Wing, No. 5, for nine weeks. So must begin a little road work to toughen me up.

Before going off to this course, I had the good fortune on February 2 to meet my former university roommate, Hughie, who, in order to get Overseas, had transferred to the Infantry. The first thing he said to me was "Sandy, old cock, I have a date for you tonight." It turned out that Hughie had one round too many for his magazine and the result was that I escorted Julia Sloane, one of the loveliest of Nursing Sisters, to a nurses' dance that evening—after Hugh and I had had dinner together in his Mess. My good deed had consequences later on, for, remembering there was to be a dance after Fred's wedding, I invited this new Nightingale to the event.

Meanwhile Louise was becoming distinctly restless. In her letter of February 6, she announced that she was

beginning to take a very dim view of trying to plan weekends, even though I know there's nothing you can do about the courses you are sent on. If you can, however, think of any way we might spend some time together this weekend you can phone me. My leave has come through.

If you are stationed someplace near where I could stay and are not working nights, maybe I could spend the last two or three days of my leave there, and we could at least see each other.

A week later I made some amends by finding an evening at Bordon, when I was free, to entertain her as she was on her leave. She paid for her room, and I took her to dinner after which I was sick, possibly from rum and coke. In a cab on the way back to her hotel, she held my throbbing head on her breast, trying to comfort me in my distress. I cannot now understand how, in a letter to my brother the week after, I could describe Louise as a real stickler and pronounce that from then on I intended to play the game in a more delicate manner.

At Freddy's wedding, as best man, I performed my duties flawlessly in church but have to admit that my performance became defective at the reception, where I drank joyously of both rum and gin. The description of my condition varies according to the person I am writing to. Ellen read that I managed to be quite merry, Iain was told that I was fairly well out to sea by late afternoon when I went to get Julia for the dance that followed the reception. She was very excited as this was the first dance away from her unit that she had attended in England.

My diary written up three days after the wedding probably gives a reasonably true account of what happened:

> I was, I am ashamed to say, still very fuzzy, if
> not downright incapable, when I went to get
> Julia at the hospital. She came along, however,
> and was charmingly insouciant about my condi-
> tion, which must have been obvious to her. At
> the Mess she very graciously agreed to dance
> with several of my acquaintances so that I could
> disappear and be disgustingly sick for two
> hours. I tried everything known to me as barrack
> remedies for alcoholic poisoning but with little
> success.
>
> By midnight, when the dance ended, I was
> just able to be respectable enough to join Julia
> and take her home in the back of a 30 hundred-
> weight, where, for a short time in the cooling
> darkness, I fell asleep—something she may not
> have noticed.
>
> Of one thing I am certain and that is that our
> roles that evening should have been reversed: in-

stead of my escorting her to a dance, she should
have been escorting me—probably to a hospital
bed. And I am now so embarrassed by all I did
or did not do that I doubt I'll have nerve enough
to go to her and apologize—and I don't see how
I'll ever convince her to go out with me again.
Hope Hugh doesn't find out. 'O, what a rogue
and peasant slave am I!'

Back on the windy verges of the manse, Ellen in February
was complaining about the monotony of her life. And she was
still upset by the suffering being inflicted on the Berliners:

Imagine Berlin has been pounded three times in
four days, and the *Globe* states that the Allies intend to obliterate it. How dreadful for the poor
people in the ruins! I don't suppose you get a
chance to see the daily paper. London has had
its 701st alert, at least 26 people died in that
bombing.

Then she went on to speak of her quilting:

Yesterday I put those quilt blocks I made in the
winter all together, pressed the seams out, made
the lining ready, and got the quilt on the frames
for quilting. It will take up most of my time for
the next two weeks. You'll remember this is the
quilt I want Elizabeth to have. What have you
heard from her recently?

I sidestepped Ellen's question by saying that I seldom heard
from Elizabeth even though I had answered the few letters she
sent to me promptly.

A week later I was back in Louise's arms dancing until 3:45
on a Sunday morning in her hospital's large Mess Hall. My
diary reports that I "was agreeably surprised at ten that morning when Louise brought me my breakfast in bed: an orange, a
fried egg (fresh), bacon, heaps of buttered toast, honey, coffee,
and a jam tart." I also noted that I intended to drop Julia Sloane
as two Nursing Sisters were one too many.

117

From February 6 on, I was at Canadian Training School, No. 5 (Battle Wing), where I became an Infantry officer in training forced to face situations as close to battle conditions as my somewhat sadistic instructors could make them. During the nine weeks on this course, I was allowed out of camp just three times. The first, a short weekend, I spent with Louise at her unit. The next was a pass for one evening to meet Louise again who was staying at a nearby inn.

After a very good dinner of breast of pigeon, brussels sprouts, roast potatoes, coffee, cheese and biscuits, we sat and talked. Louise very generously said I could spend the night with her as there were two beds in her room. She even showed me the room which was very attractive with low dormer windows looking out on a garden. My bed was a single one. The other was a high double bed which, opened up, looked invitingly comfortable with white cotton sheets, the usual bolster and pillows, and with Louise's sky-blue gown across it. Her offer was a tempting one which I had to decline as I kissed her goodnight for it was then after ten o'clock and I had a four-mile walk back to camp where I had to report in at midnight. At 0630 hours the next morning in the grey light of dawn, I was present and accounted for on the P.T. roll call.

Whatever I told my old friend McRuer in the air force about this trial to my flesh, his return letter was an outspoken attack on my apparent gentility:

> I really must round upon you, my dear fellow, for your treatment of Louise. When are you ever going to discard your idealism and face the facts of your sexuality and hers? How could you leave her alone, late at night, frustrated in such a completely adequate location? What did you get out of ten English courses at Queen's? Didn't Daun Chaucer rub off on you at all? Have you forgotten Sir Toby's injunction: 'Board her, woo her, assail her!' And can't you recall, sirrah, 'those deserts of vast eternity' where only worms try 'long-preserved virginity'?

You do distress me, Sandy, old boy, and sometimes I think verily you are a kind of Puritan.

The next time I saw Louise was on the forty-eight-hour
leave which separated Parts I and II of the Battle School's
programme. And it was she who arranged the details of travel
to Canterbury and booked separate rooms for us in a rather
drafty, mousey, old hotel in the High Street. She had chosen
wisely for I found the city endlessly fascinating. On the first
morning of our leave, while Louise slept in, I discovered the
Eastbridge Hospital almost next door to our hotel. What particularly appealed to me was the idea that Chaucer's pilgrims
might have stayed here in the Undercroft, which is a low room
with stone vaulting below the chapel.

After breakfast the two of us walked away from the Hospital to where Mercery Lane intersects the High Street. "It's hard,"
I wrote in my diary, "to describe that glimpse of fairy land, for
Mercery Lane is a reminder of the glories that belonged to
medieval and renaissance living and offers views of rows of top-
heavy Elizabethan timbered houses and of Christ Church Gate
with its coloured sculptures. The Gate is a kind of anteroom to
the Cathedral itself whose west entrance is just beyond."

Once inside the Cathedral, I gazed in wonder at the sweep
upward into the nave and eastward to the screen and chancel
where I stood staring up into the Bell Harry Tower which soars
in stone for 325 feet above the paving. But I could go on and on
to describe what we saw inside the Cathedral and outside
where we walked about St. Martin's Church that pre-dates St.
Augustine's arrival in 597. In the end we saw seven of the city's
churches. Louise thought that was more than enough as she
wanted to do some shopping. I agreed saying that she had endured my ecclesiastical obstacle course very commendably.

What happened next spoiled the evening, for Louise
developed such a bad sinus headache that she had to leave her
dinner uneaten at the Falstaff Inn and return to the hotel where
she went to bed. That this turn of event was largely owing to
my insistence that we tour stone-cold, musty churches all day
seems not to have occurred to me as I wrote up my account of

what we did. What did occur to me was my disappointment in not being able to share Louisa's coverlet for the night—a disaster which I attributed to my being over-educated. The next morning at breakfast Louise told me that her sleep had been very broken because of the squeaking of mice in the wainscotting; at one point, a mouse ran across the end of her pillow making her think very seriously of coming to my room for assistance. My diary entry regretted both her courage and her modesty.

Back in Battle School, the second half of my masculine education advanced ruthlessly: field craft, stalking, unarmed combat, tactical handling of weapons, assault course, laying and lifting of mines, patrol work by night, fighting in built-up areas, mortar and carrier co-operation, the use of bangalore torpedoes, and even lectures on artillery support. The course ended on Friday, April 7.

Three of the four artillery officers completed the course leaving it in fine physical condition. Some of us lost weight, but my six-foot frame gained a pound to weigh out at 154. The meals in the Mess had been well prepared and nourishing. I very much liked fresh eggs and oranges twice a week, cocoa, bread, and cheese at bedtime, and all the peanuts I could eat.

Of the various trials we faced, I shall never forget the obstacle course which was two miles long and its scariest triumph a deep flaming ditch made more hell-like by well-timed exploding thunder flashes and the stacatto of Brens firing off to the flank. Of the seventy officers I came in third. "Such a course is," I informed Iain, "easier for a farm boy than for his city cousin who is not so used to muck and dirt, the outside hazards of cold water, tunnels, cat walks, and rope climbing. I was, you may remember, very good on the hay fork rope in the barn at Eastdene." The course concluded with two examinations. Overall, I received a Q1 grading, better than 75 percent, which grade, I hoped, would impress that bleeding Major at #1 C.A.R.U.

By the time I returned to Bordon, England was richly spring-green. On the Downs I was amazed by the quantities of daffodils in the sheltered places, so dense you could pick an armful of them in five minutes. Elsewhere in the country I liked the bright yellow of the gorse in bloom. But it was the English gardens that most impressed me with peonies and bleeding hearts well up and soon to flower. I especially liked the primroses which I did not remember seeing in Canada, the small pansy-like flowers springing from a cluster of thick dark-green leaves, and the Japanese Lotus which has lovely mauve blossoms. English gardens were like little Edens everywhere on this war-shrouded island.

Back at #1 C.A.R.U., I found that I must have impressed my irate Major more than I imagined. Less than a week after my arrival, I was assigned to an advanced artillery course in Wales. If it was not the long sought-for leave, it was nevertheless an experience which made me happy. An added plus for the course was the night we had to spend in London before entraining for Wales. I was thus able to see John Gielgud's production of *All for Love* at the Theatre Royal, where I had a seat in the front row. A fine string orchestra that accompanied the Restoration songs enlivened the production. As usual I was greatly taken by the stage setting, the costumes, and the excellent acting.

Once our train moved beyond Shrewsbury, I had glimpses of hills dotted with sheep, views of the River Dee, and then bare mountain sides of granite and gneiss which shaded from a reddish yellow to a frowning black. The yellow of the broom and gorse added splashes of colour amid the russet browns of dead heather and fern. At Harlech I caught sight of the castle and ruin which made me think of Rab and his rendering of "Men of Harlech."

Our Mess was a low stone residence built in 1610. Inside, it was modern with excellent facilities: fine white linen, polished silver, waiters with the aplomb of butlers, a well-stocked bar, and a games room. I liked having my coffee served to me in a demi-tasse after dinner, just as I liked the tea and biscuits in the late afternoon when we got back from the ranges.

We were at the guns or in the O.P. all day long, and when it rained—as it did most of the time—we were often wet and cold, but our sergeant instructors, who were back from North Africa, treated us very humanely. All the personnel and all the officers on course were British except for five Canadians. I was a G.P.O. on several occasions, sometimes a gun number, and often at the O.P., where the Welsh mountains made ranging on a target difficult because so many of our rounds simply disappeared into valleys and gullies beyond our vision. So far as I know, my performance was a credit to my past training.

Throughout the course, letters and parcels were not forwarded to me so that I was almost as eager on my return to Bordon to check my mailbox as Rab was on the other side of the Atlantic. "I can always tell," Ellen said, "by your father's walk, as he returns from our mailbox at the roadside, whether or not we have received a letter from you." As winter and a slow spring gave way to summer, Ellen's letters reflected a variety of interests: the hens were now laying well; a jeweller in Stratford had assured her of the genuineness of the cairngorm in the brooch I had sent her from Edinburgh; Stephen Leacock had died on March 24; the English pound was trading at $4.4; and she'd been able to buy a $100.00 bond with her own savings.

At Bordon, I managed to see Hughie again and, with his encouragement, renewed my acquaintance with Julia Sloane. On May 2, she and I made an excursion to Hindhead where we rambled along paths into a valley, the vegetation of which reminded me at first of Petawawa: poplars, scrub pine, and brush. But as we descended, wild flowers and shrubs in bloom appeared all round us. Cowslips, wild daffodils, yellow gorse, purple heather, wild violets, forget-me-nots, primroses were just a few of the flowers I could name. Thrushes, chaffinches, cuckoos, larks, blackbirds—all were in song.

At the bottom we came upon a series of ponds, neatly cropped to their banks whose still surfaces netted in reverse the setting sun. We strolled on with little regard to direction or to private property until a particularly offensive little terrier convinced us it was time to make inquiries at a nearby cottage. To our surprise, a burly farmer and his plump wife came to the door and invited us in to their home for a glass of beer, milk, or lemonade.

Theirs was the type of English cottage which I'd only seen on postcards. It was set in a mass of garden flowers kept in by a neatly trimmed hedge and almost hidden away in the valley among the trees. We entered the cottage through a low door into a small living room which had a deep fireplace at one end where an old man with white whiskers sat dozing. Soon we were introduced and our host brought forth numerous bottles of Friary Ale, as well as lemonade for Julia and his wife. The grandfather in the chimney corner had his pint, and we all talked till nearly midnight.

The lady of the house, a Lancashire lass, had served as a nurse in World War I and quickly made friends with Julia. The husband was a Cockney. We talked about Canada, of holidays, of Threadneedle Street, of farming, of corn on the cob (a delicacy unknown to them), of cathedrals, and of nightingales, which they assured us we could likely hear on our way home.

And all too soon we were on our way back, hand in hand, under a full moon and the roar of our Lancasters winging their way to continental targets. The distant noise filled the heavens, disturbing sleeping birds into song. I am sure we heard nightingales, but, in such a setting and with so pretty a lady, I could have heard the angel Gabriel himself trying out a few trills on his horn.

But once more the truth was that I had one too many Nursing Sisters to occupy my attention. And my propensity for such company was jarred toward a kind of reality when I received at this time a letter from Elizabeth who apologized for the gap in her letters offering good reasons:

> I've fallen down pretty badly on the job of keeping you supplied with mail, haven't I? My only excuse is that I've been too dashed busy and in a foul temper from overwork!
>
> The 'At Home' was no sooner out of the way than up loomed a War Savings Stamps Campaign, a public speaking contest, and Easter examinations. My home form sold the most stamps of those in the Collegiate. As a reward we got a picture of a Hurricane!
>
> And then I've been visited by the Inspector. Words cannot describe my emotions when he

walked into my first lower-school history class. I was reviewing, since there was no point in taking new work with examinations to come as soon as the Inspector left. He went straight to the sloppiest boy in the class and looked at his notebook. Then he began his interrogation; 'What other books did I use besides the authorized text? What historical magazines did I take? Did I encourage the pupils to make scrap books, collect pictures, do individual projects?' Having had to answer a flat 'no' to most of the questions and feeling too crushed to justify my own method of teaching history, I skipped lunch and retired to my room in tears.

He saw four more of my lessons including Health, Art, and English, and on the final day took me quite by surprise by stating that 'I don't want to flatter you, but I think you show great promise'. And to the School Board he was apparently even more lyrical.

She ended by saying, "Doesn't this letter make you glad you are a Lieutenant and not a pedagogue? Cheerio, and all my love, Elizabeth." I made no reference to this letter in my diary, and I wonder what I told her when I replied. As for me, it was time someone in authority sent me a long, long way from Bordon and two nearby Nursing Sisters.

Chapter 9

I Stop At Eboli

A thousand miles away from Bordon two armies, the American
Fifth and the British Eighth had driven the Germans from Sicily
after thirty-eight days of fighting. Attached to the Eighth Army
throughout the fighting in Sicily was the First Canadian
Division which waded ashore on the mainland of Italy at Reg-
gio di Calabria on September 3, 1943.

On September 9, the Allies effected the landing at Salerno.
By October 1, the American Fifth was at Naples and the Eighth
had taken Foggia on the other side of Italy. The war on the
Italian mainland was going reasonably well. Rome was next.
But, in this hope, General Alexander was thwarted by the cun-
ning of his opposite, General Kesselring, who managed to swell
his German forces from six to twenty-six divisions and establish
a formidable defense line running from Ortona on the Adriatic
across the Abruzzi Mountains to the Gulf of Gaeta on the Tyrrhenian Sea.

The most promising approach to Rome was via the Liri Valley on the west side of the mountains. Here the Allies faced the
Garigliano and Rapido Rivers and the Gustav Line of defense
which, in turn, was backed by another known as the Adolph
Hitler Line. Preparations for the offensive took time. The failure
of the Fifth Army to break through the Gustav Line in January
1944 and Kesselring's success in bottling up 50,000 Allied
troops, who had landed sixty miles farther north at Anzio be-

tween January 22 and 23, 1944, meant that the offensive, when it came, had to be massive. To that end the Eighth Army was moved from the Adriatic sector to the Monte Cassino area. By this time, too, the First Canadian Division had been augmented in November 1943 by the Fifth Canadian Armoured Division from the United Kingdom. In early May 1944, the Allies were poised for the assault on the German defenses.

Seventy-five miles behind their front was Salerno and, fifteen miles south of it, the small town of Eboli. On its western hillside was #2 Canadian Base Reinforcement Depot, Central Mediterranean Force. Tents on the hillside attested to its temporary nature. Here, I arrived on May 17, 1944, having been struck off strength #1 C.A.R.U. in Bordon on May 2. The move was not a sudden one. I had, in a fashion, warned my parents in late April that changes were afoot: "my leave has been cancelled; security forbids me saying more." On April 29 I had packed my unwanted belongings into the "Coffin," labelled it, and left in it a letter for my parents, rather awkward and sentimental all the way to the closing: "And so dry those tears, chins up, and God bless you both. Your son, Sandy."

On the same day that I wrote this farewell, Ellen sent a letter off to me saying that a boat had gone down in the Atlantic with letters and boxes for the lads Overseas. As usual she was concerned about my welfare. "It's all very well," she said, "to tell me not to worry, but you know not what you are asking. And I do pray every night and in the daytime, too, that you will return safely."

I did not get this letter until I was in Italy—very pleased that our troopship and its convoy were spared enemy attack as we moved through a calm Bay of Biscay and the Strait of Gibraltar where, during the night, we caught sight of the lights of Algiers blinking off our starboard side. The Mediterranean by day was calm and blue beneath a warm sun, too warm we soon found when we docked at Naples and marched off in our heavy wool battle dress to waiting three-tonners.

Exactly six months earlier on November 8, 1943, my future Regiment, the 17th Field of the Fifth Armoured Division had also docked at Naples before going on to its camping area at

Afragola, five miles north of Naples. Two months later, on January 14, 1944, the Regiment fired its "first shot in anger" near San Leonardo, three miles south of Ortona on the Adriatic front. For the next two months the Regiment moved from gun area to gun area enduring snow, rain, mud, and intense enemy opposition.

At 0530 hours on January 17, near San Vito, the guns put down concentrations in support of the Perths and Cape Breton Highlanders for the advance across the Arielli River. On that day alone the 17th Field fired 10,960 rounds of high explosive which included a Mike Target, Scale 90. From San Vito the Regiment moved south and west to the Orsogna area on the headwaters of the Moro River where rain and sleet created seas of mud. The same sort of weather prevailed on the next position at La Torre, where the "War Diary" reported no end of rain and snow and where the gun pits and dugouts had to be bailed out. Here the 17th remained until March 7, for the most part, under cold, wet skies with ammunition expenditure restricted to forty rounds per gun per day. It was a miserable time for all ranks but especially for the gunners for whom keeping dry was nearly impossible. Casualties, too, occurred throughout this period of action, the Regiment losing three killed and sixteen wounded—a sad prelude to the outcome of battles that lay ahead.

In pouring rain, on March 7, the 17th withdrew to a rest area, where it remained until April 14, when it moved into action at Acquafondata north-east of Cassino, moving again on May 5 to a concentration area at Capua prior to the assault on the Gustav and Hitler Lines of defense. If the men were not as battle-tried as their brothers in the 1st Division, they had, since firing their first shot in anger, demonstrated very commendable powers of endurance, technical efficiency, and courage.

On May 17, the day I arrived in Eboli, advance parties from the 17th Field moved up to reconnoitre gun positions for the attack on the Gustav Line. The Regiment's "War Diary" on May 19 tells briefly of the opening battle:

Early this morning the 78 Div (Br) breached the Gustav Line, the infantry have continued to advance. Consequently our guns were almost out of range and early in the afternoon we were given prepare to advance. . . . The devastating effect of our concentrations and barrage became more and more apparent as we advanced. Most houses have been demolished and the others have at least been hit by our Arty. Even the trees are uprooted and mangled branches are everywhere. We advanced approx 5 miles on a heavily congested road to arrive in our new position just after dark. Jerry must have seen the concentration of vehs in this area because he used his artillery extensively throughout the night. One of our gunners was blown out of his slit trench and one of our F.A.T.'s was destroyed.[3]

By May 23, the Gustav Line was military history and the "War Diary" moves on to describe the

full scale attack on HITLER LINE launched today by 1 Cdn Corps. After a full day of fierce and bloody fighting the 1 and 2 Inf Bdes of 1 Cdn Inf Div and some 5 Cdn Armd Div units smashed their way through. To do this they had to overcome a veritable wall of pill boxes, concrete emplacements, fortified hull-down tanks, anti-tank guns, and ditches, and numerous mine fields. It was a brilliant victory and paved the way for our armour which should go in tomorrow. Within our own Regtl area, we were again subjected to heavy enemy shelling and mortaring which was more concentrated than ever before.

---

3. The "War Diary," 17th Canadian Field Regiment, Royal Canadian Artillery, is held in the National Archives in Ottawa.

For the 17th Field, the advance brought heavy casualties, especially on May 21 at approximately 1800 hours when E Troop position was heavily shelled. Two slit trenches received direct hits killing three men instantly and mortally wounding another. It was a sad day for the Regiment. Throughout the slow advance and, despite our smoke screens, the Germans from their observation posts on the hillsides to the east of the Liri Valley laid down very effective harassing fire on our tight columns moving up in clouds of dust. Between May 16 and May 31, the 17th Field lost seven men killed and thirteen wounded.

The Globe and Mail on May 23 made Ellen and Rab at home vividly aware of how desperate the battle was:

> Canadian infantrymen hacked through 20-foot deep barbed wire entanglements into the inner defenses of the Hitler Line northeast of Pontecorvo today as the Germans threw the last of their immediately available reserve strength into a desperate counter offensive against the Allied advance.
>
> Fierce fighting raged along the entire front as the last of 17 Nazi divisions (perhaps 170,000 men) south of Rome and immediately north of the Roman capital were pushed into what may prove the climactic struggle for Italy.

On May 29 my parents saw a picture in their newspaper, with the caption "Back from Battle," showing British soldiers escorting wounded German prisoners past a ruined Sherman tank in the shattered Nazi stronghold of Cassino. Three days later another picture displayed an Eighth Army 25-pdr. gun in action during the current offensive in Italy; the readers were told the gun had fired 400 rounds each hour for four hours in the battle. Even if the facts might be misleading, Ellen and Rab may have known better than I did at the time details of the Liri Valley offensive.

Ellen's letter of May 18, for example, informed me that she'd just heard over the radio that morning that Cassino and the monastery had been taken. I doubt very much that I knew this fact any sooner than they. As I think now of my admonitions to them not to worry, I realize how puzzling such advice must have seemed to them. And I wonder what I would have thought had I known then that, between May 15 and June 4, 1944, the 1st Canadian Corps in Italy lost 789 killed, 2463 wounded, and 116 taken prisoner.

Certainly such starkly vivid statistics were far from my mind on May 26 when I told Iain in a letter what I was doing on Eboli's hillside:

> What am I doing? Nothing, just lounging by
> Tent 22 on a hillside covered with volcanic ash,
> tents, and olive trees. A little while ago I was flat
> on my back on my safari bed eating filberts
> which I crack open by placing them on the
> buckle of my web belt and whacking them with
> a stone—caveman technique.
>
> My tent mate is Freddy and for that I give
> many thanks: he's always unruffled, tidy, and
> unflappable. Both of us by now are getting used
> to this Italian sunshine. Still it's worrisome.
> When I left England I was, I thought, hard and
> fighting fit. Now I shuffle about and yawn and
> even have spells of self-pity as I look at the
> angry glow of sunburn on my arms and legs. A
> most unlikely soldier.

From Hampshire's green and pleasant fields to Eboli's arid and gritty hillside was as culturally shocking as the difference between the regulars at the Red Lion and the terribly lazy and dirty Eyties whom I dismissed as a harmless lot.

My criticism, however, of southern Italy and its people suffered a slow change attributable at first perhaps to the landscape. Across the valley from our camp I could see the sides of a volcanic mountain that was always spectacular in the setting sun. Strangely shaped, it was for two-thirds of the way up, dark brown with purply splotches, while above, it was a light pearl-grey in colour. Its craggy peak was often obscured by a wreath of cumulus cloud that assumed spectacular hues in the evening light. Though it was more than twenty miles away, the peak would on a clear day seem deceivingly close.

Nearer at hand was the cold, green water of the Sele River where Freddy and I went swimming and saw the irrigation ditches that helped produce huge crops of sweet melons. And nearer still, just below our camp, were fields of wheat, their golden yellow splashed with the red of poppies. All this we could see, without effort, from the entrance to Tent 22. If you could set aside the poverty of its people and their dwellings, the Italian countryside was visually very attractive.

In the camp, between courses on mines and the ever predictable one for gun position officers, Fred and I spent much time lying under a silvery-grey olive tree beside our tent eating melons, writing long letters home, discussing the mail we received, and attending to such household chores as getting six pairs of cotton shorts tailored to suit our tastes. We said, on first inspecting them, that they must have been made for Limeys— too long in the leg and three inches too big in the waist. We took them to the Italian seamstresses in the camp for the necessary remodelling.

Another complaint we made about the khaki drill was that it was much too khaki coloured. We found out that we could eliminate much of the khaki by having Italian women wash the drill and leave it to bleach in the sun. As a consequence, we began to look like the veterans we saw on occasion coming back from the Liri Valley: faded bush shirts open at the neck with sleeves rolled up correctly; faded shorts, knee-length stockings with puttees half way up the calf; a deepening tan, and smartly trimmed moustaches.

In my letter home on June 8, I referred to the Second Front and to the excitement in the camp where everyone congregated at breakfast and dinner to listen to the radio and to watch the widening beachhead pinned out in a variety of colours over the map on the bulletin board in the Mess. I went on to say that the night before last we'd heard the King speak over the radio in one of the nearby tents. At the end we'd all snapped to attention as the national anthem was played. I also told my mother she could be thankful I was in Italy and not in France. On what basis I made this observation, I cannot now say.

My letters from home were, as usual, greatly supplemented by those of other correspondents. On June 1, Dr. Bradwin sent me the news of Frontier College and praised my last letter as one of the finest that had ever come to his office.

> I could not help thinking when I read your letter how different it would seem in your mind when you compare the vastness of the back places of the Canadian hinterland with the crowded cities, villages, and countryside of Italy, so much of it now in ruins. I have said to myself more than once that all through the lifetime of reading I have pictured Italy almost as a paradise, yes and Greece and the Aegean—but I have learned more this winter from press reports about the inclement weather—not bitterly cold, of course, but foggy and rainy, with mud and filth and dirt—that are a part of Italy, that it seems to me I can never conjure it as a beauty spot again.
>
> All the world stands aghast at this moment not knowing what the next fortnight may mean. I have only one wish in my heart and that is that Hitler and his whole cult can be beaten to their knees, and then, with sleeves rolled up, this world can set its face anew to greet a rising sun— not just in the nature of a New Day, when all troubles are past—but to greet a widening of human understanding so that we are all prepared to buckle down to what is most required for peace and for goodwill towards our fellows.

If Dr. Bradwin thought he could never conjure up Italy as a beauty spot again, Julia in England had no such misgivings as she gave way to romance and breathlessness trying to imagine what Italy was like:

> I'm sure there are many lovely senoritas and you

won't know Italy at all until you know them.
They love music, and I'm sure they dance beauti-
fully. As you supposed, the horses, mules, and
donkeys would fascinate me. Have you done
any riding yet? Oh, Italy must be very, very fascinating.

After this outpouring, she became practical and told me she
hoped she was just as conscientious about security as I, adding,
"I could make you whistle were I to talk!" Then she warned me
to be scrupulous about taking my mepacrine tablets for malaria
which was rightly called the accursed fever.

Louise, too, wrote for I had told her in a previous letter
about Julia. She thanked me for doing so, "though, as you say,
I'd probably have heard about it anyway, there's just one thing
I'd like to know. I know I shouldn't ask but are you writing to
her? (I really won't say another word about it)." She did not
write to me again until August 1 when she had little to report.

Elizabeth had not written since April 23. It was a letter
which Ellen had read—as she did all the letters I sent home—
and which she referred back to when I complained about the
long waits I had between Elizabeth's letters: "I do not think,"
Ellen told me, "that you do her justice. You know the pressure
of preparing and marking examinations and all that teaching
means. You know, too, that she is not one of the frivolous, fishing kind." That advice tendered, Ellen turned to the subject of
her turkeys: "A little one died yesterday—too many lice. I did
not think there was a louse on them so, after breakfast, I disin-
fected the rest of them lest they get droopy and die, too. Now I
have just ten left, and I must watch them for I would like to
raise them."

Meanwhile in Eboli I had decided to learn some Italian. To
that end, I went every other day in the evening into the town to
meet a high school boy who had agreed to teach me. By
devious streets and alleys I went to his home which was above
a long winding staircase from the street level. "On the first landing," I told Iain, "is a tethered donkey—a more morose-looking
beast it is hard to imagine. At the top of the stairs against the

133

hillside is a kind of backyard in which a hen and her brood are kept in a wire enclosure. As well, there's a cat tied to a chair by a piece of string—a precaution against its appearing in a family stew. As it spends much time scratching, I suspect it has fleas." My school setting was rounded off by two fig trees, a pile of rubble, and an old man who always asked me for cigarette papers in the hope that I'd give him cigarettes instead.

Inside, through a beaded curtain on the doorway, in a very bare room at a long bare table, we had our lesson. I liked my tutor and found Italian to be a pleasant, soft, very rhythmic language, easy to acquire because of my background in Latin. Before I knew it the lesson time would be up, and I would be saying *grazie* and *buona sera* and making my way past the hen and the donkey and the cat to the street below.

The road from the town back to camp ran by a fruit stand whose occupants Fred and I knew well for they supplied us with nuts and oranges. Lucia, the mother, was the owner and her daughter, Mafalda, the helper. Mafalda was darkly pretty and much taken with Fred even though she knew he was married—but then, as we discovered, she also was married; her husband was fighting with a special German division on the Russian southern front. One consequence of our friendship was that we accepted an invitation to visit their town lodging. It was, I reported, an interesting outing:

> The family live partly below ground level. The living room with its stone floor, its blackened fireplace, unpapered walls and sparse furniture serves also as a dining room and bedroom, for in one end of it is the big bed in which Lucia, Mafalda, and the three children sleep. There are no men because Lucia's husband and her eldest son are prisoners of war.
>
> They made us very welcome and pulled the shutters to so as not to attract the attention of the 'Red Caps', the military police. While we made the acquaintance of the children: Raphael, Pietro, and Luigi, their mother in an adjoining grotto

134

that served as her kitchen, fried eggs in olive oil for us, and Mafalda cracked a bowl of hazel nuts using her strong white teeth as nutcrackers. With the eggs, and nuts, and black bread, we had a bottle of Moscado from which Lucia wiped layers of dust with her apron. The Moscado contributed much to the evening, so that, feeling little pain, Freddy and I just managed to get back into camp in time to avoid interrogation.

One desirable consequence of my closer acquaintance with the Italian people was my becoming considerably less arrogant toward them—even a bit caring. I told Ellen that I felt sorry for Lucia and Mafalda as I saw them at the end of a day with their unsold fruit and nuts in baskets on their heads and backs making their way barefoot over the Vesuvian dust and clinkers down the hill to their unheated cavern at 22 Garibaldi Street. From now on both the landscape and its inhabitants interested me.

Although we had little need of leaves at 2 C.B.R.D., the authorities were pleased to make them available. On our first forty-eight-hour one, Fred and I went to Salerno to an Officers' Club, a rather swank place, formerly a gambling den for the Royal Italian family. Here we bought litres of Spumante for seventy-five lire a bottle, and learned to pop the corks at the genitalia of the naked cherubs decorating the ceiling, and to ogle at the big-breasted, Rubens-like women dallying with foppish admirers on the walls of the Salon. The stringed orchestra belted out "Lili Marlene" for us just as it did for the Jerries before us.

On the beach we saw beautiful Italian girls and a miserably scab-ridden child in the arms of a dirty old woman, who all the while lavished terms of endearment upon it. This is Italy, I told Ellen, a land of violent contrasts where beauty and misery are seldom separate for long. To Iain, I spoke of the caves farther up the beach where for a couple of bucks you could have a woman for the whole afternoon. Those experienced in this practice recommended sea bathing afterwards as salt water was supposed to be an excellent disinfectant for the old pecker and less embarrassing than a short-arm inspection at a Pro Station.

On our next "48" we went to Naples finding its streets dirty, narrow, swarming with people, ragged children, and traffic of every description, all moving or just existing underneath lines of the citizens' laundry. In one square I saw on the pavement a still form covered with an old army blanket, while crowds of curious Neapolitans milled about. But, once out of the lower city, the view from the heights north across the harbour to Vesuvius was splendid, not as golden and misty as J.M.W. Turner made it, but still a flowing scene in the setting rays of the sun. "Vesuvius," I wrote on, "is still smoking, a reminder of its last eruption in March of this year when it dusted Eboli with its debris."

Both of us spent part of a day shopping, Freddy getting a jewel box for his wife and I an ivory brooch for my mother. Later on I bought a dozen lemons nicely boxed to send to Julia while Freddy got two pounds of mixed nuts for his wife. In the evening we saw the San Carlo Opera House where *Rigoletto* was playing. I wanted to get tickets not, I am sure, because of the music but because I wanted to see inside so old an opera house; my companion voted the idea down.

On Sunday we toured the ruins of Pompeii. First, however, we saw the cathedral in the modern town, fascinated by its elaborate decoration. The matched Milan marble, the painted domed ceilings, and the glitter of gold and silver in the altar area seemed, however, oddly incongruous with the sombre women kneeling here and there in prayer. A guide took us in a lift to the top of the tower where we could see the ruins of the old Roman city, the Via Roma, ancient viaducts, Vesuvius smoking quietly, and, to the west, the blue, blue Tyrrhenian, and the outline of Capri.

I denounced the Pompeian tour as a racket describing the swarms of ragged urchins at the gate pressing upon you pamphlets and postcards of doubtful value, nuns and friars begging alms, and sharp-faced youngsters tugging at your sleeve and offering you the services of their sisters for two dollars with a nearby carriage handy for your transport.

Eventually, for ten lire we gained admission to the ruined city and were able to walk about and view the awful devastation that fell upon it in A.D. 79. Here I saw my first Roman amphitheatre which brought to mind Browning's lines about the burning ring that "the chariots traced as they raced," while "the monarch and his minions watched the games." For over an hour we wandered up and down the excavated streets, entering a restored Roman home where we admired the courtyard and the surprisingly clear colours of the wall paintings. We also inspected a Roman bawdy house wondering how the girls ever got their customers into the short stone cubicles. Finally, we saw in a museum-like building the stone outline of a man and woman smothered by the burning lava while they were asleep. Other such outlines testified to the cataclysm that had overwhelmed this ancient city.

When we returned to the entrance, I had the feeling of walking from one civilization into another. But the poor wretches outside bothered me more than the stone forms I saw within. One forlorn, rather dirty Italian woman seated on a stone at the gate was suckling her baby—utterly tired she seemed, with no sign of embarrassment as the crowds of curious soldiery passed, their boot plates crashing on the ancient thoroughfare.

A week after our return to Eboli, we were on a live shoot in the mountains. On the way climbing up from our valley, we met farmers going to their fields in great clumsy two-wheeled carts drawn by white oxen, passed several mud-caked water buffalo, and the occasional herd of goats which scrambled out of our way into the ditch to look at us with their yellow eyes. For two hours we followed a precipitous road, the gun tractors growling along in low gears. At the top it was cool and fresh, and we could see for miles down into the sunlit plain and then on out seaward. Not far from our gun position were charcoal burners tending their fires; I thought they looked rather like gypsies.

The shooting was even more tricky than it was in Wales— just one bottomless valley after another into which rounds disappeared. I had my turn at the O.P. and did well enough, although another ranging round would have put me more squarely on the target. On the return we saw an Italian family at work building a house. One of them, a strapping, very handsome woman, was carrying a flat rock on her head which must have weighed seventy pounds. She walked erect and barefoot up a steep slope with her burden as if it were a part of her. She and the others never even looked at us.

By June 24 I was admitting in my diary to my delight at being in Eboli. "Tonight I saw a glorious sunset over the hills. It was a rich crimson sky with a low-lying mass of dark storm cloud on the horizon. Just above the cloud appeared the most wonderful shades of mauve, purple, and indigo." I assumed it must be the moisture from the sea and dust particles which contributed to this heightened colouring. To the east was our mountain undergoing its daily revelation of shade and light upon its rocky countenance. And near at hand, below us among the olives, thousands of fireflies gave our slope a festive appearance.

With such scenery about me, I said, such good meals at the Mess, so little arduous work to do, and so much entertainment when leaves come up, "it would not be asking too much to have me pay room and board. And it's safer here than in Bordon. I've almost forgotten what an air raid sounds like and forgotten, too, the regulations attendant upon it. Here there's no blackout and very little restriction upon our movements and obviously no demand for our services in the forward areas."

The mail nearly always brought letters and parcels either for Freddy or for me. A letter from Jeanie, my Kingston nurse, thanked me for the most beautiful sea-shell lamp I had sent her for a wedding present and posed a teasing question: "Did you ever think once, Sandy, that you had won me?" In the same mail was a letter from Ellen whose bank account showed a healthy balance of $175.75. Hired hands for haying were "now being paid $5.00 a day, imagine!" Another letter was from Julia, who was obviously under orders for France and was probably stationed in Whitby. She was annoyed because she was unable to go walking—"one of those damned inventory checks, blankets and pillows this time." What she wanted to do was wander through the narrow, twisting streets and climb the cliff again to where the old abbey is, an enchanted spot, truly, for that old abbey is where Caedmon sang thirteen hundred years ago. "Magic always lingers, you know". A letter from Louise said I could expect no sympathy from her if I had what she described as "Nursing Sister complications." From McRuer, now stationed in England, came a small parcel containing a tobacco pouch, a pipe, and a collection of Montaigne's essays.

On July 5, Fred and I were agreeably surprised to learn we had been given a seven days' leave. It was about the last thing we really needed, but then, I said, "it's never wise to turn down such well-considered intentions on the part of the military." We left on a Sunday for the vicinity of Sorrento. For miles along the coast we had breathless views of sheer rock walls above us and then, a thousand feet below, the Mediterranean where it eased forward and then in a welter of effervescent foam fell back from the rocks, only like Sisyphus to begin all over again. It was a terrifying road especially at times when the driver had to stop and back the truck up to get round some of the hairpin turns. For miles the truck seemed to climb steadily and then in a matter of minutes, slipped down to a whitewashed tourist town with a long sandy beach and terraced vineyards that clung to the slopes above the sea's edge.

And then we arrived at San Agata above Sorrento to find our hotel where we had soft beds, white sheets, very appetizing meals, marble floors throughout the ground level, and a barber to shave us in the morning. Here we sat under palm trees on the terrace, seven miles by a twisting road to Sorrento, and about two thousand feet above it, but less than twenty minutes from the town if we walked straight down. The walk back, however, was a real endurance test.

Our hotel was on the tip of the Sorrentine Peninsula that divides the waters of the Bay of Naples from the Gulf of Salerno. The view, particularly in the evening, was a flood of slowly changing colours: below, mauve, purple, violet, indigo; above, the dull reds and browns of the craggy hills; around us, all the bloom of the garden and the dark green of the palms; and, of course, far away, the shimmering blues of the sea.

For two days Fred and I went swimming every morning,

my first experience of how buoyant salt water is. On Wednesday we took a diesel-powered boat to Capri. It is a truly beautiful island, precipitous and offering surprises at every twist of its winding roads. How I wished for Norman Douglas' *Siren Land*, a book I read at Queen's. I could remember little of it then except the author's reference to the Blue Grotto, which I was so determined to see that I made a second crossing to the island by myself. On our first trip the sea had been too rough to admit us to the entrance which is so low that only a small rowboat can pass in.

Inside, the effect stilled me to silence. The water was the clearest blue, while the light from the setting sun sent a quivering, hazy, bluish light over the walls. The water ran off the oars like liquid silk. The only sound was the sea's lap at the opening. Even though it was all largely a visual illusion, I liked it very much just as I like scenic deception on the stage. On the way out of the Grotto to the landing, the Italian boatmen sang "The Isle of Capri" and "Lili Marlene." They were a happy, bronzed lot of local navigators.

By making two trips to the island, I managed to see most of it for it's only about four miles long and barely a mile wide. From Tiberius' Villa, where the sea is a thousand vertical feet below and the Italian coast a hazy outline in the heat and moisture, it was an easy walk to the west side of the island, where Monte Solario rises about two thousand feet above sea level.

At every turn of the road something new rose before me. The villa of San Michele, built by the Swedish archaeologist, Axel Munthe, attracted me, not so much for the artifacts within, as for what I saw from its colonnaded walks shaded by dark cypress trees. Nine hundred feet below, the sea came gently in over some sort of crystalline rock, which gave the island a light-greenish margin rather like the ones some people used to outline the coasts of old maps. And the flowers were paradisal: huge hydrangea, bougainvillaea, geraniums, oleander, and daisies, and others I couldn't name. On our first trip there we had a meal of steak and corn on the cob at an American hotel. On the next trip I did without eating so that I could have time enough to see all I wanted to see.

On the return crossing, I met a British Nursing Sister. She and others were staying at the Y.W.C.A. well down below our hotel. She was another Ross, a Scot from near Inverness, who had had most interesting experiences. She had been evacuated from Dunkirk, served in Africa and Sicily, and was now with the Eighth Army in Italy. She made the rest of my leave very pleasant. We went swimming, sight-seeing from a jeep, and shopping in Sorrento. We saw a movie and spent one evening just sitting on deck chairs under the palms, gabbing away like children in the face of a cooling sea breeze. Vesuvius was just a dim outline amid the stars along the horizon.

Alison was very good company, not as pretty as Julia but considerably more mature and intelligent, not at all cloying. I hoped I'd see her again. The leave had been the best one I'd had so far in George's Army.

Back in Eboli, Fred and I were surprised to learn that we had been singled out as instructors for a course designed to convert no longer needed anti-aircraft gunners to field artillery personnel. "It is as if I am fore-ordained either to be taught or to teach while others fight," I complained. The course went on for six weeks. At first we thought we wouldn't like the work but changed our minds as most of the Ack-Ack personnel were sergeant majors or sergeants, an altogether good lot of chaps who worked as hard as we did at logs., antilogs., trig. functions, and the artillery board. Since there was now little likelihood of our being taken off this instruction, we made improvements in our canvas household. We now had a little petrol stove, a frying pan, and a pot so that we could have snacks at night. One night we had two fried eggs apiece.

Mail was plentiful and frequent, sometimes disturbing, as when Julia warned me to be more careful:

> Do you know what I found inside your last envelope which was addressed to me? You will be surprised, Lieutenant Ross, to know that the letter inside had for its greeting, 'My dear Louise', which compels me to ask some questions. What happened to my letter—if there was one? And

who, pray tell, is my dear Louise—such a pretty name! Is she by any chance in this hospital unit? What fun to meet her and discuss *you* as a person whom we both know. Should make the tea cups rattle! A kind of character autopsy!

It was embarrassing, and I had to confess. Later Julia told me that Louise was in a nearby hospital unit, but she had not yet had the pleasure of meeting her. She was, however, anxious that I continue writing to her "for I find your letters very interesting—at times a bit scandalous!" As usual, she was careful to suggest that I never meant more to her than, as she put it, "a comrade-in-arms."

In Eboli, the Conversion Course which we were running went on smoothly despite the heat. Both of us had some homework to do at the end of each day as we prepared for the next one. It was good review especially the training we gave on the artillery board and on the director, the instrument for passing line to the guns. I admitted that I'd much rather be giving this course than offering talks to bored gunners in camp about the perils of venereal disease. On one Sunday afternoon we even managed to requisition two motorcycles on which we travelled fifteen miles south to see the Greek ruins at Paestum. We were amazed at the extent of them but disappointed as we knew too little to identify what we saw. Only goats, foraging in a wilderness of weeds, patrolled the ancient relics washed over by the cool sea winds. After an hour of aimless walking in and about broken temples, we returned to Eboli and the preparation for Monday's classes.

If the two of us grumbled about our "inactive role in this bloody war," we had little cause so far as the activities of our future regiment were concerned, for the 17th Field had moved out of action on June 6 to an area south-east of Pofi below Frosinone. After two weeks here, it moved again to an area a half mile from the Volturno River, where it stayed until August 1. After this date, it moved north and east by slow stages toward the Adriatic coast—and battle once more. Men and officers meantime had had rest and leaves to Rome, where they admired the clean spacious streets, modern buildings, and, most of all, the beautiful women. As well, the Regiment took part in numerous training exercises, had its guns calibrated, and endured several inspections of men and equipment. The "War Diary" for July 13 refers to one of the reasons why it was sometimes difficult to maintain unit strength: "Learned today that the C.O. has malaria. Our regret was mixed with amusement that the one who was the Unit Malaria Officer should be the first to fold!" But such emergencies did not as yet require replacements. And so with no demand for our services in the 17th, Freddy and I were, although we didn't know it, sensibly occupied in Eboli training men who, it turned out, were to be urgently needed before the end of the year.

Our work on the course was not so demanding that we had to spend all our time in camp. On July 27 I wrote to my parents about the first opera we had ever seen. It was *Aida*, put on by the San Carlo Company in Salerno; directed by Franco Patane, it listed names like Silvio Santarelli, Bianco Clemenso, and Maria Pedrini. Why Freddy and I decided to attend the opera, I do not now know—probably just for the hell of it, as neither of us had the required background or interest in classical music. But regardless of our cultural poverty, we were seated expectantly in a box in the theatre at the hour advertised. Promptness was hardly necessary as, for some wartime reason, the show was an hour late in beginning. Some of this time we spent admiring pretty signorinas and their vigilant mothers through our opera glasses. More time was gleefully given over to watching an altercation that developed over a lady who was either in the wrong seat or whose ticket was for another night. In the end the management brought in the *carbinieri* who attempted to remove her. To this treatment she objected volubly and vigorously, cursing, kicking, and struggling as she was pushed down the aisle to the exit. This helped the Canadians and Americans forget their long wait. We added our cheers for the oppressed one as if we had been watching a wrestling match.

My letters to Ellen and Iain reveal that I was impressed by the singing. The acting, I thought, was amateurish, the timing poor, and the interval between acts languidly long. The scenery and the costuming suggested empty splendour; the orchestra, especially the string section and the brass, was very effective. Once or twice, when the troops became restless, the Italians in the audience filled the theatre with snakelike hisses which restored decorum. It was, on the whole, I told Ellen, something different and an exposure to better things.

About this time I received two letters, one from Hughie and one from Louise. Hughie, in England, had been on an infantry course for five weeks. "The south coast," he said, "is nice, too nice, perhaps. I sometimes have difficulty determining whether I am in the army or on holiday. Labrador was never like this. Last week I met a farmer who has a beautiful hunter which he let me ride for two evenings."

Louise, somewhere in France, had had her first experience of "going to a cinema when it was raining and the tent leaked and dripped on my head and down my back, must say I got very wet but stayed on and saw the show as it was very good, *A Guy Named Joe*, I think that was the name of it." Rather ominously, she told me there was a friend of mine "in the same camp that I am in, but I haven't met her yet!" She was not pleased at their location: "The towns are very dirty, no waterworks to be seen, a stream runs down either side of the street."

Then on August 18 I had my mother's news of home where two more turkeys had died, only six left; they had lost three little pigs when the sow lay on them shortly after birth; ten white shiny little fellows lived on. Altering course, she reported that three Woodstock boys have been reported killed, one in Italy. "And oh, I do hope that this war will soon end and that you can come back to us."

Toward the end of the letter she referred to one I had sent home as I had told her again she could read anything I sent back to her. This was one of Elizabeth's letters written on April 23. The letter had impressed Ellen whose sense of propriety was disturbed by what she said was my constant carping about the infrequency of Elizabeth's letters.

> I cannot see why you are so down on her—simp-
> ly because she does not write frequently, you

say. If there are no promises between you, how can you expect her to be over-anxious in writing often.

I wonder if you have not been carried away by those nurses and others who are looking for a man, and who do not possess the steady and fine qualities which Elizabeth has. I cannot say from reading Louise's letters that I find much of interest; they are shallow. This is not a lecture, but if Elizabeth writes again, do not by any means stop writing to her. That would not be a gentlemanly thing to do.

But Elizabeth did not write again until November 12. Both Louise and Julia did. The latter gave her impressions of France and some advice.

If Italy is the land of lemons, oranges and nut trees, then France is apple land. Every field is an orchard. Herds of cattle pasture under apple trees, and horses and donkeys roam at will among them. Our tents are pitched among them, and we walk through an apple-shaded road to leave camp. The apples are for cider, not eating; they are a hard, tasteless pulp.

I have not met Louise yet, but she must be in the immediate vicinity. I do assure you, comrade-in-arms, that when we do meet, we shall enjoy dismembering and comparing!

And may I ask if you are writing long letters to that 'agreeable Nursing Sister' you met on Capri? If so, do be careful how you stuff your envelopes!

From this point in time, there's little question that my letter writing should have been approached with greater circumspection. But, of this need in August 1944, I seem to have been blithely unaware. What mattered much to me each day was the mail I found waiting for me in the Mess. Epistolary niceties had to be balanced against loneliness and the desire just to talk and to know.

Chapter 10

Becoming A Soldier

But my life in Tent 22 in Eboli, with its evening snacks of water-melon or fresh peaches, its kilograms of nuts and oranges, its NAFFI entertainment, its gossipy correspondence was soon to end as higher military considerations elected for an Allied assault along the narrow coastal route leading north from Ancona between the Etruscan Appenines and the Adriatic Sea. For this offensive, units of the Eighth Army had to be transferred back from the west to the east side of Italy.

The 17th Field Regiment was one of many which made the move going north from the Volturno to Rome and then on to Lake Trasimeno. Passing by Assisi, the Regiment went on to Foligno and Fabriano, coming to rest on August 18 in a concentration area near Iesi, fifteen miles west of Ancona. The move was the prelude to General Alexander's plan "to drive the enemy out of the Appenine positions and to exploit to the lower line of the Po, inflicting the maximum loss on the enemy in the process."[4] The stay at Iesi was brief. Recce parties were soon on the move. The Regiment's "War Diary" catches some of the drama of August 23, 1944:

> Weather heavy with heat waves and no sign at
> present of a let-up. . . . Recce parties again went

---

4.   G. W. L. Nicholson, *The Gunners of Canada* (Toronto: McClelland and Stewart, 1972), Vol II, p.220.

forward today at 1200 hours to our position near
Monte Maggiore. The Regiment is to occupy the
forward gun position on the F.D.L.'s and expected to move approximately 2200 hours
tonight. . . . The move progressed very happily
to a point turning off the main route to our gun
area. This route proved to be a long, tortuous
way in and, we soon had one 3-ton lorry, two
15 cwts. and a quad (F.A.T.) rolled over in the
ditch or broken down. The night was fairly dark,
and we were, of course, not allowed to use
lights. The enemy harassed our occupation by
frequent spasms of shelling. It was during one of
these periods that a round found its ugly mark
and killed Lt.-Col. F.T. McIntosh, L./Cpl. T.A.
Kennedy, and seriously wounded Sigmn.
Grunau, H. . . . This is the second C.O. we have
lost in a period of three days, making a total of 3
officers and one O.R. killed, and one O.R.
wounded since Exercise Olive began [August 16].

As well as enemy action, sickness in the form of malaria and
jaundice were also taking their toll of personnel. As early as
August 21, the Intelligence Officer noted that "unless reinforcements arrive very soon, we will go into action short of officers."
Some were, however, already on their way to the unit.

Two such officers, Fred and I, had received orders on
August 17 in Eboli to join the Regiment. During the night, when
the guns were moving along the treacherous access roads behind Monte Maggiore, the two of us were bumping our way
northward in the back of a covered 3-tonner laden with a mis-
cellany of supplies. As it was really not possible to sleep, we
waited and watched over the tail-board as the driver, with
dimmed lights, moved along the Up Route. Beyond Pescara a
storm over the Adriatic simulated a violent artillery duel but
died out as we neared Ancona.

Some time after dawn, I was on a camouflaged gun position
and being told to take a roll call of the Battery, as that was a

good way to get acquainted with some seventy men whom I had never seen before. "It was rather strange," I remarked to Iain, "trying to sort out all the locations where I might find a man answering to his name on the roll. Altogether an unorthodox procedure as compared with the rigid proprieties of a drill square." Eventually all were accounted for, and I found time to stow my gear and begin adjusting to life in a dugout with my "Ack," my signaller, and the ever-present Zero Line on the artillery board. A month later, in one of my letters, I told of seeing my first dead man, the Regiment's Commanding Officer, wrapped in a grey army blanket secured with signal wire, just his carefully polished high boots showing, while a piper from the Toronto Irish played that saddest of laments, "The Flowers of the Forest."

My transition from Tent 22 to Map Reference 159613 below Monte Maggiore jarred me loose in jig time from lecture room preconceptions. From the entrance of Fox Troop's Command Post, I could see the four lean 25-pdrs. showing their muzzle brakes from under the green and brown of their camouflage nets. The position was a shallow shelf of perhaps half an acre at the bottom of a deep valley. Four hundred feet above the guns was the hill village of Monte Maggiore. Just ahead of the village was the Metauro River where the Romans over 2000 years before had defeated Hasdrubal. Between the village and the troop was a hillside made picturesque by groves of gnarled olive trees. Well behind the four guns—spread a hundred feet apart like the claws of some giant predator—was a dried stream bottom where the cooks had set up their burners.

The shelling Fox Troop had endured as they moved into position guaranteed deep slit trenches and heavily revetted gun sites. The Command Post, a rectangular hole in the stony ground, had a rough cover of planks and odd timbers scrounged locally over which at night a tarpaulin made it possible for a light to be used for the artillery board. To preserve secrecy, no firing was to take place until H-Hour, which was set for 2300 hours plus 59 on August 25. Later, when I thought security less urgent, I described my introduction to battle to Iain:

At times I couldn't see my own guns for the dust caused by high explosives bang on our position. Obviously Jerry knew where we were to the last yard, but thank heaven his guns were not always accurate; many of the rounds meant for us exploded up the slope among the olive trees. But it was at night that I found the shelling even more unnerving than in the day. And it was during the night that Jerry really dusted us off—in the course of which exercise he managed to set the camouflage netting on one of our limbers on fire. It was a real effort for me to leave the safety of the dugout and race over to the gun to offer assistance. Inside the limber, its doors open, were rows of cartridges filled with H.E. and, round about us, exploding mortar bombs. I was damned scared and perhaps not very helpful, but I'm glad I managed to show, as initial impressions mean much, as you try to justify your existence in a regiment as seasoned as ours. Fortunately no one was hurt.

For a time I worried lest I became 'windy', but gradually I simmered down although I still got awfully close to the bottom of a slit trench when Jerry was right on target with his mortars or his guns.

I must give great credit to my gunners: big prairie farmer-types, strong and spare of speech, gun-centred, who waited defiantly for their turn. It's just as well they were not the ones who found two Italians in the village above us who had maps, binoculars, a mirror, and radio set for directing the German fire on us. No damned wonder the fire was so accurate. I heard we shot them.

At last, however, I was where I thought I should be. My consciousness curtailed, my actions the result of other men's initiatives: the enemy firing at my map reference, my own superiors passing orders to me. No time to imagine the composition of war as it extended beyond the twenty-four guns of the Regiment, although I noticed farther up the slope dug in among the olives, infantry with blackened faces waiting for darkness, when they were to move forward to the Metauro River and there await our artillery concentrations and the uncertainties of combat.

The next day, August 25, was a long, hot hell for the Regiment while the gunners waited under the burning Italian sun and counted the three hundred rounds of ammunition, which the R.C.A.S.C. had delivered to each gun, and while officers checked fire plans and synchronized watches. The intermittent shelling was now a nuisance which merely whetted hatred and a longing for that one word over the Tannoy, Fire! And so we waited in gun pits,or slit trenches, or dugouts, until driven by our own needs, we moved cautiously to latrines or field kitchens. Only with the wounded was there reckless haste as stretcher bearers made their way to regimental aid posts.

As the noise and movement of Day 1 merged into that of Day 2 on the hill slopes leading to Monte Maggiore, I began to be a soldier: to know what it was like to endure, to survive, and to be afraid—even while making calculations designed to destroy those trying to destroy me. Some of my tenseness, I told Iain, began to disappear as I watched the minutes and then the seconds on the sweep hand of my watch move closer to the H-hour and my first fire orders to the gunners of Fox Troop.

The drama of the night of August 25 did not escape Lt.-Col. G. W. L. Nicholson as he prepared his official history:

> It was a quiet night, the air was mild, and by half-past eleven the moon had gone down and the sky was full of stars. After the uninterrupted rumble of traffic behind the front on previous nights a breathless silence held. The heavy processes of concentration and assembly were over. The planners had done their work. Everything was ready. A few minutes before midnight

officers and men at General Burns' headquarters stood watching in the darkness. The infantry would be across the river by now and making their way up through the olives to the Roman road. Then at one minute before the hour the guns opened up, their flashes playing over the sky-line like summer lightning, their thunder arousing the coast and disturbing the slumber of the inland mountains. The assault had begun.[5]

Unknown to me and the sweat-streaked gunners silhouetted by the blinding flashes from the overheated barrels of their guns, a visitor watched at a distance leaning on his cane and smoking a cigar. The visitor's own account tells of his flying into Loreto, near Ancona, on August 25 with General Alexander, whence the two of them went to Sir Oliver Leese's headquarters behind Monte Maggiore.

> Here [says Churchill] we had tents overlooking a magnificent panorama to the northward. The Adriatic, though but twenty miles away, was hidden by the mass of Monte Maggiore. General Leese told us that the barrage to cover the advance of his troops would begin at midnight. We were well placed to watch the long line of distant gun-flashes. The rapid, ceaseless thudding of the cannonade reminded me of the First World War. Artillery was certainly being used on a great scale. After an hour of this I was glad to go to bed, for Alexander had planned an early start and a long day on the front. He also promised to take me wherever I wanted to go.[6]

---

5. G. W. L. Nicholson, *The Canadians in Italy, 1943-1945* (Ottawa: Queen's Printer, 1966), Vol. II, p.504.

6. Winston Churchill, *Triumph and Tragedy* (New York: Houghton Mifflin, 1953), pp. 118-119.

Churchill never suggests that Operation Olive had anything but his approval, even though he knew how the requirements for Operation Overlord in Western Europe and the need to support the ill-considered Riviera campaign in southern France were, as he put it "skinning the whole front [in Italy] and holding long stretches with nothing but anti-aircraft gunners converted to a kind of artillery-infantry and supported by a few armoured brigades."[7] But did he as he watched the battle on August 26, remember that just a year before he had argued that the Allies should stop their advance at the Leghorn-Ancona Line and fortify it so as "to seal off the north of Italy"? Did he also remember his warning words to the Chiefs of Staff at the same meeting: "I remain strongly convinced that we should be very chary of advancing northward beyond the narrow part of the Italian peninsula?"[8] Overruled by the military strategists, Churchill was soon to witness the neglect of this advice as Alexander and his forces pushed northwards. Ahead of the Canadians in Italy from Monte Maggiore to Bagnacavallo lay the flat lands of the Adriatic littoral hemmed in by the foothills of the Appenines and intersected by many short rivers like the Metauro, Foglio, Marano, Ausa, Marecchio, Fiumicino, Savio, Montone, Lamone, and Senio all of which made natural defense lines for skilled and desperate German defenders and created a litany of hardships and death for Canadian infantry.

But this was the future, not 0300 hours on August 26 when our guns, their barrels blistered and recuperators dripping hot oil, fell silent. By daylight we were all trying to catch up on sleep, assuming that the enemy would leave us alone, for our infantry were across the Metauro and quickly moving out of range. But in mid-morning our peace was shattered when Jerry sent over some 17 cm stuff which killed one of our gunners and made us wary and edgy for the rest of the day.

The freedom of movement that I had known with the guns in Canada, England, Wales and Eboli was a thing of the past.

---

7. *Triumph and Tragedy*, p. 123.

8. Annex to Minutes of Meeting held at the White House on September 9, 1943, pp. 6-7.

And it was disconcerting to me to realize that one enemy shell
in the right place could badly disrupt all the theory and lecture
room tactics I had stored up in my mind. In those first few days
of action, I also found out that I could be the only officer in the
Troop Command Post. On Regimental Rolls I might be the
troop leader, the junior officer, but again and again in action
what I found in practice was that sickness, leave, or duties elsewhere in the Regiment meant that the senior Command Post
person, the Gun Position Officer, was missing, and I assumed
his duties in addition to my own. This meant that I often slept,
ate, and worked by the artillery board and the telephone in the
Command Post. That this occurrence was not the trial it might
have been was owing to the quality and the high degree of training that characterized the men of the Regiment. You were often
helped along, as it were, by unseen hands for everyone knew
his job and could perform it equally well by day or night. "They
are," I told my brother, "a splendid lot of men, and I hope I
never let them down."

It was not until August 28 that the Regiment's "War Diary"
noted our move to a new position. At 0400 hours on that day,
the drivers in the F.A.T.s growled their way up from the Wagon
Lines so that the gunners, having opened up their gun pits,
could limber up and get their bedrolls and equipment stowed
away in the tractors. Then, with the sergeants peering from the
hatches through the grey light, the drivers took their orders and
spacing behind the George vehicle and set off, guns and limbers
jolting behind, to cross the Metauro and to disappear in clouds
of dust northward from Monte Maggiore, already christened
"Death Valley."

By 0900 hours, when the Regiment had taken up its new
position, the enemy were already out of range. And so the advance continued as the Germans slipped away toward their
Gothic Line, whose defenses stretched from Pesaro on the
Adriatic across the Appenines to a point in the west just north
of Pisa. With each move I gained confidence, as I told Iain: "You
should see me, take my own bed apart when we move at 0300
hours. I can undo, tie up, and roll my safari in seconds before
chucking it in my George vehicle—and all this in darkness and

some confusion." The safari bed with its slender steel frame was a luxury which I had found in Flight's in London for £2/9/4. When I had time, I even dug my slit trench deeper and longer to accommodate it.

I soon found, too, that the Command Post could be placed in an Italian farm building so long as we were careful not to use the upper storeys and so long as we accepted the risk, for buildings gave Jerry easy map references for ranging on us and his 88's gave precious little warning of their arrival. I told of this accommodation in several of my letters home:

> The last *casa* we were in had tremendously thick walls within which it housed humans at one end, cattle, oxen, and huge casks of wine at the other. Inside we were dry and comfortable and very hospitably treated by the signor, the signora, and their family. Jerry had just moved out and taken most of the oxen with him to pull some of his guns, the memory of which action being enough to send the signor into very dramatic speech and gestures.
>
> The gunners were particularly happy with that lodging because it had fresh hay in which the three men off duty from each gun by day or night could sleep. Fleas which infest both the house and the barn sections of the 'casa' are an itchy inconvenience. We watch them through the night in the light above the artillery board, very agile little blighters.

Meanwhile the Regimental Rolls suffered deletions. Jaundice and malaria claimed on August 21 an Acting Battery Captain, the Medical Officer, and the Signals Officer. From August 24 to August 31, casualties from enemy action included one officer and a gunner killed and nine gunners wounded. My comment to Iain was tinged with fatalism: "I think I am learning to be careful, but sometimes no amount of care seems to keep a man intact."

Throughout our spells of firing and movement forward, other military concerns were passed on to us through the Orders of the Day that filtered down to Fox Troop from R.H.Q.[9] The breadth of the "do's" and "do not's" was wide. All ranks were informed, for example, that "the only information which a P.O.W. may give to the enemy is RANK, NAME, and NUMBER." This warning came about because "British P.O.W.s were reported to have given valuable information to the Germans."

A less serious topic was given more space, perhaps because the Colonel himself had been a witness: "It has been observed [the Order began ominously] that various types of unauthorized head dress have been taken into wear, such as bowler hats, top hats, straw hats, etc. This practice will cease immediately and in future approved military head dress ONLY will be worn."

Another clothing abuse was also serious enough to find a place in Orders on September 8:

Socks—Wastage
The wastage rate of socks has risen during the past three months at an alarming rate, as shown by returns from laundry and bath exchange.

A large proportion of socks returned are fit only for salvage and show evidence that the soldier is not exerting any effort to keep this item of clothing in repair.

As socks are becoming in short supply in the theatre, sub-unit cmdrs. must impress on their men the necessity of 'sock maintenance'.

Alive to the even more pressing necessity of conserving his unit's strength, the Colonel on October 13 drew the Regiment's attention to the effect of careless drinking habits: "All troops are warned against the dangers of arsenical poisoning from drinking Italian anti-fly solution in mistake for wine. Within the past month eight cases of arsenical poisoning, with four deaths,

---

9.   See "The War Diary," 17th Canadian Field Regiment, R.C.A. , held in the National Archives of Canada.

have occurred amongst troops from this cause."

From a very different command level, far removed from the great casks of vino and the smaller containers of fly dope to be found in any Italian *casa*, was the directive from the Commander-in-Chief to the effect that the neutrality of the Republic of San Marino, just a few miles north west of the war zone, was to be "respected." Then Orders referred to a regimental need that eventually concerned me directly: "Reports from the Unit Maintenance Inspectorate reveal an unsatisfactory state of maintenance of vehicles held by Canadian units. Commands at all levels will give personal attention to the means by which the standard of maintenance can be improved."

Of all these "do's" and "do not's" the only one that appears in my correspondence at this time is the one touching on head gear. I told Ellen, "It must be some love of sartorial elegance which compels some gunners to pick up unusual head gear belonging to some Italian grandee and then, of all things, to wear it when it can be seen by the C.O. Hard as a top hat is, it's scarcely a substitute for a steel helmet." In the end I turned the problem over to the Troop Sergeant-Major who had a way of dealing with such theatrical display.

Poor roads, demolished bridges, and accurate hostile shelling delayed the advance northwards. But, by August 30, the Regiment was in position to support infantry preparing to assault across the Foglio into the Gothic Line. Writing to my brother at this time, I requested he send me a pair of motorcycle goggles: "You have no idea," I told him, "in what clouds of dust we move, rather like being in an Ontario barn at the height of threshing." As he had asked me about Freddy, I reported that I had not seen him since joining the Regiment. "We simply have no time for visiting. Anyway that's dangerous! Stick to your own hole is sound advice." The last sentence of my letter was suggestive of the strain of continuous activity: "It's now 4:00 a.m., and I must give over this writing. What I need most is twelve hours undisturbed sleep in my very own bed."

Not until September 4 did I write to Ellen to tell her not to worry as life in action was not nearly as dangerous as some people make it out to be. Who the some people were I did not say. The food, I told her, was good. "Last night we had potatoes, diced carrots and beets, boiled chicken, and raisin pie without a crust on top." The chicken, I confessed, had an Italian origin. The next day I told Iain that I had received six letters and two numbers of the *Maple Leaf*, the Canadian newspaper which first appeared in January 1944. This letter was more informative than others I'd sent in August:

> It's 0200 hours, and I have little to do as the
> troop is on a harassing fire task at given inter-
> vals, which means all I have to do now is stay
> awake beside my phone. No trouble staying
> awake with all the racket from the guns.
>
> I've got a nearly ideal set-up for writing. I
> use my map case for a board and a battery-
> powered electric light which shines over the artil-
> lery board; it's a great improvement over the
> candles we used in Tent 22.
>
> Due to unexpected enemy action, I've lost a
> kit bag containing my whole supply of food
> saved from parcels I've received. And even
> though Montaigne says, 'There is nothing so
> hampering, so cloying, as abundance', I still
> want some of the things I had in that kit bag. So
> will you please send me Sunlight soap for
> laundry, some pepper and salt, and a pipe with a
> strong mouthpiece that I can't easily chew my
> way through.

I ended by saying that "the Germans are formidable foes, make no mistake about that. Occasionally, they emphasize their prowess accurately and loudly on our gun position."

Tied up in this bundle of letters was one from a man named Owen, who had at one time shared a tent with Fred and me in Eboli, and who had gone with us on the Sorrento leave. He was now with the 2nd Field Regiment and obviously not so censor-conscious as I:

> I am fine and healthy although the climate and
> surroundings here are not conducive to long life.

The grim battle is on, have been on several rec-
ces and on one night recce found myself and
another fellow out among blackened faces, the
22nd boys getting ready for an attack. About
turn for us and away in a jeep.

Have experienced everything—almost, 88's,
17 cm, 15 cm, 21 cm, mines of all kinds but none
on our gun positions. Even had Jerry planes
dropping anti-personnel bombs and strafing
with M.G.s. Heard the snipers working at times,
too, and infantry small-arm fire from about 400
yards away.

News about the weaker sex is very poor, am
definitely on the prowl! And no vino at all. But
you should see the vineyard of grapes we're in
now. Ye gods of war! As big as (was going to say
eggs), but forget how big they are. Meals are really O.K.

Tonight it's raining, hope it isn't the rainy
season. Can hear Jerry with his big bass drum
landing them ahead of us right now.

What Owen said about the war was applicable to Fox
Troop; the Regiment's "War Diary" on September 3 spoke of
two persistent Jerry planes that dropped several anti-personnel
bombs and did a good deal of strafing. The Regiment escaped
without casualties.

Other letters that the Regiment's mailman brought to me at
this time included a rather sad note from Fred's wife saying
that, although she had heard from him, he hadn't had any letters from her for several weeks. She had been very ill for five
weeks and his letters had helped a lot—"and, oh I do so look
forward to receiving them. And I hope the war won't go on
much longer so that we can be together again. It's getting on for
eight months since we were married, but to me it seems like
years." She signed off asking me to "take care of my Freddy for
me, please."

Owen wrote again in mid-September saying how much he

liked a recent Herbie cartoon in *The Maple Leaf* in which the irrepressible Herbie is filling his water bottle from a barrel of wine in an occupied *casa* while saying: "Must be purty tough on the lads in Holland, all they've got to put in their bottles is water." Owen had also seen a sign on the road saying "Reserved for 83rd Gen. Hospital," which put him very much "in mind of those attractive Nursing Sisters we met in Sorrento."

Then he recurred to battle:

> Do you remember the chap, Gibeault, whom we
> met in Bordon. Well, he was killed. Just arrived
> on our gun position and hadn't even got his stuff
> unloaded when Jerry shelled us. Gibeault dived
> under a F.A.T. just as a mortar shell hit beside
> him and blew his head right off.

My letters home give little indication of the death and destruction which marked the advance northward in Operation Olive. Aware of censorship, I made no reference, even to Iain, that we had suffered losses between 4 and 15 September. Two officers and two gunners had been killed, and two officers and eighteen gunners wounded. On one occasion I had served as officer in charge of a burial party, a fact I passed on rather curiously to one of my high school teachers, the one who had taught me to appreciate Herrick's "To Daffodils." It was well I had had to memorize the poem for in battle its elegiac note often came back reminding me of how "short a Spring" some of us seemed destined to have. And certainly, as the struggle for the Gothic Line raged on, death and fear of death—or worse— were ever present. Weeks after the battle, I recalled occupying a gun position in late afternoon on the edge of a long valley, where I could see all about me the panorama of war: to the right, one of our batteries which had leap-frogged forward earlier and was already firing; behind us, great clouds of dust as an armoured unit came through partly hidden by the valley's crest; and to the far left in front, the area of the F.D.L.s, only visible because of mortar bursts.

What bothered me here was not the proximity of battle but certain puffs of black smoke from Jerry's air bursts in the sky to my immediate right. Such aerial goings-on I knew were the tell-tale signs of the enemy ranging in on targets. Why I assumed that the target had to be me I'll never know. But the impression was so strong that I swear cold fear almost numbed my body as I stood alone in the field by my director waiting for the sergeants to take line from me. And I don't suppose I waited any longer than two minutes—perhaps less. It was ridiculous of me to feel afraid because common sense should have reassured me that Jerry had a hundred more worthwhile targets across that landscape than me and my director. But that is how fear can engulf you, even destroy you. I was lucky and stood my ground. And all those G.P.O. courses in England served me well because my director drill was almost a reflex action. But not until I rejoined my Ack and Signaller, busy digging at the Command Post, did I settle down. Just to dig was an enormous relief. Thank God, I have never felt the same again as I did that day.

Gradually our advance slowed. I had, of course, no way of knowing that what was to be "a headlong pursuit," after our breakthrough on the Gothic Line, would turn into a "bitter, creeping battle"[10] that would last from September 3 to September 22. From high points on the Coriano Ridge, the Ripabianco Ridge, the Frisoni Spur, and the San Fortunato Spur, the Germans had excellent observation of their foes on the narrow coastal plain. German shelling of the Regiment's O.P.s was particularly effective. Life on the gun positions was also very unhealthy as high explosive hindered movement and made personnel edgy and fatalistic.

It was some help to me at this time when I was given or found a batman who proved to be a forager of rare abilities. Not only could he find Italian hens, but he could behead them, pluck and eviscerate, and boil them up very satisfactorily in hard tack cans. This expertise was most acceptable to the Ack, Signaller, and me in the Command Post. Our only complaint—too many pin feathers which looked very unpalatable. Although both Owen and I seemed to think our meals acceptable enough, the Regiment's *History* for this period states that "The

---

10. Nicholson, *Canadians in Italy*, Vol. II, p. 526

ration situation during the whole Gothic Line operation was grim. There was no issue of fresh meat or vegetables, and the meals consisted of a steady diet of M & V."[11]

At 0100 hours on September 13, the "War Diary" for the Regiment notes the attack on the Coriano Ridge had begun:

> The Cape Breton Highlanders were on the right flank, Perths on the left and the Irish, when the other two were firm on the Ridge, did a left hook into Coriano. The artillery support was probably greater than any single brigade had ever had. The 1st Canadian Corps artillery, consisting of ten field regiments, six medium regiments, two heavy regiments and two heavy Ack-Ack regiments, was in support and the artillery of the 5th British Corps was on call.

Not until noon on September 14 was the Ridge in Canadian hands. The Germans had fought well and denied Coriano's houses one by one to the attackers.

Word now came for the Regiment to move to the river bottom below Coriano, which had been heavily mined. The guns limbered up at 2045 hours and made a fine run on a pitch black night without mishap, arriving at 2245 hours. At 0015 hours they were on Theatre Grid, and I was bent over the artillery board plotting targets and fire plans and noting the vital statistics for each if they were called for. In the early morning just to the rear of the position, one of the gunners on his way to a latrine found a shoe with a foot in it, a grim reminder of the hazards on the slopes about. Farther away, German shells were exploding amid the clouds of dust raised on the Up and Down routes by Allied traffic.

That day, September 17, was a Sunday, and the Padre held a succession of small services at each battery. I told Ellen about the one at Fox Troop:

---

11. *History of the 17th Field Regiment, Royal Canadian Artillery, 5th Canadian Armoured Division,* (Groningen: Niemeijer, 1946), p.61.

One gun was placed out of action with a Union Jack draped over its breech, while skeleton crews manned the other three guns. The Padre read from the Bible, gave a short talk and prayer. Singing of hymns was a melancholy failure as my prairie gunners seem to have neither music nor voices for such an event. In view of something that happened during this day, I think religion must have seemed somewhat incongruous to the Troop. Whose side the Almighty's on is at times not at all certain.[12]

The next day at 0400 hours, everyone awake in the Regiment, saw for the first time anti-aircraft searchlights illuminating enemy targets on the San Fortunato Ridge so that medium bombers could find their targets. Later, on the same day, the gunners saw a Spitfire ablaze and spiralling downward until, with a great roar, it ended in a black smudge in the Regimental area. The pilot parachuted but unfortunately landed among the Germans.

As the battle surged on, the Germans retreated north to put the Marecchio River between them and their pursuers. Allied hopes rose with the expectation of an armoured breakthrough into the Romagna Plains, for the defenses of the Gothic Line were in ruins. After a month of savage fighting, Operation Olive was over. But Monte Maggiore was only thirty miles behind, a grim reminder that the advance had averaged little more than a mile a day.

Between September 8 and 21, the army's 25-pdrs. had fired 1,200,000 rounds as compared with the 1,000,000 rounds fired over ten days at El Alamein. "Canadian losses," states Nicholson, "were heavier than for any period of equal length either before or after during the Italian campaign." The 5th Armoured Division lost 1385 officers and men, including 390 killed, but it was, as General Sir Oliver Leese (who had succeeded

---

12. The "War Diary" for this date speaks of "a heavy concentration" and of a shell that "landed right in 'A' Troop gunpit killing Sgt. T. J. Stewart and wounding the other five members of his crew."

Montgomery as General Officer Commanding-in-Chief of the Eighth Army) told his troops:

> ... a great victory. By the bitterest fighting since El Alamein and Cassino you have beaten eleven German Divisions and broken through into the Po Valley. The greater part of the German armies in Italy were massed against us and they have been terribly mauled. I congratulate you and thank you all. We must now hit hard day and night and force them back over the Po.[13]

But the army Commander's enthusiasm and/or optimism rested very much upon two conditions: one, that the German ability to fight brilliant withdrawal actions was no longer a decisive factor; and, two, that it would not rain. As it turned out, neither condition offered grounds for much hope.

---

13. Nicholson, *Canadians in Italy*, Vol. II, pp. 562- 563.

Chapter 11

Grim Days

"I was asleep in my slit trench when rain began on the night of September 20." The rest of my letter to Iain described what happened.

Since I had no protection from the wet, I took my safari apart, rolled up my bedding, tossed it into the George vehicle, and returned to the Command Post. I was disappointed because I had counted on having a good night's sleep as we were then definitely out of range and had been told to get rest. My G.P.O., Ack, and Signaller were already bedded down in the Command Post which meant it was a bit crowded.

By the time I entered, it was pouring rain, and the clay soil was getting sticky. The dugout was a well-constructed hole in the ground provided by some comfort-conscious Jerries who must have had little chance to use it. As it was on the side of a ravine, we had dug steps leading down to it. In the rain these were turning into a viscous and decidedly slippery stairway. Once inside, I forgot the weather as the dugout was both dry and safe from stray rounds. I found a seat, wedged myself upright, and began to wait.

About 11:30 p.m. the second of our Acks slithered down into our midst, drenched from head to foot. He had dug an oversized slit trench and built a make-shift shelter over it using his ground sheet and an arrangement of scrounged wood and his rifle to hold it in place. The rain had gradually filled his ground sheet, causing the underpinning to collapse so that he received the flood in bed. He was very disconsolate as he contemplated how he was ever going to get either his bedding or his uniform dried out.

His gloom eased when the next visitor, having lost his footing on the steps, arrived on his bottom in nothing but his undershirt and his white briefs, clutching his very wet uniform in his hands. Unlike the Ack, he had undressed before getting into his slit trench. What made for much hilarity was the intruder's rank; he was the Troop Sergeant Major. Then, as if we were not already crowded enough, the Bdr. Signaller joined us. He had escaped the fate that overtook the others and was reasonably dry. Now we could offer standing room only until the G.P.O. went off duty at 1:00 a.m., when he eased the congestion by retiring to the George vehicle, not always the safest place but at least dry.

> So, here I am writing a letter at 0300 hours trying to kill time until dawn when I hope this bloody rain gives up. Everyone else is asleep in various uncomfortable positions. For a time the Sergeant Major chattered away to me about his past and of all things wanted to know what de la Mare's traveller meant as he called out 'Is there anybody there?' It is interesting how our memory work from school sticks with us—probably well worth the effort. But at last the Sergeant Major has fallen asleep, sitting bolt upright with one of my blankets wrapped around his naked frame. He used his briefs to wipe the clay off his feet. His other clothing is somewhere back in the Wagon Lines, a quarter mile of water away.
> I'm glad you are learning some first aid. Wish I knew more than I do. Here, it's just a tourniquet, a shell dressing, and back to the R.A.P. Seeing my first casualty was unhinging, but I am much more used to this happening now.
> The latest was an Italian peasant lad who

got, by some misfortune, into the minefield on
the Coriano hillside, where he stepped on a Schu-
mine. It blew his foot right off and burned his
other leg black. He was in considerable pain
when they got him to the Command Post. I shall
not for a long time forget the look on his face
and the piteous *Mama mia's* he uttered. The last I
saw of him he was lying back in a jeep ambulance on the way to the A.D.S., his bloody
stump in the air, and still calling on Mary, the
mother of Jesus, to help him. It was my first experience with what a mine can do to you. I was
impressed.

On September 23 the Regiment moved at 0200 hours to a
new area. The night was black as Erebus and the road twisting
with deep ditches and gullies on one side; on the other, sheer
walls of rock. We were all tired so that keeping our vehicles a
safe distance from each other and keeping them on the narrow
road required exhausting alertness on the part of the drivers.
Not until 0745 hours were we in our new position and on
Theatre Grid.

Tired and awaiting fire orders, I was surprised to find the
Troop Sergeant Major coming to me an hour later with a long
face and, very unlike him, a hesitant manner. He told me that
he had bad news. When it came out, it was to announce
Freddy's death. He had been accidentally killed during the
move that night, when a vehicle he was on strayed from the
road, rolled over, and crushed him.

It was the cruellest blow [I wrote] and nothing
whatever left for me to do for one who had been
so good a friend. By now we were firing, and I
was alone with the troop and unable to leave the
Command Post to attend the funeral which was
at 1100 hours. Death seems to me now so much
more intimate. That some of us must become so
suddenly forever silent suggests the machina-
tions of the 'Purblind Doomsters'.

By October 1 Ellen had the news from Iain now living in
Guelph. "Oh, Sandy," she wrote, "I just cannot believe Fred is no
more; I feel so sorry for his English bride and his parents. All
day long I have been thinking of him, which is strange as I
knew him only from your letters, and, my son I have been thinking of you, too. Oh, do be careful." From Fred's father came a
letter dated October 24: "We received official word on September 29th, and it was certainly the most tragic and heart-breaking
news that we have ever had to bear." Later in the letter he asked
me, if I could, to visit his son's grave.

Early in November I heard from his wife:

> I never for a moment thought anything would
> happen to dear Freddy. We had planned and
> longed so much for the day we would start life
> together in Canada. I just cannot believe I shall
> never see him again. I was ill for a long time
> after his death and am only now recovering.
> That's why you have not heard from me before
> this.
>
> If only I could have seen him once more, for
> we had such a few weeks of married life
> together.

She had received the box of mixed nuts which he had sent
her from Naples. These she was keeping for Christmas. The
jewel box she intended to keep forever by her. She had had a letter from the King and Queen "offering their heartfelt sympathy
in my great sorrow." Nine of her letters to him had been
returned to her unopened. "I only wish," she continued, "he
could have got my letters more quickly. I wrote to him every
day." She closed asking me to try to visit Freddy's grave and
say a prayer for her.

The day following his death, the Regiment moved at 1330
hours. "With his usual nasty touch," the "War Diary" reported,
"Jerry took this opportunity of shelling all the roads in the
neighbourhood of the Marecchio River. There are a good many
lads in the Regiment who won't forget that trip for a short
while." Later that afternoon three of the ammunition trucks

belonging to my Battery were hit, one gunner killed, and four more wounded. By 1615 hours, Fox Troop was on Theatre Grid, and I was bent over the artillery board preparing the Troop's portion of a thirty-two-line barrage that required 350 rounds per gun. According to the "War Diary," the plan was fired from 1940 to 2235 hours and went off without a hitch. I had little time to grieve.

Rain continued to thwart the advance as the Regiment moved beyond the Marecchio. On September 29, the Intelligence Officer noted in the "War Diary" that there had been

> about ten Army Service Corps vehicles bogged down this morning, but F.A.T.s and a lot of hard work saw them all back on the road by 1100 hours. Where they are going to move next we can't figure out, as the bridge immediately behind us has flooded out. The road situation is almost unbelievable, and all routes practically defy all traffic except jeeps. Communications were ripped and torn all over the place, and for the better part of the day the only communication beyond the Regiment was by wireless. ... Heavy shelling and mortaring all day, but the passing of shelreps and moreps was almost impossible owing to the heavy traffic on the air.

At 0300 hours on Saturday, September 30, I wrote to my parents saying I wished I could tell them what happened during the nights of September 28-30. "I doubt if so much drama was ever packed into any movie. I shall never forget those nights." What happened in part appears in the Regiment's "War Diary" on September 30.

> Heavy harassing fire carried out by the enemy all day with Nebels and guns which naturally brought a stream of shelreps. We must be passing at least one hundred per day, if not more. At 1910 hours reports came from all O.P.s of signs of a counter attack. .... Sixteen D.F. and D.F. (S.O.S.) tasks were fired, also one Uncle Target,

three Mike Targets, and two Battery Targets. The enemy attacked with infantry and tanks. Enemy planes were bombing and strafing the F.D.L.s and gun areas at the exact moment the attack began. . . . A Coy. of the Perths has not been heard from since the attack started.

Two days later the "War Diary" announced that one of the Regiment's officers serving as an artillery observer with the Irish was missing, presumed P.O.W. As well, fifty-three men of "A" Company of the Irish had been taken prisoner.[14]

I made no mention of these troublesome days until November 20 when I sent a long letter to Iain describing what happened within my perspective of the battle; I was alone, I said, with the troop as my G.P.O. had been evacuated with an infected arm. On arriving at the new gun position, we placed our Command Post at the bottom of a deep ditch which was dry, offered excellent protection, and spared much digging. But, alas, the decision lacked foresight.

An hour after we had reported on Theatre Grid it began to rain heavily, which brought a trickle of water creeping round our feet. That trickle soon became a small stream, and it in turn a big one which convinced us that if we stayed where we were, we would be swept out into the Adriatic. Reluctantly, we turned out into the downpour with our shovels and constructed a proper dugout on the bank above the stream, just getting our equipment out in time and managing throughout the exercise to stay in action.

The next day the Regiment was shelled repeatedly, but we were lucky because many of the rounds disappeared in the mud before exploding, so that we had less shrapnel than usual and escaped casualties. By nightfall all was so quiet that I decided to put my bedroll under the George vehicle, which we had parked beside the dugout, and try for some sleep. But at the last moment I changed my mind and put the bedroll, minus the safari, on a narrow shelf in the Command Post. My batman

---

14. Nicholson, *Canadians in Italy*, Vol. II, p.572.

then decided that he'd adopt my original plan.

All went well until midnight, when Jerry sent a round over—probably an 88 mm—that exploded just in front of the George vehicle. I heard the batman cry out and went to see what had happened. He said he'd been hit in the leg. I pulled him out on his blankets, which were wet with blood, and tried to see where he'd been hurt, but the leg was such a mess that all we could do was apply a tourniquet above the knee and yell for the stretcher. He and his bearers disappeared back into the rain and the darkness, and that was the end of the best batman I'd ever had.

I remembered the message from one of my signallers about 1910 hours on September 30 to the effect that the enemy had crossed the Fiumicino River, which we referred to as the Rubicon (probably the same river that in ancient times formed the boundary between Italy and Cisalpine Gaul, the same river that Julius Caesar crossed as he marched against Pompey in 49 B.C.). That both German tanks and infantry were coming our way instead of our tanks and infantry going their way was a distinct shock to me. But in seconds fire orders came, and for two hours we smothered the Hun with fire and steel so accurately that his counterattack fizzled out.

Either that night or the night before I had my first experience close up to Nebelwerfers shelling our troop position. I thought their moaning, screaming flight a real horror. Fortunately for us all the rounds struck about three hundred feet ahead of the guns, but even so I was mightily impressed by the fiery ball they made on impact. For a few minutes I began to have the same feeling in the pit of my stomach as I had had from time to time at Monte Maggiore. It was, however, soon over. Once we had regained what the enemy had tried to keep, our intelligence reported only light shelling and mortaring all through the day and night of October 1 but no casualties, and that sort of activity continued for several days.

Throughout October, November, and December, the Regiment set its face towards the Lombard Plain, inching its way northwards over hundreds of map squares to gun positions in the mud. Opposed by rain, swollen rivers, and von Vietinghoff's

76th Panzer Corps, General Alexander admitted as early as September 26 that his forces were "too weak relative to the enemy to force a break-through and so close the pincers."[15] Also, the supply of reinforcements for the infantry regiments was drying up. In Canada, Colonel Ralston was clashing head-on with Mackenzie King over the necessity to send NRMA conscripts overseas. Such a move, in effect, amounted to conscription and, for King, this would mean the end of the Liberal Party, success to the C.C.F., and the possibility of "two nations warring in the bosom of one state." On November 1, 1944, the Prime Minister dismissed Colonel Ralston from his Cabinet.

In the Regiment, reinforcements were needed. On September 27, the "War Diary" noted that forty-three badly needed reinforcements had arrived which included some more of the converted Light Anti-Aircraft gunners. Two days later the Regimental Orderly Officer observed that it was "almost a physical impossibility to keep the Regiment up to strength." On October 4, our ranks fleshed out when another draft of nineteen O.R.s and two officers arrived. But, by October 18, the Regiment was again considerably under strength.

One man who would never come back to us was my batman, Rowe, who wrote to me on October 8:

> Dear Mr. Ross;
>
> Well Sir I'm feeling pretty good now; I've had two operations and two casts put on, it was quite a large hole but they made a good job of patching it up.
>
> I'm finished for this war, but in a year should be able to walk without a limp.
>
> If you haven't already done so or turned them in will you see what you can find of my large pack and send anything personal like my New Testament to my sister?
>
> Give my regards to everybody and keep ducking at the right time.

---

15. Nicholson, *The Gunners of Canada*, Vol. II, p.238.

If you do drop me a line, let me know how
close that shell was, I never heard it.
Best of luck Sir.

I never mentioned the shortage of personnel in my letters.
Shortages at the time to me seem to have meant a pair of "Duck"
rubber boots which someone had stolen from me. Ellen was
very concerned: "However do you get along without your high
boots in such wet and mud? Iain has sent another pair on to
you—just when you'll get them, one cannot tell." Later on she
told me that "we have sent off your Christmas parcels; they are
all eats as I did not know what else to send you. Iain sent a
Christmas cake to you; it was from Fred's mother, who wanted
you to have it."

To Iain, on Sunday, October 8, I reported that the weather
on our sector was damnable—rain, rain, and mud everywhere.
On that day we had had a very successful evening church service in a barn because the Padre had timed the event to coincide
with the issue of rum. Parcels had arrived to cheer us in the
Command Post, "where we all share such loot at once rather
than hoard it and run the risk of its destruction by enemy action."

I went on to say how much I admired the ingenuity of my
gunners as they coped in the open with mud and rain. They
had become masters in the art of shelter building in their gun
pits, some of their efforts resembled the sod huts I'd seen in pictures of early homesteading on the prairies. Recently daily existence for the men had been an even greater tribulation because
the ground was now so sodden that it affected the accuracy of
the guns: the ground on which the gun platforms rested was
simply not stable enough, so we had to take up alternate positions, and the men had all their house building and digging of
gun pits to do over again.

But despite the weather and the appalling condition of the
roads, mail arrived regularly at the Battery Command Posts. E.
W. Bradwin sent on a message of cheer and good wishes. From
Louise came a letter revealing that life for her was full:

Running a 90-bed ward is a full-time job, but I

like every minute of it and wouldn't have
missed it for anything.

Saturday night I was to a dinner party at a
hotel just around the corner here. Was really
wonderful. We had chicken, lobster, apple pie
and ice cream, tomatoes, stuffed celery, pickled
onions, salmon, hard-boiled eggs, etc., and coffee. Some really good cocktails before dinner,
champagne and wine for dinner, and Scotch
after. Had a Belgian orchestra which was really
super. I danced miles.

Before closing she said she'd like very much to meet me in Paris
for a few days' leave even though she admitted that Paris and
leave were rather a distance away at present.

From my batman's sister came a note thanking me for sending on her brother's possessions. He had been the only boy in a
family of five sisters, and he had a wife and son in England.

Another letter of October 21 was from Owen in the 2nd
Field:

Got your letter with the sad news about Fred. I
had heard about it at the time while on a recce,
but as the G.P.O. was on leave, I couldn't leave
the troop. I was damn sorry to hear about it,
though: it always seems to happen to the best fellows.

A week ago I had a hell of a rough time. Was
all alone in the troop. A wounded chap standing
beside me was killed, I got away with a nick on
my eyebrow and a bit in my eye. Never saw
such concentration before—and all day long,
too. Things have improved considerably since—
even sunshine now.

From October 1 until October 21 the map reference for the
Regiment's location never changed, a certain indication of how
successfully rain and a stubborn enemy taking advantage of
dykes, swollen rivers, stone farm buildings, and the unending
screens offered by vineyards could stop an armoured division

in its tracks. But during those three weeks the old hazards of active service were present. Six gunners were wounded and two killed in the Regiment. One of the dead belonged to Fox Troop:

> He was one of my best gunners, a big prairie
> man, strong and even-tempered, who bled to
> death inwardly as we carried him on the
> stretcher through mud and Jerry's shelling to the
> R.A.P. Nothing at all heroic about such an end
> from a piece of shrapnel you never see and one
> that left just a small blue bruiselike opening on
> his chest.

A less deadly chore came on October 12, when Part 1 Orders carried a note about a Field General Court Martial to be assembled for the purpose of trying a gunner charged with desertion in the face of the enemy. I served as the Prosecuting Officer. The only detail of this event that survives in my yellowing correspondence is the one sentence: "The poor simple bloke got six months in the digger."

What I still remember of the circumstances is sitting in my Troop Leader's vehicle, jacknifed over sand bags on the floor boards, and watching a straight gravelled road ahead that was screened on one side by jute sacking strung on poles. In the back of the vehicle under a tarp was one of our French-speaking gunners who could see the road as it unrolled behind us. The Germans had the entire length of it under observation and were shelling it while we made a run for it, "getting the hell out of there," as my driver would say.

With the accelerator to the floor, we were roaring along trusting that our number was not yet up, when a shell burst on the road about one hundred feet ahead of us compelling my Jehu to brake furiously into a cloud of dust and flying debris and then, in low gear, to get round the crater in the road. As he brought his vehicle back on the road, Jerry bracketted, and the shell burst behind us but off the road and harmlessly as we roared into high gear and away.

Back at the gun position, we missed the gunner in the back of the vehicle. Nearly a month later he returned to us, having

174

presumably become disillusioned with the Italian family who had sheltered him, after blind fear drove him from our vehicle while we were being shelled. His knowledge of Italian had served him well with his rescuers, and he spoke with warmth of their kindness to him, especially of their fresh eggs, homemade bread, and *vino rosso* which had been his daily fare.

Why I had been chosen to be the Prosecuting Officer for his Court Martial, I do not know as I was quite innocent of the role I was expected to play and had to be prepared for the task by a senior officer sent in to preside over the case. But, of course, the evidence was such that my legal inadequacy mattered little, and our gunner disappeared from his Regiment. I don't suppose that his punishment was really merited, but by adhering to army protocol, we had acted as we were supposed to act for such offenses and had reminded all ranks of their bounden duty and service as we battled northwards through rain and German resistance.

Chapter 12

Addio Italia

With his guns and transport bogged down in Italian mud, the Colonel of the 17th Field may have had time to remember that he had to react to the complaint made by the army's Unit Maintenance Inspectorate regarding the condition of Canadian army vehicles. He acted quickly. And I was the first officer singled out to be sent on a Motor Transport Course held in Benevento, four hundred miles south of our position on the Fiumicino:

> All I have to go on [I told my parents] is the name of the town where the course is held. So here I am in the corner of a small railroad box car travelling south: shades of my Frontier College days.
>
> I am the only officer on the train and am vaguely in charge of fifteen British soldiers and a mixed lot of Indian troops: Gurkhas and bearded Sikhs. We had to take our own rations with us which brought about a real chow-row in the neighbouring car where the Indians were. A deputation came to see me, very respectfully, to say they had nothing to eat but hard tack. The reason? Well, only the army could send an Indian detachment off with cases of bully beef to eat! Fortunately we had tinned fish in our rations which we did not want, so we were able to ar-

range a swap, and the Indians were happy.

At the rate we are travelling, it's going to take us days to get to Benevento. Our cooking arrangements, however, have just been resolved by one of the British lads, a Somerset man, who, when we were stopped at a siding, scrounged a supply of bricks and built a fireplace just inside the door of our box car. Our mobile residence at mealtime resembles a wigwam in all but its rectangular shape. Whenever the engine gets any speed up at all, the fireplace blazes merrily, and the smoke and sparks are sucked out the open door.

We expect some railroad official will put a stop to this catering service, but meantime we have hot tea and a kind of pudding which the British lads make by putting hard tack in water, adding sugar and anything else they think suitable, and boiling the whole mess up in a hard tack can.

And there you have a sketch of my new life. Just now I haven't the slightest idea of where I am in central Italy. And I must stop this run-along letter as our car is bumping about in all directions. One good thing about this trip is that I'll get caught up on sleep as we do not travel at night.

A day later I told of a long wait at a siding when, going for a walk down the track, I found a fierce-looking Gurkha brewing up a pot of tea over a small fire. He turned out to be a very agreeable chap who immediately insisted on giving me a tin cup full of his tea, saying, "Here, Sahib, is a drink I make for you." Fancy Sahib Ross's pleasure! And it was excellent tea, much better than I got from the "Brits" in the car, who made theirs too strong. I also told Rab and Ellen that the Gurkha had showed me his kukri knife. "Razor sharp it was. No wonder the Jerries fear the attention of the Gurkhas on a dark night."

After four days and nights in the box car, I and three British N.C.O.s arrived in Benevento three days late for the course. Even the scenery through the mountains was by then becoming monotonous. The hills were barren and the similarity of the towns and villages offered no variety, except the scars inflicted by bombing and shell fire. And the people were so miserably poor:

> And that reminds me of something that happened about a month ago on our gun position. About four in the morning, I heard voices coming towards us in the distance. We all stood to with cocked weapons waiting. And guess whom the voices belonged to! A group of twenty, maybe thirty Italians, the women shrouded in black shawls and black dresses, the men in ragged coats and trousers—some with no shoes. The women carried bundles on their heads and most of the men battered suitcases tied up with twine. One man pushed a kind of handmade barrow piled high. Ignoring our challenge, they came out of the dark on to the gun position. They were a very tired lot of desperately poor people who begged some bread from us and then trudged off into the grey light of dawn. We could not understand their dialect, making out only the word *Tedeschi* (Germans). What a frightful task awaits a country like Italy once this war is over.

Although late for the course, we were given extra tuition in the evenings so that we were able to catch up on what we had missed. As it turned out, this course, run by the British, was all that I could have hoped for. The workshops were large and offered all sorts of opportunity to work on a wide range of wheeled vehicles. As well, the British had a way of providing comforts which I really liked: dinner plates instead of mess tins, tea at 10:30 a.m. and 4:30 p.m., and, when you awoke in the morning, an Italian batman was standing by your bed with a cup of tea for you, while in a corner of the room stood your boots, polished and ready to wear.

I shared a room with a South African and an Indian, Kishan Singh, who spoke English fairly well; he was a devout Hindu, a small, wiery man. I became used to seeing him at his prayers in the evening when he lit a sandalwood taper which filled our room with the most pleasant odour as he seated himself cross-legged before it.

We had several talks about his religion when we were alone in the room. To my query as to his feelings towards Occidental missionaries, he replied that good was done, but those of his people who adopted Christianity became outcasts. He said rather firmly that India should be able to send out its own missionaries, an idea which had never occurred to me. Although I listened carefully to him as he talked about his beliefs—about Brahma, Vishnu, Siva, and Krishna—I became sadly muddled up. As far as I could tell from the complexities of his account, his religion had a great array of gods and their consorts. As a faith, however, it seemed as all-encompassing as my own. Certainly he practised it much less self-consciously than I did mine.

Nothing of the warrior was at all obvious in Kishan Singh. His kindness, his quiet otherworldliness, seemed quite at variance with the reputation his fellow countrymen have won for themselves. I could not imagine him using a bayonet.

My other roommate, the South African, was a big man, at least six feet two inches, broad shouldered with a chest like a sherry cask. What attracted me most was the appearance of his back when he was getting ready for bed or shaving in the morning. It looked like the face of the moon on a very clear night, deep pits and scars shadowed it from the nape of his neck to his buttocks. I asked him what had happened. It turned out that he'd tripped a German jumping S mine in the desert and survived—after weeks in the hospital. He was part black, although he had few negroid features. I liked him very much, and his descriptions of his homeland near Algoa Bay made that country seem most attractive to me.

My two weeks on course went very quickly. The instructors were among the best I had ever had in the army, and the

Officers' Mess was a lively spot where Kishan and I spent several evenings just talking and one getting maudlin drunk on my bottle of issue Scotch. It seems strange to me now that we never talked about the troubles in his homeland: about Nehru, or Gandhi, or agrarian reform. If we did, I've forgotten, and there's no mention of them in my letters that survive.

During those two weeks, I was too busy to have time to see much of Benevento, although I mentioned Trajan's Arch in one of my letters to Ellen and told her I could find nothing in the impoverished shops in the town to send her for Christmas. Instead, I said, I was sending her a cheque—one not to be banked but spent just on themselves. My M.T. course had ended well considering the late start, and I was pleased to receive an A grade.

My return from Benevento was almost as unusual as my trip there. I was sent by Army Transport to Bari, where I took ship to Ancona. Here I found wheeled transport to the Regiment. Despite the life-boat drills we endured, the voyage from Bari was really very interesting. With us were perhaps 150 black Basuto troops. I had never seen these men before, big chaps, coal black, tremendously happy and inordinately vain of their clothing, especially their fancy hats which, one of their officers told me, they would lose or deliberately damage beyond repair if they were not quite satisfied with them.

Most of the Basutos were Roman Catholic. Regularly in the evenings they gathered on the deck to hold a service with Scripture reading, prayer, and singing. Their singing was deep and rhythmical. I could have done, I remarked "with one or two of them in my troop for our own services." Although simple, their act of worship was affecting and reminded me of something I had read about Highland regiments in the Peninsular War, when regular religious services were carried on by enlisted Catechists. No priest was present at the Basuto service. What they celebrated seemed spontaneous requiring little direction. To me their gestures and singing indicated a really joyful faith, one I'd never recognized before but which impressed me very much.

By November 6, I was back with the Regiment, now in a rest

area in Fossombrone on the Metauro River, where a plan to house men from one battery in the local jail miscarried when part of that building collapsed sending one of the gunners to hospital. Fortunately, safer billets were found for them. On Sunday, following my return, I wrote to my parents. I sat in the Officers' Mess keeping close to the one stove, as it was much too cold to write in my quarters. Even here, any distance away from this stove, I could see my breath in the air; the whole end of the Mess had been bombed out and over the gaping hole we had strung a huge tarpaulin to keep out the wind which came whooping in from the snow-covered summits of the nearby hills.

Curiously it was the little necessities of life that troubled me here. It was really bleak, I complained, getting out of a warm bedroll at dawn and knowing you had to queue up with village women at the fountain in the square to get water for shaving. Once I had the water, it had to be heated in one-half of a mess tin over a primus stove. The process at least kept the mess tin clean against the time when we would be in action again. Breakfast in the Mess, where the temperature compared favourably with that around the fountain, made me think longingly of the comforts of another Mess in Benevento. Of course, had I had a batman, my early mornings would have been a bit more agreeable, but a batman was becoming less and less a possibility as reinforcements became scarce. The gunners, too, disliked Fossombrone but for other reasons. I overheard one of mine wishing heartily that he was back in action because he "was damned well fed up cleaning and polishing guns and equipment."

Having told my mother about my voyage and the shortcomings of Fossombrone, I turned to sorting and reading the correspondence which had been held at the Regiment. One letter was from Hughie who was then on a "Battle Course" in England:

> If I survive this six weeks, I will be a full-fledged
> infanteer. I was, as you may guess, rusting away
> doing nothing so decided to volunteer for the in-
> fantry. If I had not done so, I would probably

have been sent anyway. As you know Ack-Ack
is pretty well done.

I rode in a fox hunt a week ago, Sandy! It
was a swish affair—about twenty-five hounds,
huntsmen in red coats and white breeches,
topped off with horn and whip, beautiful ladies
and beautiful horses. We rode from 10:30 to
16:30 and got one fox. It was a day to be remembered—much better than anything in Labrador.

Along with Hughie's letter was another from Ellen who
referred to Colonel Ralston's retirement and the mud slinging
that attended the Presidential election in the United States. She
went on:

My how I would like to talk to you and to see
you. Somehow your last letter made you seem
very near, I suppose, because you were not in action; then you seem so far away. I wonder if by
now Elizabeth has written to you and what the
verdict is. As yet we haven't a phone, but am
going to see about it soon as it's pretty lonely
here especially in the evenings. Glad you took
out another $200.00 bond; I got one for $100.00. I
liked your box-car letter.

If there was no letter from Elizabeth in that batch of mail,
there was another from Louise who had had two from me since
she had last written. She began by wanting to know "in
heaven's name" what I had been drinking "the night you slept
on the floor in Benevento instead of in your bed." Then she
went on to say how busy she'd been:

This was one of those days, evacuating, trans-
ferring from one ward to another besides nursing, and the desk work, it's a full-time job but
don't have all day to spend at it. I would much
rather be doing bedside nursing and looking
after the boys any day. One thing I can do is lay
down the law. I try to do it as tactfully as pos-

sible, but when some Limey lad asks you fifty times to get him back to his unit instead of a Reinforcement Depot, when you can't do a thing about it, it does try one's patience a bit.

However, for all that, I enjoy every minute of it, as the boys are so good about things and never complain. One Limey lad who was very ill yesterday said this morning that he was 'just smashing' today. Really makes one think one's doing something worthwhile.

Haven't been out very much, about once in ten days lately. Went to one English party and the Brigadier and I discussed the seriousness of the servant problem after the war. Needless to say he is much more worried about it than I am.

The day after Louise wrote from France, Julia wrote from Belgium to say she had given up Tent 38 among the cider apple trees for a very modern apartment in a Belgian city: "deep arm chairs, wall lights, cream tiled kitchenette converted to a bedroom, large living room." The apartment had been occupied formerly by German naval officers. "When I am married," she announced, "I want an apartment like this one." She was very, very busy and on duty from 7:30 a.m. until 7:00 or 8:00 p.m., with little or no time off. The hospital had been in German hands, and they were still using up German medical supplies which, she said, were very good.

The hospital is very large, splendidly furnished and equipped, warm with lots of hot water. Belgian girls help us in the wards as V.A.D.s; Belgian nurses work with us, too, while their doctors come with our M.O.s. Boy Scouts help also as well as Belgian ambulance drivers and clergy.

My ward is the one for face wounds. No doubt you've seen enough face wounds to realize what some of the cases must be like. As ever the boys are always wonderful. They want only your care and understanding, and I think they fear pity. We have some P.O.W.s too, of various ages, wounds, and resentments. In all fairness, they are brave, too.

I hope this war is finished soon. Sometimes, after seeing these boys, I wonder if it's worth all this sacrifice. ... Soon Armistice Day will be here. Remember the parades? And the bands? The wreaths and the Last Posts? I am not disillusioned, but there's so much pain and irony that my heart aches at times.

Eileen of Woodstock days also wrote; it was the last letter I ever received from her and contained her reaction to Freddy's death; she had known him for some time in England before his marriage.

To say it was a great shock is putting it mildly. I still don't believe it. My co-worker on the ward asked me if the chap was a close friend of mine and in my stupor I said, yes, then, no, and then, yes, he was a friend of a friend of mine, Sandy Ross.

And guess what my dear, you old sly boots! My co-worker is Julia Sloane. Does her name ring any bells in your belfry? I have been working on the same ward as Julia now for two weeks. She seems like a good egg and is full of fun.

Must run now, Sandy, I'm still full to the eyes, and I realize how you must feel, too.

What may be inferred from my correspondence with my clutch of Nursing Sisters was that they regarded me only as a friend, a little eccentric, possibly devious, but someone who could be depended upon to write to them regularly. I was not, as I may have thought, their idea of a really suitable husband. Even Louise's letters have a sort of neutrality about them which made my assertion that she was chasing me seem downright self-deception. Whether I knew it or not, I could at this date

depend upon only one woman and that was Ellen w.
mitted only one competitor for my place in her affection
that was Elizabeth.

But here again I was mistaken for on December 4, when we
were back in action near the village of Godo, six miles east of
Ravenna, I received a letter from Elizabeth that explained much:

> This letter may be a very bad mistake, but ever
> since I received your last letter I've known I had
> to write it. I just hope I can state the facts plainly
> without sounding like a melodramatic ass.
>
> When I was seventeen, and before I met you,
> I fell in love. You made me forget him—almost.
> The times when I wanted to call us quits and
> stopped writing for weeks on end were the times
> when the ghost of this former love returned to
> haunt me. Two years ago I thought I had it lick-
> ed, but the last few months have proved how
> wrong I was.
>
> It's something, Sandy, over which I seem to
> have no control—believe me; if I had, I should
> soon cease to be miserable. I thought I could
> keep on writing to you as one sweetheart to
> another, but the words stick in my pen and
> won't come out. This other person doesn't know
> how I feel—and won't—in fact, none, but you
> now knows what a complete fool I am capable of
> being! I can't kid myself any longer that it is
> simply a passing fancy, and so I am writing now
> to ask you to leave me to my misery, Sandy, and
> try to find happiness with someone else. Does
> that sound heartless? Forgive me if it does.

There followed a lengthy account of her teaching and her
worries about the attitude of the new generation of restless students whom she found in the classroom. It was an honest but
sad attempt to come to terms with the accidents of her life in a
rapidly changing society. It was the last letter I ever received
from her. I told Ellen about my loss in a letter in which I posed

185

as the "gentleman" and then tried to shrug off the happening: "I told Elizabeth, if my releasing any claim to her would make her happy, that she had my consent for I did not want to be the cause of any unhappiness to her. But at one time I was so sure she was mine. Well, heigh ho! It's all over now, and my love has fluttered away. I don't think I'll worry much, although I'm sure I shall never really forget her."

Now, I wonder why, at the time, I did not protest and insist she not be such a fool. Ellen's reaction was to fall back on an ancient placebo: "Well, Sandy, maybe for you it's a blessing in disguise—just wait and see. There are many fine girls yet who perhaps will make an ideal mate for you. Until then, bide your time." That advice tendered, she turned to her own affairs. Rab had bought another cow, a purebred Jersey three-years old for sixty dollars. "She is easy to milk and will freshen in March." They needed the additional stock to keep the stable warm enough in winter. For their own warmth, the Tavistock dealer had brought them fourteen hundred-weight of coke for $9.10. "We can now save our hard coal for the really cold weather."

The manse, Ellen found out, had many shortcomings, not least of which was the uncertainty of having rainwater in the cistern available for bathroom purposes. The cistern was more often dry than full of rainwater. The bathroom should have been connected years before to the well which was five hundred feet away from the manse. "Of course," Ellen said, "we can't expect our close-fisted church elders to agree to do this for us. I suppose they think we pay too little rent. But in winter it's dashed hard having to go out to the Parliament House, especially when it's stormy and cold."

From the livestock and the outhouse at Harrington to France must have seemed a bit incongruous to me at Godo as I opened a letter from Louise. But she, too, had problems. She was "teed off" with French plumbing which, she maintained, was on a par with that in England. None of the radiators on their fourth floor worked, and they were heating their rooms with a coal oil stove. On the social side, things were poor too. "I had one date with a Commando officer, who walked me all over town—not in the least romantic, I can assure you." She was looking forward to Christmas. "Remember last Christmas at Horley, we were so happy then. I'll be glad when this war is over. Really don't think I should write what I believe about things. Am afraid it wouldn't pass censorship."

Sometime before we left Fossombrone, I met Owen and the two of us went to see Fred's grave. It was very peaceful on the wide hillside, not at all as it was when we had a gun position a half mile away from the cemetery. All that remained of the battle for Coriano were a few burned out hulks of tanks, ruined farmhouses, and the town which was a complete shambles.

Fred was buried with about twenty-five men from the Cape Breton Highlanders. A white railing ran around the cemetery, and plain crosses marked the graves. I remembered his wife's request that I make a prayer for her, which I tried to do, but found the words difficult to find and the process embarrassing, which made me feel ashamed and annoyed. Instead of praying, I gave some money and some cigarettes to two Italians who lived nearby and asked them to plant grass and flowers on the grave in the spring. As well I took down their names and addresses intending to write to them later.

The "War Diary" for the Regiment, once we were in action again, refers repeatedly to unsettled weather, drizzling rain and, of course, mud. The one cheering happening during the day or night was the arrival of mail and parcels. Occasionally, too, our accommodation improved. The *casa* in which we had our Command Post on December 6 had a large living room with a stone floor and an enormous fireplace where all the cooking was done—most of it, I thought, in a large black kettle. The walls were plastered but had never been papered; representations of saints and the Virgin Mary served as decorations. The ceiling had rough beams across it; bars and shutters on the windows were meant to keep out cold and heat. The smell was a damp mixture of animals and humans for the stable was at one end of the house. Water came from an outside well by means of a chain, pulley, and bucket.

Farming methods here would have seemed primitive to my old boss, Simon Munro. He would, of course, have accepted the role of oxen had any of these beasts with their wide curving horns been left in the possession of the signor. But, thanks to the efforts of the Desert Air Force, the Germans were so short of transport that they had commandeered our host's oxen. He, poor man, was reduced to putting yokes on cows when he wanted to move his big two-wheeled cart. Actually, we saw very little of him as he went about his everyday chores.

It was his signora who showed us how to make a fire in the fireplace from green twigs and brush. Once it was going, we toasted our bread over the fire while she sliced the Spam Ellen had sent me and fried it in one of her pans. As well, she contributed a huge pitcher of red wine from one of her vats. Her concern for our welfare took our minds quite off the mud and Jerry's erratic shelling.

For the first two weeks in December, I had, what I told my brother, was "one hell of a dose of diarrhoea which made my comings and goings most uncertain:

> Until a few days ago I was able to cope, but three nights ago I failed to make it to the latrine. The poor old sphincters simply gave up all at once, with the result that what was supposed to be inside was outside—all the way to my ankles—a revolting slimy mess! Fortunately I had long Johns on, and I was able to get out of my battle dress trousers before they became contaminated.
>
> But you can imagine the not too well restrained mirth that greeted me on my return to our Troop's nerve post. Nothing like an intestinal disaster and nakedness to remove the barriers of rank.
>
> So there I was drawing water from the well and washing myself and my underwear. I might have thrown the long Johns away, but I have only two pairs and the other pair was back in the Wagon Lines with the George vehicle. And, of course, no batman to come to my assistance. Actually my immediate needs were beyond any duties a batman could be expected to assume.

Finally I got the underwear clean and for the rest of the night they hung limply from a cord in front of the fireplace while the gunners tried out various brands of wit such as 'Have you ever seriously considered, Sir, the possibility of setting up a laundry or dry-cleaning establishment on your return to Civvy Street? I understand there's good money in it and people often have dirty clothes that have to be cleaned. You should think of it, Sir, it could be the answer to one of your problems.' And more of the same.

And that did it. I went to the M.O. and described my condition. Guess what he gave me. Three tablespoons of castor oil and twenty whacking great white pills! But I do believe he's not as mad as his remedy suggests because at this time of writing I do feel much better.

This illness was fortunately the only one I suffered while with the Regiment so that, save for the course in Benevento, my tour of duty was unbroken. As time passed, I grew more confident of my role as Troop Leader and quite used to seeing my Gun Position Officers come and go: one to the Battery Command Post, one to hospital, one to R.H.Q., and one to another regiment. In the absence of a G.P.O., I was the officer in charge. Gradually it came to me that I was accepted by the men in the Troop for whom I began to feel increasingly responsible. Discipline was never a problem, and, if there were any disputes, they were resolved out of my hearing.

My superiors were the sort who never hesitated to tell me if I was not up to the mark. For the first month their favourite chastisement was to be abusive if my Troop was slow in reporting "Fox Ready!" to the fire orders we received. But once I learned to steady one of my "Acks," who was extremely nervous when plotting targets, our tardiness disappeared. We were never the first to report "Ready," but we were never the last which made for better relations with the Adjutant.

I nearly always worried about my map reading skills when

we moved at night, and I was the lead vehicle responsible for bringing the troop to its new gun area. Once, when I mistook a crossroads, I ended up turning the guns around in an Italian farmyard not far from the F.D.L.s. Perhaps this shortcoming came about in part because I had never driven a car until I was in the army so that I had a poor sense of distance covered at various speeds. This sense, I told Iain, was not helped at all when it was pitch dark, no headlights, and the sergeant-major not on point duty.

I'm sure, too, there were other occasions when I failed to measure up, but of these I have no record—possibly because I was too embarrassed to admit them or too anxious to avoid causing disquiet at home. The learning process went well beyond the pages of the military manuals. Regardless of enemy action, mud, or movement forward, I did, however, continue my letter writing. Early in the new year, E. W. Bradwin answered one of my letters which he had received on December 10. "How I wish," he said, "I were closer to you so we could sit down and have a cup of coffee. Yes, even in a dug-out, for I feel ashamed to think I am not sharing in some way the privations that men have undertaken, particularly those I have come to know as labourer-teachers."

Along with the letters came parcels, one I noted was from the Knox Church ladies of Harrington who sent me three hundred cigarettes and a pretty Christmas card. Two others were from Iain and Ellen; hers contained a Christmas cake, a jar of honey, two jars of crabapple jelly, and several spy apples—all edible. In my reply to her, I said I was taking a chance and keeping the cake and jelly for any celebration we may be permitted on Christmas Day. Motorcycle goggles and rubber boots with insoles arrived from Iain, the first no longer needed, but the second just the ticket for this mud that encircled us. It was excellent mail service.

Meanwhile Fox Troop inched its way along the Adriatic coast past names that sang as you pronounced them: Piangipane, the Valli di Comacchio, Villanova, Osteria, Bagnacavallo, Mezzano, and Alphonsine; and over rivers that were small but desperately difficult to cross and hold in the face of incredible German resistance. To the Allied right was Ravenna with its ancient Byzantine churches and Dante's tomb; to the left, the city of Bologna; and, in front, the battle for the rivers: the Montone, the Lamone, the Fosso Vecchia, the Naviglio, the Fosso Munio, and the Senio.

The "War Diary" describes a corner of the battle's patch-work quilt of death and destruction: of armoured thrusts on most unfavourable terrain beneath weeping skies; of thick mist at night when tired gunners peered anxiously over their gun shields for any enemy patrol that might blunder upon them. Elsewhere, records tell of fearful infantry casualties on the dykes where the Perths alone in the Fosso Munio action of December 19-20 lost thirty-two killed and forty-nine wounded, and of patrolling at night until a roused enemy called for artil-lery fire and opened up with Spandaus that could spit out 1200 rounds a minute. On December 17 the Regiment prepared a fire plan of 160 Stonks and Murders to support the Irish and the Perths as they attacked toward the swollen waters of the Fosso Munio with its five-feet high dykes sheltering German infantry.

Progress in December was brutally slow. By the time the Canadians were on the Senio, they had advanced but nine miles in the twenty-one days since the offensive began on December 2. The 1st Canadian Corps had lost 548 killed, 1796 wounded, and 212 taken prisoner.[16] On December 30, Field-Marshall Alexander abandoned the assault and established a winter defensive line facing the Senio River.

Fox Troop was quick to take advantage of a little perma-nence. Gun pits were soon elaborately strengthened and, except for the field of fire, protected overhead from the frost and flur-ries of snow that took the place of rain. As well, the gunners built their own shelters using sods for the wall above ground and scrounging lumber for roof beams. Within their *casas* they placed stoves of various homemade brands that could burn either oil or wood and provide heat to warm them and dry damp clothing. Around the walls of these shelters they made sod shelves on which they could lay bags of cordite that had be-

---

16. Nicholson, *Canadians in Italy*, Vol. II, p.640.

come damp in the cartridges. Within these rather explosive structures, the gunners of Fox Troop slept or whiled away the long hours off duty until the day before Christmas, when they fired two hundred propaganda shells over their enemy.

Christmas was unlike any I had ever celebrated. Our Battery cooks made use of an outside Italian oven where they performed culinary marvels. We had a makeshift Christmas tree on which the lads put gifts of cigarettes for the adult Italians and candy and gum for the children. The officers served the men what I thought was a very good dinner. The turkeys were perfectly cooked in the outside oven. Altogether I managed to assemble six pints of beer, two bottles of Scotch, and a bottle of Portuguese port. Of this I drank one beer, sharing the rest and my Christmas cake with the Command Post people. The Scotch I gave to the gunners who were visibly appreciative.

Throughout the day, the guns were silent on both sides. The Forward Observation Officer came in, and, as always, we were relieved to see him and his signaller and to hear how much worse things were with the infantry than with us. The F.O.O.'s party polished off the port.

The day after Christmas I left the Regiment for seven days' leave in Rome. With the exception of my two weeks on the M.T. course, I had been in action for the better part of three months. My Officers' Advance Book shows that I drew fifteen pounds, the equivalent of six thousand lire, from the Paymaster on December 24. What my feelings were as our three-tonner set off south and west with its quota of men on leave, I don't say. Nor do I seem to have written home while I was on leave. If I did, the letters have been lost.

While in Rome, I told Iain, I saw as much of the Eternal City as I could—from a smoky den of vice to the Palace Room at the Vatican where the Pope gave us his blessing. It was a colourful, rather Renaissance-like affair with Swiss guards, fanfare of trumpets, and colourful dress. The Pope got down from his sedan chair and walked along the lines of people giving blessings. He seemed a very gentle soul. I wished I had bought a set of beads before going in as he would have blessed them, and I could have sent them to my old Catholic friend, Sweeney. Some of the R.C.s had as many as five or six rosaries to be blessed.

Can't say I liked St. Peter's itself, I went on, as it's so huge that it's hard to get hold of mentally, and it's too baroque for my tastes. I was perhaps more impressed by the museum and the art galleries where I saw works by both Raphael and Michaelangelo. Marvellous marble stairways, columns, and wall facings. I came away impressed, too, by Bernini's Piazza with its wide curving lines that direct your eyes to St. Peter's itself.

From piety to vice in Rome is a very easy decline. When I set out on this leave I was interested in finding out if what some of the less inhibited of my gunners said about Roman night life was true. I wasn't at all sure of how far I intended to go, but I had the necessary safeguards with me.

I did manage to spend one evening in a night club where there were floor dances, masses of service people all rather noisy with drink, and, I swear, an Italian girl for nearly every one of them. I found a tall, rather pretty girl who came to the point very quickly just after midnight: $25.00 or my white wool winter jacket. To speak the truth, I thought her price high.

But sometime later two or three of us with our bargains sallied forth into the nearly deserted Roman streets to escort our ladies to bed. My wench proved to be indecisive, as if she were not keen at all on the venture. Then to my astonishment she suddenly moved to the edge of the sidewalk, lifted her skirts, and relieved herself rather noisily in the gutter, thereby smothering the fire of my lust. Dismayed, I left my dark siren and fled. Fortunately I did not know the other men so my running away could not be advertised. But that was the end of my search for sex in Rome.

The rest of my leave during the day was spent tramping streets and gawking at old ruins, churches, and monuments. Architecturally I found Rome full of glorious sights. Beside St. Peter's is the Castel San Angelo, originally built in A.D. 136 as Hadrian's tomb. It has been both a fortress and a prison and stands guard just where the Tiber performs one of its meanders.

Then I saw even older sites: the Colosseum, the Circus Maximus, the Roman Forum, the arch of Septimus Severus, and

193

other antiquities I'd never heard of before. One afternoon I walked along the Appian Way, so straight with its varied ruins, its lovely pines and cypress brooding over its tombs. While on this hike, I came upon the entrance to one of the catacombs, but it was closed.

I wandered alone by night through a maze of ruins, coming out in bright moonlight upon the Colosseum in its cold, circular stillness. I tried to get the feeling of centuries past, but the ruin, the fact itself, was too much. It made a prisoner of my senses— so I just stood amazed at this Roman amphitheatre that could, in A.D. 80, seat fifty thousand spectators.

On my last morning in Rome I went out to see where Keats and Shelley have stones commemorating their sad, strange existence. To me this Protestant cemetery was a melancholy place, so many British, many of them young people of the eighteenth and nineteenth centuries lay buried there. It was not far from this cemetery to St. Paul's Without the Walls where originally Constantine built a church over the tomb of the Apostle. Today's church, a huge, cold monument, attracts, I surmised, more tourists than worshippers.

During most of my evenings I saw concerts and plays: the *Barber of Seville* at the Teatro Argentina was great fun. I liked Paolo Silveri, who was the barber. I also saw *La Bohème*, but I didn't like it as well as the *Barber*. At the movies I watched *Murder in Thornton Square* and *Two Girls and a Sailor*. Later, I sat through a very entertaining comedy called *Someone at the Door*, by Dorothy and Campbell Christie.

> As well [I told Iain] I attended an 'Eccezionale Concerto' on Sunday, which featured artists like Maria Caniglia, Franco Mannino, and Ruggero Ruggeri. It was in aid of ambulance work. On New Year's Eve I was at a dance in the Officers' Club and had a great time after midnight with a Canadian Nursing Sister attached to the South Africans; you'll be relieved, no doubt, to know that I can't remember her name now, and I do not have her address.

And that, *fratello mio*, is the account of my
leave in Rome, which certainly strengthened my
legs even if it left my brains in a ferment. I'm
afraid I slept most of the way back to the Regiment. It was a good leave. I've sent my map of
Rome and all my theatre programmes home to
mother.

A week later I told Ellen that we were all excited about the
advances being made by the Russians, who were just 250 miles
from Berlin. "If this rate of advance continues," I said, "we'll all
be home for next Christmas." Then I turned to her last letter to
say how pleased I was that she now had the telephone installed
and how glad, too, that she liked the painting I had sent home
from Sorrento and which Iain had framed.

You ask if I ever see captured Germans. We
often see them, and the lads grin at them very
suggestively as they are marched to the rear. As
a rule they are husky fellows, dirty, and battle
weary. I think I know how tired they must feel—
but to be beaten as well! Many of them have
been bombed by our planes mercilessly. About
the time Freddy was killed, I knew something of
that when we were on occasion both bombed
and strafed. But that's all over now; we control
the air completely.

Actually I have only one worry now and
that's because I have fleas which I picked up in
our last command post. The little devils are hard
to combat. I don't know which is worse—the
fleas or the flea powder we use to discourage
them.

Later, writing to Iain, I spoke of Julia as someone who I
thought was becoming interested in me as perhaps more than an
engaging correspondent. She had sent off to me a bottle of Scotch
packed in cotton wool and encased in straw. As well, she had sent
on a box of chocolates and a whole flock of good wishes.

> Do you remember that it's just over a year ago
> that we sat down, strangers, before a meal?
> Remember what we talked about? Isn't it inter-
> esting how the warp and woof of another's life
> gets woven into the pattern of one's own. What
> do you suppose we'd talk about if we were
> together to-night? Maybe I'd tease you about our
> first time together when you fell asleep—or did
> you?

This letter must have pleased me although I told Iain that Julia may still "be more interested in my letters than she is in me. I guess you never really know women. And she is so con-foundedly pretty!" Then I reverted to the old worry of provid-ing for Rab and Ellen in their old age. "By the time they're secure I can forget about my Belgian beauty for by then she will have faded away from me into the arms of another man."

Two weeks later Julia's friendship was not so apparent as she referred to my account of my visit to the den of iniquity in Rome:

> You met some dubious dames, didn't you? They
> would be just other women to me, you know. Of
> course, I have opinions about them, but I im-
> agine you can guess what they are. And is all
> that the real Italy? You know it's true—all that—
> everywhere, though in Canada to a far less de-
> gree, I think. Because I despise cheapness,
> wantonness, and—being a girl—rarely meet
> either, I for my part would have just a lovely
> leave in Rome, and there would be no blots in
> the remembrance.

Roused by my trespass against her finer nature, Julia con-tinued making quite clear her disapproval:

> I'll never succeed in understanding how people
> who have any pride or caring for themselves, or
> who appreciate cleanliness and beauty, can find
> amusement or entertainment, much less tempta-

tion in anything at all so offensive as vulgarity, cheapness, and evil.

No record survives of my reaction to this stinging lecture on my intended descent to Roman iniquity.

Meanwhile I was in action, having returned from Rome to the Regiment in time to take part in a roaring do on January 4 when the 5th Division artillery helped break up

> 'the strongest counter attack the Division [had]
> ever contended with'. Through the joint efforts
> of the Canadian infantry, the Desert Air Force
> (which kept German armour from getting for-
> ward), and the devastating fire of the 5th
> Division's three field regiments (together with
> the 142nd Field Regiment (S.P.) R.A.), an initial
> penetration was sealed off, and the enemy
> thrown back with costly casualties.[17]

Writing to me on January 5, Ellen reminded me that it was my birthday and that I was now twenty-eight years old and "what a pity it is that you have to be in the army when you should be in a classroom in Canada." That said, she reverted to the headlines of the the day in *The Globe and Mail* and the reports of Allied casualties.

> Just think how horrible life must be for the Ger-
> mans. Last night the Allies had 2750 planes over
> northwest Germany. And the 770th Casualty
> List for the RCAF has appeared. I counted the
> names of the Killed, Missing, and Presumed
> Dead. There were twenty-one of our own boys.
> Did you ever meet Allan Laughland from
> Guelph? He was one of those listed. And a ship
> the Lady Nelson has just arrived in Halifax with
> 500 wounded and sick veterans on board. Oh,
> how I wish this awful war were over and you
> were home with us.

---

17. Nicholson, *Gunners of Canada*, Vol. II, p.256.

As for me, the war in Italy was drawing to a close. On my birthday, the Regimental "War Diary" reported that a rumour was going about to the effect that the Regiment would not be in the line for very long. As it turned out, this was our last gun position in Italy, very near Mezzano. "We're not far," I told Iain, "from Bagnacavallo, where Allegra, Lord Byron's child died, and not far, too, from Ravenna, where he lived with his mistress, Guiccioli." On January 23, 1945, the Regiment limbered up once more and made its way through a heavy snowstorm to Cattolica, where it remained in rest until February 17.

Chapter 13

Belgium And Action Again

Far beyond the bounds of the Regiment, men in government
and the services had decided that it was wrong to have divided
the Canadian army so that one part had the priviledge of being
wounded or dying in sunny Italy whereas the other part had
what was conceived to be a greater privilege of being wounded
or dying in France. And so, with as much determination as it
showed in March, 1943, when the Canadian government insisted that Churchill find a place for Canadians in the battles for
Italy, the same government now insisted that the Canadian 1st
Corps in Italy be reunited with the First Canadian Army serving under Montgomery in Western Europe. This reversal of
thinking can, says one historian, "only be called a silly chapter
in Canadian war policy."[18] The result was that with as much
secrecy as possible, the Canadians in Italy were readied for the
move to France, leaving behind them an excellent reputation as
fighting men and 5764 comrades who had given their lives in
the battles from Pachino in Sicily to the dykes of the Senio in
the Romagna.

But the silly reasoning behind the planning that moved our
divided forces from one country to another was greeted cheeri-
ly by Fox Troop who were mightily stirred by the prospect of a

18. C. P. Stacey, *Arms, Men and Governments: The War Policies of Canada,*
1939-1945 (Ottawa: Ministry of National Defense, 1970), p.54.

move away from the cold and everlasting mud. Because of the security blackout, no letters could be mailed so that, between February 15 and March 15 of 1945, only one of mine to Ellen survives. I began it on Sunday, February 25, in Harrod's Staging Camp near Leghorn and mailed it from Wervicq in Belgium.

> This letter will come to you in dribs and drabs, and heaven only knows when you will get it as we are very much under the heavy hand of security. But great things are happening. We are leaving Italy, no doubt about it, as we are now loading guns and equipment on to American L.S.T.s. My gunners are really excited as they welcome the end of Italian mud and snow. And I, too, share their feelings although I've only been here nine months. And yet I'm afraid we have no very good grounds for our enthusiasm as war in France is probably just as barbarous a process as it is in Italy.
>
> As I sit in the sun and warmth here looking out to the blue of the Ligurian Sea, I am forced to admit I have had a wonderful if, at times, savage experience. Even the trip across the Italian Appenines was something a traveller might pay for gladly. You should have seen the Regiment: one hundred and forty vehicles, all gleaming in the sun, as they went up and over the mountains. From the greasy mud and rain of Cattolica to the snow and cutting wind of Foligno and on and down, grinding in bull-low at times, we came out in the valley of the Arno, where I got my first view of Florence and, through a 30-power telescope, of the leaning tower of Pisa.

The next day our convoy went through Florence and past Pisa to a staging camp where I stood and writhed in delight under a hot shower. That evening I saw two shows: *The Ghost of the Cantervilles* and *Lassie Come Home*. But what stuck in my mind was my sight of Florence. How I wished the whole convoy had got quarantined in that city for a week. But no such luck. Without a waver in our line of march, we rolled through the city, past fascinating towers and churches and then by Pisa, so white in the sun.

I wished at the time I could remember more about Shelley. I was sure he had lived for a time in Pisa near the Arno, and I knew it was from Leghorn that he and his friend Williams sailed before they were drowned. I remembered, too, how James Roy liked "Adonais" and how he linked the poem to the drowning as he quoted a verse I memorized later, thinking it might come in handy for the final examination. Life, for Shelley, made a kind of stain on "the white radiance of Eternity," something, it now occurred to me, that war was very good at promoting.

When I returned to Ellen's letter I was a member of an advance party for the Regiment, helping make arrangements for its accommodation at five staging areas between Marseilles and Wervicq on the Belgian frontier.

> I shall not spend long on this letter today [I wrote from St. Rambert d'Albon] for it's bloody cold in this tent. I shall take nothing off but my shoes when I crawl into my bedroll tonight. Although we have had bright sun ever since we left Marseilles and its great harbour with its whitish cliffs, we have always had a cold wind behind us. I think the French call it the mistral. Whatever its name, the French are welcome to it.
>
> For miles along the lower Rhone we saw hundreds, if not thousands, of burned out German vehicles which must have been there some time as they are badly rusted. I expect Allied fighter planes must have caught Germans retreating. That's why they are so evenly spaced. Maybe they are the aftermath of the landings at Hyères and Cannes last August.
>
> This is going to be a long jaunt—someone said at least a thousand miles if you count in the

crossing of Italy. Imagine! I'm having a tour of western Europe with a Mediterranean cruise thrown in—for nothing. No, it's better than that—I'm being paid to do it. Must not then complain too much about this drafty, cold tent where I could certainly do with some heat and hot water. And, while I am listing my needs, a nice pair of flannelette pyjamas would be far less itchy than dear old George's battledress.

No more writing was done until March 9, when I appended a postscript in Wervicq:

It's been a wonderful trip, a thousand miles in convoy and, happily, no serious mechanical trouble. I'd like to take both of you over the route after the war. Do you think we can plan on it? And you'd like Belgium for it's clean, warm, friendly, and interesting at every turn.

I am billeted with an elderly Flemish couple who have a milk and cream business. They have given me a large comfortable bed in a room that smells of hundreds of house-cleanings and airings. The bed has snowy white sheets and big soft pillows.

Every morning before I go to breakfast in the Mess, they insist on my having coffee with them, which mine host grinds himself and then brews with great care. With his cream, it's delicious, far better than what our cooks can come up with. And my bustling little hostess insists on doing my laundry, which comes back to me so clean and so nicely ironed and folded that it seems a sacrilege to use it.

All these Flemish folk seem possessed by the demon Cleanliness. They even scrub their sidewalks as well as the outside of the front of their houses for a distance of at least a yard above ground level. The lower floors of my

house are tiled and just gleam, even on a dull
day. The upstairs rooms are of wood and plaster.
Coal is scarce, but they seem to have plenty of
electricity and natural gas. Each morning from
my bedroom window I am awakened by the clat-
ter of wooden clogs over the cobbled streets.

The weather is mild, like England's at this
time of the year. Spring is definitely here.

Further letters home elaborate on how much I liked the
country and its people. Even the farms I saw seemed attractive:
small, intensively cultivated to the very road's edge, and many
displaying a well-cared for draft horse. Unlike the French
farmers, who seem to have some sort of feudal hangover that
compels them to live in villages surrounded by vast fields, the
Belgians, I said, have their houses on their own small holdings.
Livestock was scarce in both countries. As to the people, they
were as a rule either very young or well on in years, not many
in-betweens.

Within a week, I had concluded that the Belgians were really happy to have us in their midst. The older folk remembered
Canadians from the Great War. Actually, Wervicq was just a
few miles from fields where many of our own fathers had
fought and died: Ypres, St. Eloi, Menin, Armentières, Poper-
inge. Some of these I visited.

As a rest area for the Regiment, Wervicq offered bags of
entertainment: ENSA shows, danses, symphony concerts, and
pubs open every night. I asked Ellen not to send food parcels as
our rations were quite adequate: white bread, fresh meat,
vegetables, and even fresh eggs. Italy was soon just a bad experience on a distant horizon.

On my first free weekend I went off to see Louise—a second
choice. Her reception was chilly as she asked why I had not
gone to another hospital close by. My explanation that the town
was out of bounds for this weekend should have caused her to
send me packing, but she didn't. Before many minutes we were
friends as formerly, and I was invited to a wedding for one of
the Nursing Sisters. It was quite a celebration that lasted until

four in the morning.

Mail to the Regiment caught up with us almost as soon as we arrived. I had news of Hughie whose mother said he'd crossed the Channel; she gave no other details. She had sent a parcel to him and one to me. From Ellen came a less cheerful note than usual. The hens were laying, but the grades were poor; she was tired because it was 8:30 p.m., and she'd just finished cleaning nine dozen eggs after a busy day on which she'd done a laundry. She had, however, read through my bundle of travel items from Rome.

She was still blunt about Louise who was, she was sure, someone she could not like. Julia seemed too kittenish for her tastes. And Rab was in her bad books for having signed exemption papers for a neighbour's boy on the grounds that he was the only son, whereas, she asserted, everyone knows there is another brother at home. By the letter's end she was worrying about me: "I often wonder just what you will be like when you return home. I think you will not be the same boy you were before enlisting—something just tells me that."

From my Queen's friend, McRuer, now in England, came lines extolling life in far-away Tahiti: the fare from London was only £29.1.1; you could live there for $10.00 a month, and "there's no law against what we, who suffer still from Puritanism, call promiscuity. What would you say, my good fellow, to disappearing after the war, like Gauguin, for a sojourn in Paradise?" He was pleased that I had received the copy of Montaigne's essays.

Julia told me on March 16 that she was sure I did not describe my escapades to my mother in the same detail that I relayed them to her.

> And I am sure you never mentioned that dreadful party you had in the Irish Mess in Italy. Good grief! Whatever possessed the Irish officers to play touch rugby in the Mess at two in the morning? And how big was the tub they mixed the rum punch in? I can't imagine officers and gentlemen throwing one another out of win-

204

dows—and in their kilts too. Are you sure this
happened? And how do you know if you were
hiding behind the piano? I presume—I hope—
that the party was a stag affair.

Julia went on to say she'd been off duty for two days with an in-
fection in both eyes, which an M.O. thought was caused by one
of the diptheria patients coughing in her face. The M.O. was in-
sisting she stay off duty for the rest of the week.

"Haven't heard any news about leave," she continued, "but I
have applied to go to Paris. Paris in the springtime is like an old
dream that's been hidden away for a long time." Her postscript
was to the effect that she was enclosing a photo of herself in
which she appears sitting in uniform by the bole of a huge tree;
her legs are drawn up under her apron, her veil, elegantly
coiffed, is well back, drawing attention to a remarkably pretty
face, eyes far apart, cheeks dimpled, hair boyishly short at the
edge of her headdress. A smile parts her lips.

Julia's letter arrived at the same time as one from E. W.
Bradwin to whom I had been confiding rather much, even telling him about my interest in a career in journalism. Ellen, I
knew, was opposed: "It's a poor way to make a decent living,
and, my boy, you won't have the security that you can expect as
a high school teacher." Dr. Bradwin was more tactful and far-
sighted:

> I read between the lines just a little touch of un-
> settlement. I could but admire the tribute you
> pay to your good father and mother. ... By all
> means, do not forget your loyalty to them, for as
> they get older they will be dependent upon you,
> and after all they have a claim that is not to be
> entirely ignored, no matter what relationship is
> assumed in life.
>
> You mention in your letter that you were not
> clearly decided whether you would go back to
> teaching or would take up writing. However, do
> not try to make a decision on the minute. These
> things will beset you maybe for months at a

time. Meantime, I should advise you to take advantage of every opportunity offered by the army so that you can get credit at London or Oxford for additional study that might lead toward an M.A. and help you one day if you decided to take a doctorate.

I earnestly hope that out of this war, with its destruction, and danger, and havoc, you will come back unimpaired and bigger in life and heart, to be of service to men and to your country.

Aside from the practicalities of gun and vehicle maintenance, Wervicq sustained the initial impression I had of it. The town burghers were generous and their daughters attractive. Beer was abundant. The Regiment was ready to be entertained. A dance I attended was a private affair in a small château which only broke up at 6:00 a.m. because the R.C.s wanted to attend mass.

It was just as well, however, that religion did put an end to our capers because in the early afternoon of that Sunday we had to line up in a casual display of interest—and cold sober— to greet Field-Marshall Montgomery who drove up in his jeep, gathered us around him, and, after a few words, told us why we were in Belgium. His statement was a bit of a surprise as some of us were beginning to think we were in Belgium to be entertained. Monty destroyed that illusion brutally by asserting in measured tones that we had come from Italy to Belgium "to kill Germans." After that announcement, it required a little deceit to give the old chap, with his black beret and bomber jacket, three cheers as he waved to us from his jeep and drove off.

Monty's visit was a clear indication that the Regiment was to see action. I even tried to prepare Ellen for this eventuality. "You must not worry too much if my letters seem far apart at times especially when we are on the move. If anything does happen, you'll hear very promptly. Always no news is good news, so don't worry." But Ellen was quite alive to the possibility of the dreaded final official notice which but a few days before had come so close to her as to chill her very heart: "I've just heard," she wrote on March 29, "that Hughie has paid the supreme sacrifice. Oh, I just can't think about it. How awful to think he has gone! I have written to his parents, and you must do so too. And, oh Alex, do be careful. I do hope you won't have to go into action again. I am praying every day for your safe return."

Hughie's death bothered me more than Freddy's, for I had known Hughie for so long and so intimately. "I wished," I told Iain, "I had seen more of him than I did after our first year at Queen's. He was truly a gentle person with both intelligence and quiet charm—more mature than I. How sad to think that so good a person had to meet his death in a ditch from a sniper's bullet and is now no more than a blank file, an intermittent ghost in the lanes of memory. What evil lies all about us!"

Ignoring the prevalence of evil, and taking a chance that the Regiment would not move the next day, I travelled ten miles away on the evening of March 24 to see Julia at her hospital. I found her tired and drawn and not the cheerful girl I had known in England. I apparently told her so because, in a letter to me on April 2, she said she was sorry I had found her so different from the person I'd expected. And then she rounded on me sharply for an incident I had mentioned in which I'd been short-tempered with a lumpish Flemish girl who had sewn my Div. patches on crookedly. I had left the girl in tears. Julia told me I should be even more penitent than I was and then rather surprisingly quoted Hilaire Belloc's lines:

Of Courtesy—it is much less
Than courage of heart or holiness;
Yet in my walks it seems to me
That the Grace of God is in courtesy.

To Ellen, I admitted that my meeting with Julia was disappointing and all the more so as the fault was mine for having been so outspoken.

That my letter writing was getting me into what I called fixes was becoming ever more obvious. Their confessional side left me open to criticism from the Nursing Sisters and to Ellen's criticism of them in turn, especially her deep-seated dislike of Louise which no amount of assurance from me could allay. But Ellen's opposition to any woman but Elizabeth for me was, whether I knew it or not, a kind of common-sense ballast for my coracle as it bobbed about on my short odyssey. Ellen's will and determination to have a home of her own instilled marital caution and very little chance of my ever marrying a Nursing Sister whose biological needs could not afford to wait upon the rhythm of my future convenience.

Leaving Julia at her desk just outside her ward at 2000 hours, I returned to Wervicq at midnight only to find that reveille was at 0300 hours and the Regiment's departure at 0500 hours. I had only two hours' sleep. By 1000 hours that day my guns trundled by Julia's hospital. It was a tiresome move. I remembered especially going through a very long tunnel in Antwerp and meeting tanks in convoy going the opposite direction. In the eerie, yellowish, half-light of the tunnel, which seemed to me much too narrow for the traffic in it, I was more than a little anxious for I had taken the wheel of the vehicle to give the driver some rest.

And we were no sooner out of the tunnel than we met a huge two-wheeled cart with traffic hemmed in for a block behind it and some peasants busy trying to repair a broken belly band on the horse's harness. I was much relieved when my driver woke from his nap and took over in the city traffic.

That experience reminded me of another night when I drove twenty miles with no headlights in a forward area on the Rubicon. It was pitch black with only the lights on the "babies' bottoms" ahead of us and the gun flashes somewhere behind. Jeep ambulances and ammo trucks were forever contesting the right of way. Either side of the road was a quagmire and, with his usual foresight, Jerry was plumping the odd shell into the area. In one ruined village, my left front wheel dropped into a shell hole, and I had to get nearby Aussies to pull me out. It should be, I reflected, a mighty simple matter for me to drive a car once I'm back home.

At 2000 hours on March 24, Fox Troop arrived in an area

near s'-Hertogenbosch, where we saw our first V1s flying over-head—noisy, venomous, little sky wagons. Four days later we were in action on the "Island" between Nijmegen and Arnhem. The first rounds the Regiment fired in anger on the Western Front came down on a harassing fire task on March 29. By April 7, Fox Troop could look directly into the outskirts of Arnhem which unsettled the gunners as it was quite obvious that Jerry in turn could see us. But to our surprise he did nothing about so obvious a target. So little was happening that to fill his daily report the Intelligence Officer noted that all officers had turned in their .38 pistols in exchange for 9 mm semi-automatics.

A week later the Regiment left the "Island" for Arnhem by crossing the long Bailey bridge over the Waal at Nijmegen, the Rhine at Emmerich, and on to Elten and Arnhem. I was a member of the advance party and was most happy to see the guns move in as we had waited for hours for them to arrive. As a regimental area, the centre of Arnhem was much better than the "Island" where we disliked looking at dead, bloated Holstein cows in the fields and even in the barns—the consequence of Jerry having flooded the area.

In Arnhem the mail caught up with me; it was now moving more slowly than formerly. A letter from Ellen written on March 24 did not arrive until April 16; she hoped I was still in Wervicq. I did not tell her until April 21 that we were again in action. In this letter I alluded to close fighting:

> Due to the fortunes of war, I have had all my clothing, foodstuffs I had squirrelled away in-cluding, alas, a bottle of whisky, all my letters, a picture of Julia, the one I had of Elizabeth, and other mementoes destroyed. All I have left is the clothing on my back and my bedroll. The loss was due to Jerry—damn him. You'll hear about it eventually—for the Regiment bore the brunt of the fighting; just now I cannot give you details other than to say I am well.
>
> We are now in a very pretty bit of country, little touched by war, and the towns, I do

believe, are as pretty and modern as any I've seen. Some fruit trees are in blossom, trees are leafing out, and the countryside smells of spring—green and fresh.

The war cannot last much longer. In one day we moved 130 miles forward. You should see the way the Jerries are surrendering, droves of them, often dirty, scruffy, hungry, with that P.O.W. look so hard to describe—sullen, impassive, hopeless.

The delay in the mails was compounded by the security measures that enveloped the move from Italy. On April 26, two months after the Regiment had left Leghorn, Ellen wrote to me saying that "just the other day the news came over the radio about your move in convoy from Italy. Everyone is amazed, it surely must be one of the great events of the war."

On the day we arrived in Arnhem, my G.P.O. left Fox Troop to go on leave, and I was alone once more in the Command Post. Our next move was called Operation Cleanser; it was to be a fast armoured thrust of thirty miles north to the Ijsselmeer at Nijkerk.

Chapter 14

Otterloo And After

At first it was the old armoured razzle-dazzle that we'd almost forgotten in those rain-drenched Romagna flats along the Adriatic: in and out of gun positions, surging north, and no necessity to dig gun pits or dugouts. But Otterloo, our Waterloo, was upon us. It's not possible to write intelligently about what happened to us because what happened was like the sinking of the Titanic, very much a matter of being in the wrong place at the right time.

My C.P.O. and I were on the advance party which arrived at the village of Otterloo,[19] ten miles north-west of Arnhem, at about 1400 hours on April 16. The village was in the hands of the Irish, and all sorts of traffic jammed its streets. Our second-in-command allotted us our gun area just north of the village limits in an open field that bordered on a pine forest. A dirt road with a ditch on one side served as a boundary between the two troops of the battery.

As the guns did not come in until after 1900 hours, the C.P.O. and I had all sorts of time to take stock of our location which alarmed us to the extent that we took a jeep to have a look about. We were certainly sited ahead of the F.D.L.s which seemed to be vaguely defined by the village boundary. That there may have been some doubt as to where the enemy were

---

19. On Dutch maps, *Otterlo*

became apparent when we learned that our arc of fire was to be 360° which meant that gun pits could be a drawback. As there was no activity whatever in the immediate vicinity, the C.P.O. and I drove about two miles north on the dirt road but found no evidence of any living person. The road was dusty, unused, and unmarked.[20]

Back at the Battery position, the C.P.O. chose his Command Post about 600 feet ahead and east of mine and across the road. E Troop was about the same distance south of the Battery C.P., and directly across the road from F Troop. My own Command Post was some two hundred feet ahead of the guns in a small brick house which had a lean-to at the side where we set up the artillery board and the signals equipment. The pine woods were almost at the back door, so we hid the George vehicle among the trees. The rest of our vehicles were in the Battery Wagon Lines about 1200 feet to the rear of the guns, next to a cemetery on the outskirts of Otterloo.

The Regiment's other two Batteries were scattered behind us and somewhat to our left, while R.H.Q. was to our right and behind E Troop. By early evening the village streets were crowded with troops and vehicles of the Irish, even Divisional H.Q. was there. As the Regiment had no screen of infantry in front, we had to establish as best we could our own all-round defense. I gave orders for the Bren, rifles, and small arms ammunition to be brought to the guns of my Troop and for the gunners to dig slit trenches sited so as to give us as much defense as possible. No gun pits were dug, which left the guns exposed. That may have been a mistake—I'll never know. It may even have saved lives as gun pits are dangerous places when shrapnel is flying about.

By 2100 hours we were on Theatre Grid, and by 2200 hours I had prepared our D.F. tasks on the artillery board. For the next hour I checked what had been done at the guns by way of

---

20. Further confirmation that no Germans were in the vicinity may be found in the "War Diary" belonging to the Irish Regiment of Canada for April 16, 1945. Their Intelligence Officers reported that "The town of Otterloo and surrounding area were cleared of enemy by 1400 hours."

making us as secure as possible and found, as usual, that my gunners needed little supervision. They even had the Bren mounted on the flank with a clear field of fire from a weapon pit. I was somewhat relieved when three members of the Irish arrived and set up a 2" mortar and a Bren in front of our command post. It was a thin screen but better than none at all.

Some time after 2300 hours I put up my safari at the door of the lean-to and lay down on it fully clothed. It was a quiet, moist night, no moon, warm—very like a spring night in the country in Canada. From my safari I could see on one side the outline of my No. 1 gun in the field and, on the other, the shaded light over the artillery board and the dim form of my signaller by the telephone. Inside the house on the lower floor some of the gunners off duty, one of the "Acks," and a signaller had commandeered the living room and were asleep on the floor.

I, too, had just dozed off when something woke me out of a crazy dream in which I heard mother calling my name very clearly. The next impression was equally ridiculous: the sound of horses and wagons on a dirt road very like what I'd heard so often at Simon Munro's in the evening when we would be bringing the last loads of hay or oats to the barn. Having decided the sound was no part of my dream, I told the signaller to alert the C.P.O. By the time he came on the line I heard someone yell out the challenge which that night was "Hockey." There was no reply, "Puck," and in seconds a Bren somewhere fired.

And that's how it all began a few minutes after midnight on April 17. To give a coherent account of what followed is nearly impossible because the fighting was so confused. By 0100 hours one thing was glaringly obvious, the Regiment had been caught where an artillery unit ought not to be—ahead of the infantry and in the way of a determined enemy attack supported by mortars, machine guns, and even anti-tank weapons.

It was our Battery Command Post that took the brunt of the initial fighting. By 0130 hours I had my last words with the C.P.O., who was able to assure me I was on my own. By 0200 my telephone link with E Troop was cut, which meant that any further communication with other units of the Regiment had to be on foot, for I assumed—and incorrectly—that my George vehicle with its wireless set was by now in the hands of the enemy in the woods before us. The nearest unit accessible to me was C Troop, about 300 yards behind my No. 4 gun. It was no use trying to go to E Troop because by this time the Krauts had infiltrated between our positions using the ditch along the road as an approach. We could see them from time to time because, shortly after 0200 hours, they managed to set fire to the Battery Command Post, which created a huge glare lighting up both friend and foe.

The Jerries next went after my Command Post, wounding one of the Irish so seriously that their defense crumbled, and wounding one of my signallers when they sprayed the living room with a burst of machine gun fire. But at this point, and for some reason beyond me, some of the attackers decided to surrender, which meant we had frightened, sour-smelling German prisoners stuffed inside the Command Post seeking safety, and German soldiers outside the house determined to kill us.

The greatest scare came when, within the Command Post, we heard the sound of breaking glass and saw the muzzle of a machine gun appear past the blackout curtain we'd draped over the one window of our lean-to. Captors and prisoners alike froze in silence as the muzzle made a slow evolution round the room and then to our relief quietly withdrew. I slipped outside and around the C.P. hoping to find and shoot the intruder, but he had left.

It's difficult to be clear about what happened next. For one thing, on my return from the circuit of the house, more Germans appeared with their hands up so that I had to gather them and those in the C.P. and take them to the gun area where I made twenty-one of them lie down in a shallow depression and put one of my gun sergeants in charge of them while I went back to C Troop Command Post to get assistance to evacuate both the wounded and the prisoners.

C Troop put me in touch with both R.H.Q. and the Irish: R.H.Q. were informed of my position and the Irish asked to provide a stretcher party and some men to escort the P.O.W.s. I also asked for tank and infantry support, but that was not to be had—

presumably because my gun area must have seemed to them altogether too unhealthy a place for either infantry or armour.

Back at Fox Troop C.P., with the Irish stretcher party, I soon realized how hopeless it was to hang on to the house. The signaller in the living room had died of his wounds, and the gunners, awakened by the din, had decamped to the guns where they were energetically digging straight down. I then gave orders to close down the C.P. and accompanied the remaining personnel, the stretcher bearers and the P.O.W.s, back to C Troop C.P. and again requested tank support frcm R.H.Q. because I knew the G.G.H.G.s were in the village. But no dice—so I walked, ran, and crawled back to the guns without getting shot or in any way damaged, although I was scared especially when Very flares lit up the whole area like day. You feel as if you have no clothes on, and everybody is looking at you.

What made the situation very trying was a Jerry with a Spandau who had dug himself in between Fox Troop and the Battery Wagon Lines and was creating a little hell of his own by the light of a burning Workshops vehicle which, by the time I was back at the guns, was illuminating the rear of our position and, unfortunately, our own vehicles in the wagon lines. More and more it was obvious that the best place for us was in the slit trenches. For a time I thought of firing the 25-pdrs. using air burst with a low fuse setting to get at the Germans in the woods ahead of us. I knew they were there because I had gone forward and listened. You could hear them talking but the trouble was to know exactly where the sounds originated, as there was by this time an incredible racket everywhere. And then I remembered the Kraut with the Spandau and what he might do to us if he saw the gunners silhouetted in the flash of the guns. So I returned to the gun area and gave orders that no one was to use his small arms until he could be sure of hitting his target and that no one was to leave his slit trench—not that anyone now was likely to want to. In addition I made it clear that in the event the enemy took us on, no one was to fire until I gave the order, so that we could gain the maximum surprise.

Meantime the Jerries had moved in on the Battery Wagon Lines, had engaged the drivers with potato mashers which set several of the vehicles on fire, creating a huge blaze enlivened by exploding ammunition. This fireworks was further helped by our C.P.O.'s decision to direct our own artillery fire upon the enemy using the road and the edge of the woods as an approximate target area. Eventually both field and medium guns were in on the act.[21] Their fire, coupled with the effect of German small arms fire and mortaring, made life about Fox Troop exceedingly lively and perilous. As at Monte Maggiore, my gunners and N.C.O.s were admirable in the face of so much adversity. You could not ask for better men.

I made one more trip back to C Troop C.P. for three reasons: one, to protest the rounds from our own artillery that were falling on or very near our gun position; two, to get my Browning 9 mm cleaned as I had got dirt in the mechanism either from crawling or from rubbing against the side of my slit trench; three, to ask if I could have a Bren gunner and a couple of riflemen from the Irish to help me get the Jerry with the Spandau. I saw him as a menace both to my gunners and to the drivers and their vehicles.

My plan was, if the Irish would give me covering fire from the flank, to sneak up on him from the rear of my guns. So long as his attention was fixed on what was ahead of him or on fire that forced him to keep his head down, I was sure I could kill him. With the amount of illumination available, I thought the Irish would have no trouble seeing me as I moved in. It was, however, a plan that made no appeal to the Irish, and they refused to go along with it.

Now that I know what I do, I am sure I owe my life to Irish caution, for had I moved in upon the man I wanted to kill, I should have been picked off by Jerries concealed from me by the ditch and road that divided E and F Troops. In the end we burned them out.

---

21. The 17th Field Regiment's report on operations reveals that the Regiment and the 2/11 Medium Battery, Royal Artillery, fired on twenty-two targets, many of which were in the map square belonging to the 17th Field, and some of which were extremely close or on Fox Troop's position. Altogether the artillery fired some 325 rounds of high explosive during the engagement.

Once more I returned to my gunners through what seemed to me a real inferno of bursting shells and small arms fire. You have no idea how attractive a hole in the ground about two feet by five feet by six is in these circumstances. The one I had, I shared with one of my gun sergeants, an older man who was a bit embarrassed when both of us had to pee. We contrived to do so by each of us digging out a small hole—exactly as a cat does.

None of my gun sergeants reported any casualties, and each one was steady and clear in giving response to my requests as to how each crew was faring. We could see groups of Jerries at a distance moving in and out of light from burning vehicles and explosives. They were now deep in the regimental area and, judging by the amount of small arms fire, meeting with very considerable resistance.

I found in the morning that the Battery Command Post personnel and those of E Troop C.P., as well as E Troop gunners, having run out of S.A. ammunition, were forced to yield their positions and fall back on R.H.Q. In the process, E Troop spiked its guns before withdrawing. Meanwhile, ignorant of these happenings, we crouched in our foxholes and watched the fireworks and hoped the heavy stuff stayed away from us. It was perhaps 0330 or 0400 when we were discovered.

A section of the enemy—perhaps fifteen or more, coming from the direction of the village—found, or perhaps just stumbled upon our position. We could see them more clearly as they moved toward us, no mistaking their identity especially the potato mashers they carried and their close fitting helmets. The gunners waited in silence. When the outlines seemed to tower over us, I gave the word. One burst from our weapons and the outlines changed shape and then faded. Trouble was we didn't kill all of them, and four or five of the wounded couldn't get away. I fear I must carry the cries of one of them to my life's end. We could not evacuate them or give them much assistance. That's one of the puzzling things about combat. You can kill a man and forget about him, but wound him badly and you face a quite different set of circumstances. One of our gunners,[22] ignoring my order to stay in the slit trenches, got to one of the wounded, who was calling piteously, gave him water and a blanket and put him in a vacant slit trench. It was, as I think of it now, the act of a brave, humane man, especially as the field around us was a ragged kaleidoscope of explosives— our own and the enemy's—with shrapnel singing off the steel of our guns.

And this continued until just after dawn, perhaps until 0600 hours, when greatly to the relief of our cramped bodies and weary minds we saw in the grey light and cordite-soaked air of our battlefield a Churchill tank from an Assault Squadron of the Royal Engineers come lumbering across the field towards us. As the firing had died down, I climbed out of my slit trench and waved to the officer peering out of the iron monster's hatch. The tank stopped; I climbed up the near side, and pointed to where I thought the Germans might be, whereupon the tank gunners began lobbing mortar bombs and spraying the woods with machine-gun fire.

Behind us I now caught sight of Wasp flame throwers from the Irish licking their way forward along the roadway where the Germans had dug in. It was a ghastly spectacle. The Germans died neatly, all facing the same way and nicely spaced. Later, when I inspected them more closely, I could see no marks on them—just dead men and already swelling up. I found the machine gunner whom I wanted to kill. He had tried to get away but perished in flame curled up rather like the man and woman I saw who died in the eruption of Vesuvius in Pompeii. I got the belt buckle off him for the sake of the "Gott mit Uns" on it.

And then the Germans came out of the woods to surrender, some old, some very young, and, to our surprise, a half-dozen very tough-looking women who scowled at us as they passed through. That such a rag-taggle of people gave us such a hard time all night long is past my comprehension. Of course, our own counterfire was not as effective as it should have been, but

---

22. William Bull of FB gun.

old Jerry had proved a damned formidable foe, and he'd caught us this time where we should not have been. Someone blundered a little bit.

And the shambles that was Fox Troop gun postion! The wounded Germans were in bad shape. One of them directly in front of my slit trench was, I am certain, my victim. His grey face, his helpless hands, and the blood-soaked crotch of his grey-green trousers left me much dismayed. He was still alive but no longer moaning. We sent him to the rear on a stretcher.

Back in the Command Post I found my signaller dead, with staring eyes. The gunner with me wouldn't touch him so I carried him out and put him in a Red Cross jeep. I remember him so well: a quiet, kindly man of slight build who had, on occasion, as we awaited fire orders from his set, shyly told me of his wife and wee daughter awaiting his return on Canada's west coast.

And my guns! Three of the four out of action, their aiming mechanisms twisted and broken from shrapnel. Two caissons had flat tires and damaged doors. Behind us were the skeletal remains of my troop's vehicles. But the really good news! Not one of the gunners had suffered any physical harm—not that we were that much more presentable than the P.O.W.s passing through us.

At the Battery Wagon Lines we were not so lucky, where one driver had been killed and sixteen wounded, one of whom died later in hospital. I have worried much about them as I wonder who checked on them the night before and how it happened that most of them were sleeping under their vehicles when Jerry caught them. They certainly knew how exposed our position was, and they would have seen the gunners on the previous evening returning to the vehicles for their rifles, the Bren gun, and ammunition. Furthermore, they must have seen the gunners digging in around the guns. But the example was lost on them. They prepared only one slit trench. Certainly, I never thought of them until I saw one of the vehicles blazing—which bothers me for I knew the drivers well and felt responsible for those of my own troop—and yet I do not recall ever having assumed this responsibility for the wagon lines; that was something left in the Sergeant Major's hands. But this at the best is an excuse for something I didn't do. A kind of irony attaches to this happening because my George vehicle in the occupied woods survived with only a flat tire. The driver spent the night in a slit trench beside it and was never flushed out by the Germans. And yet, a few yards away, were dead horses and smashed equipment that belonged to the enemy.

But that's war—so unpredictable—where the boundary line between praise and blame is sometimes hard to detect. You have no time to change your mind once you are committed. Had I lost all my gunners by electing to fight at the guns I should, I daresay, have been blamed for making a bad decision. I could instead have spiked my guns and withdrawn back to the relative safety of the village. That we did not do so, that we had no casualties at the guns, that we took in twenty-one prisoners, that, *pace* Montgomery, we killed five Germans and wounded at least that many more within a few feet of our position, may be matters for some praise and justification for the stand we took.[23]

But the praise, I think, should be muted. It was a freak accident of war that for over six hours nearly smothered us in destruction. It could have had no possible effect upon the outcome of the war. Friend and foe died and suffered for little reason. Had someone ordered things a bit differently, the Regiment would not have been assigned to Map Reference Otterloo 6591.

In concluding my account of Otterloo, and the longest of my wartime letters, I warned Iain that what I had written was only my own impression of what had happened. "Maybe," I said, "I shouldn't have told you what I have. It's all somewhat like a bad dream that I wish I could forget."

---

23. The Irish Regiment of Canada had 3 O.R.s killed, 3 officers and 14 O.R.s wounded. The Irish took 22 Germans prisoner. The 17th Canadian Field Regiment had 3 O.R.s killed, and 20 O.R.s wounded. The 17th estimated that they accounted for 23 Germans killed, 11 wounded, and 36 taken prisoner.

But although Otterloo was, as I put it later, "a monstrous caprice of war in which the rag ends of a German battalion came close to savaging us," I, too, may have been exaggerating just as fifteen years later military historians, trying to be coolly objective, downgraded "the so-called 'battle of Otterloo'" into a "fierce little skirmish" in which the Germans suffered "possibly 300 casualties, with between 75 and 100 killed."[24] But for the Regiment, that "fierce little skirmish" north of Arnhem will in all likelihood remain a battle honour as long probably as its gunners have memories to give it a place alongside the Liri Valley and Monte Maggiore, Coriano and the Marecchio, the Fiumicino and the Lamone.

On April 18, the Regiment moved away from Otterloo on the advance north. Jerry was just ahead of us for we found some of his impedimenta and dead horses. The blood from the horses had not had time to congeal. On the next gun position we were all a bit windy and trigger happy.

> I was really surprised, too, when one of our
> recent arrivals, I think he was supposed to be an
> 'Ack', lost all control of himself in the Command
> Post and cried for hours throughout the night. I
> talked to him for a long time but could not still
> his sobbing. And I did feel sorry for him for he
> was just nineteen and had lost a brother brewed
> up in a tank in the Liri Valley. He left us the next
> morning.

Bypassing Nijkerk, and veering northeastwards toward Ermelo, the Regiment raced toward Leeuwarden in Friesland where we arrived after dark on April 21 and stayed until April 24 on which date we pushed eastwards and north of Groningen, finally going into action at Wagenborgen on April 25, where we fired several targets for the Air O.P. The Regiment's last active role was in the reduction of German strongpoints around Delfzijl, which capitulated on May 2. Hundreds of propaganda pamphlets were fired beforehand for the

---

24. C. P. Stacey, *The Victory Campaign: The Operations in North-West Europe, 1944-45* (Ottawa: Queen's Printer, 1966), Vol. III, pp.578-79.

beleaguered to read in their own language:

An die Verteidiger von

Kessel Delfzijl

. . .

Der Krieg ist praktisch aus
Ihre Pflicht ist getan
Schickt einen Parlementär mit der
weissen Flagge herüber zum
Zeichen der Uebergabe[25]

But just before the Delfzijl defenders gave up *der Krieg* and when I was beginning to worry about what would happen if the Germans in Emden decided to range in on us with their big naval guns, I was given nine days' leave to the United Kingdom, "whither I went with as much haste and military decorum as army transport would permit." My Otterloo letter had been written in the Inverness train station over innumerable cups of tea while I waited more than five hours for a train. I was off to Dornoch, a Royal Burgh that stands somewhat aloof on the edge of the windswept sands of the Dornoch Firth. There I splurged and stayed overnight in the rather posh Castle Hotel. The next morning I set off with an Ordnance map in hand to try to find the places Rab, my father, had so often described or mentioned: Badninish, Balvraid, and Skelbo. A curious local from Pitgrudy picked me up in his old car and put me down just where the Dornoch Road crosses the Badninish and Skelbo roads. Badninish proved sandy, scrub country so unattractive that I turned about and walked east alongside the Skelbo Wood into which I went in search of a broch and tumuli that showed on my map. These ancient structures were so overgrown with whin and bracken that I gave up the search and took a footpath alongside the Skelbo Burn. The pale sunlight filtered down through the spring-green leaves of the birch and the dark need-

---

25. To the defenders of Kessel Delfzijl ... The war is almost over. You have done your duty. Send a spokesman with a white flag over as a sign of surrender.

les of the pines as I came out on a little used road above which stood the ruins of Skelbo Castle.

As a castle, it was neither large nor impressive, but it did offer a wide overview of Loch Fleet and to the east, beyond its narrow neck, the houses of Little Ferry; across its tidal waters lay dark Balblair Wood; to the north the treeless hills; and, edging up to the Castle's perimeter, the fields of the Mains of Balvraid. Warm in a sheltered corner of the ruined walls, I lay down and through half-closed eyes recalled Rab's stories of Sullivan and old Alexander Munro of the 42nd piping away below the Castle a century before my time.

From the Castle, I walked by the crofts of Knockglass and Fourpenny over the Skelbo Muir and on to Dornoch, where I spent the night. The next day I went on to Lairg to call on Alex Mackay and his sister, Maggie, distant relatives of the woman Sullivan had married in 1857. Once I had identified myself, I was made very welcome and invited warmly to stay for dinner. The first course was a bean soup with homemade bread; then we had boiled chicken and potatoes which had been prepared in a black pot over a peat fire. It was a plain meal, and I shall always remember the many apologies offered for it and the Highland courtesy these elderly remote cousins extended to me, a complete stranger.

If their croft of twelve acres with its peat bog, two cows, a horse, a few sheep, some chickens, and a collie dog was typical of other crofts, the view they had from their doorstep was not: their old eyes could see below their croft the long valley of the Shin River and, miles beyond over the hills, the country of Strath Grudie. I was reluctant to leave this landscape and the only relatives I had left in Scotland.

Early that afternoon, having made the acquaintance of the local mail carrier in Lairg, I travelled with him to Gualinn Lodge, some forty miles to the north-east, where I had arranged a "hospitality leave." My hostess was Mrs. George Ross, a warmhearted, generous lady who presided over a large AGA cooker and an ever-ready teapot. Her husband was a gilly whose main responsibility was to take his absentee landlord hunting or fishing whenever that gentleman could get away from his London employment. George was an old soldier, Black Watch, and a very good piper.

During my five days at Gualinn, I came and went very much as I liked, even climbing the nearest mountain, Foinaven, which offered, from its summit at 2980 feet, a sweeping view of the whole of this northwest corner of Scotland. Far to the west over the Minch was a suspicion of the coastline of Lewis; to the north, the Kyle of Durness and eastward, Loch Friboll. Over the empty land swept a seawashed wind, cool enough to set me off refreshed on my descent where, just below the summit, I saw my first ptarmigan, a shy, still blur of chestnut against an ochreous rock face. On my return I followed the course of the Dionard River for perhaps a mile peering in vain for a glimpse of the salmon that my host assured me lurked in the quiet eddies of the river. It was a long walk back to the welcome warmth of the kitchen, the tea, and news of the day.

On my last night at the Lodge, George took me to an airmen's dance in Durness. I told Rab and Ellen about seeing seven eightsome reels whirling about at the same time down the length of the hall. For the first time, too, I saw a dance called "Strip the Willow" that seemed to me a real rouser. The dance broke up about three in the morning. Throughout the night, George and I shared the bottle of rye I'd brought with me on leave so that by the time we left he was in good form even though he had played for several dances and danced just as many himself. The drive home in his old car with its dim lights and his determination to save gas by going down long hills in neutral seemed to me more dangerous than exciting. "Ye hae to keep a shairp eye for the ewes" was his only word of caution. Back at the Lodge, he insisted on sending me off to bed to the skirl of the "Duke of Roxburgh's Farewell to Black Mount."

I left Gualinn praising the salmon steaks that Mrs. Ross prepared, brown and delicious, from the pan on the AGA. As well, I told Iain of George's piping and how grateful I was for his hospitality. Gualinn Lodge was for me an easeful refuge where for five days I had almost forgotten Otterloo and the cries of a wounded man.

The mail carrier returned me to Lairg where I took the train to Inverness. Here in a cafe I met a naval officer touring the Highlands on a Harley Davidson motorcycle. As we were both going to Glasgow, he asked me to share the trip on the pillion seat. During that afternoon we saw Culloden and, after that ill-fated field, the quietly beautiful stretches of Lochs Ness, Lochy, and Linnhe to Fort William where we stayed overnight. The next day it was round Loch Leven and down through desolate Glencoe, stopping frequently to crane at the dark mountains above us, to admire the brown water which tumbles a thousand or more feet from the Paps of Glencoe to the brawling stream below us, and to read the inscription on the cross that marks the site of the massacre of the Macdonalds. All this time drifting masses of cloud swirled round the peaks and, eventually, on the road before us as it climbed up to the windswept Moor of Rannoch. At Crianlarich we stopped for tea at the local hotel.

It was while we were chatting away to the owner in the bar that we heard Churchill's official announcement that the war was over. The reaction of the half dozen locals in the bar was one of quiet acceptance—no cheers. Crianlarich had lost too many of its young men and women. Too many of the pint mugs in silver or pewter hanging behind the bar would never be taken down by the original owners. As such resignation did not appeal to my friend as a fitting way to say farewell to arms, we drove south to Glasgow along Loch Lomond by its green is-lands and the shouldering hills above it.

In Glasgow we shuffled along Sauchiehall Street with a mil-lion other people out to celebrate, but again it was a curiously muted festivity—nothing Harry Lauderish, or dockside, or even military about it. Just a million people glad the war was over and the lights on again. I was much too tired to stay up late. In the morning I said goodbye to my generous naval friend, wrote a letter in the lobby of the hotel where it was warm, and then set off for the station and the train for London.

Back with the Regiment in Winschoten, some twenty miles east of Groningen, all the talk was of how many points a man had and how soon he could expect repatriation. As I had just 80 to my credit, I had no worries about getting on the first ship. Most of my gunners had racked up at least 140 and many had

200 points. My own desire was—if I could wangle it—to stay on either in Europe or in Britain. That, in the end, proved easy as instructors were needed to offer education to Canadians wishing to upgrade their qualifications so that they could have access to higher education on their return to Canada.

As usual I faced a bundle of mail on my return to Winschoten. Both Louise and Julia had had their leaves in Paris. "Charm, loveliness, and everywhere romance a-plenty" was how Julia found the city. Louise was disappointed: "I did a little shopping, but there isn't anything to buy, lots of junk." She had been "to a show at the Casino and in one act, believe it or not, the girls didn't wear a thing, not even a fig leaf." Her leave offered lots of sightseeing and very little night life. Julia, on the other hand, danced and dined, drank champagne, and toured the night clubs until almost dawn. Paris could only be praised: "Standing in the Place de la Concorde at night, I could not help a verse from the Psalms creeping into my thoughts: 'There is a city, the streams of which make glad the City of God'."

Ellen's letter told me about the wounded being returned to Canada:

> One poor chap came to London minus one arm and two legs. Such a sacrifice. And some of these boys had been away for five years. I should like to go to Christie Hospital and see some of them.

A day later she continued her letter more cheerfully:

> The manse is in bright sunshine after the rain and frost of last night. I stood out on the verandah where I could hear the thrush singing from the swale. I just wanted to stay out and go with the bird song through the fields, but there was breakfast to get and chicks to care for.

Another letter was from the wife of the signaller who had been killed in the command post at Otterloo. She was grateful for the letter I had sent her:

> I will always treasure it and when little Laurie grows up and is able to understand it, she will

be proud of her brave Daddy... he was good to
us, always sending money home and writing
every day when he could. I just can't believe he
won't be back. Words cannot tell how every day
seems lonelier than the one before.

Meantime regimental life in Winschoten quickly assumed a
peaceful role. "Cease Fire" had come down at 0800 hours on
May 5. Almost at once, guns, vehicles, and gunners were subject to an all-out cleanup; officers were detailed to give lectures
about repatriation. I was given the unusual responsibility of
being Officer-in-Charge of arranging local details for the federal
elections to be held in Canada on June 11. On this matter I had
already received word from Rab, by way of Ellen, that I was to
vote for Mackenzie King.

Despite their grievously straightened means, the local
people of Winschoten did much to show their appreciation to
the Regiment, even giving some of their daughters as brides. A
memorable official reception and dance took place on June 23.
The Operation Order called for the programme to get underway by 2030 hours, for a rest period the next day from 0700 to
1100 hours when festivities were to recommence with a short
gallop with the Master of the Horse before the bar opened at
1200 hours. Lunch was from 1300-1359 hours, followed by two
hours of swimming, yachting or "just sunbathing." The twenty-
four-hour-long event ended with a tea dance at 1640 hours.
These festivities brought my brief association with the 17th
Field Regiment to an end. The war was over—but not its imprint.

I have dwelt much on my memories of it. It is, I admit, a
weakness in me to do so and to wonder so late in life about the
rightness of my choices. I can only, after all these years, take
comfort in the thought that it is our freedom to choose that
makes life so compelling or vexatious when alternatives are ignored. And wisely or perversely made, our choices with their
consequences constitute a trim reckoning—censuring, divert-
ing, and shaping us all the way to our last campaign.

But misgivings and second thoughts aside, I am so persuaded of the rightness of the decision that bracketted my life into war and history, from July 10, 1942 to June 20, 1946, that, like Sterne's Uncle Toby, I shall almost certainly end my days by inveigling the unwary into hearing "what prodigious armies we had in Flanders" and how on the night of April 17, 1945, my Regiment won distinction for itself at the "Battle of Otterloo"—not to be confused with that other battle in Flanders that took place on June 18, 1815.

Like Uncle Toby and all old soldiers we unknowingly "take our chains," as Montaigne warned, "along with us; our freedom is not complete; we still turn our eyes to what we have left behind, our fancy is full of it."[26] But, if I've turned my eyes to what I've left behind, I've done so knowingly and because I had to. What came after never resonated so splendidly or, alas, so sadly as the events of the war years—events that have left the memory so scarred, so vulnerable, so rich.

> That was another life
> a whole world different.
> That was another earth
> a cold wide ocean distant.[27]

---

26. Montaigne. "Of Solitude."

27. George Whalley, "Canadian Spring," in *No Man An Island* (Toronto: Clarke Irwin, 1948), p.42.

Postscript

For Rab (1872-1957)

Compound of mist and yellow gorse,
Badninish and Skelbo's muir,
Other ranks squared at Waterloo;
Landless, unwanted crofter stock
Bent and turned to new hopes
Across the waters.

Bound unwilling to ancestral fields,
He chafed and stood inept,
Micawber in overalls;
Unwilling instrument for Time's
Process and his country's
Market mind.

The Depression's easy touch; his
Generous hands hired out; still
He stood a granary of old tales,
An annalist for the township,
A ploughman whose violin
Summoned tears.

The man was here, and now is not,
Yet is, after the iron gates,
After the kitchen prayers and
The tears and the procession
By the hills and the gaping winds
Of far-off Thule.

GLOSSARY

A-2	Canadian Artillery Training Centre, Petawawa.
Ack	Assistant to Gun Position Officer.
Ack-Ack	Anti-aircraft.
A.D.S.	Advanced Dressing Station.
Air O.P.	Air Observation Plane.
Aussies	Australians.
Bdr.	Bombardier.
B.E.F.	British Expeditionary Force
Bren	303 British light machine gun.
C.A.R.U.	Canadian Artillery Reinforcement Unit.
C.B.R.D.	Canadian Base Reinforcement Depot.
C.O.	Commanding Officer.
C.O.T.C.	Canadian Officers' Training Corps.
C.P.O.	Command Post Officer (Battery).
Coy.	Company.
C.W.A.C.	Canadian Women's Army Corps.
C.S.M.	Company Sergeant Major.
D.F.	Defensive Fire.
Digger	Army Prison.
Div.	Division.
Div. H.Q.	Divisional Headquarters.
18-pdr.	World War I gun, shell weighing eighteen pounds.
88's	German high velocity anti-aircraft guns also used against tanks and infantry.
E.N.S.A.	Entertainments National Services Association.
F.A.T.	Field Artillery Tractor, also known as Quad.

5th Cdn. Armd. Div.	Fifth Canadian Armoured Division.
F.D.L.s	Forward Defense Lines.
F.O.O.	Forward Observation Officer.
"George" Vehicle	Gun Position Officer's vehicle.
Gott mit Uns	God with Us.
G.G.H.G.	The Governor General's Horse Guards.
G.P.O.	Gun Position Officer.
H.E.	High Explosive.
H-hour	Time set for attack.
Inf. Bdes.	Infantry Brigades.
Irish	The Irish Regiment of Canada.
Jerry	A German soldier.
Kraut	A German soldier.
L./Cpl.	Lance Corporal.
L.S.T.	Landing Ship Tank.
Limey	An English soldier.
Lt.-Col.	Lieutenant Colonel.
M. & V.	Dehydrated meat and vegetables.
M.G.	Machine gun.
M.O.	Medical officer.
Mike Target	Target calling for fire of all twenty-four guns of a Field Regiment.
Morep	Mortar report.
M.T.	Motor Transport.
N.A.A.F.I.	Navy, Army, and Air Force Institute.
N.R.M.A.	National Resources Mobilization Act, June 1940.

Nebels	Nebelwerfer, multiple-barrelled German mortar known as Moaning Minnie.
9 mm Browning	Officers' revolver that replaced the .38 pistol.
N.C.O.	Non-commisioned officer.
Oerlikon	20 mm naval gun.
O.P.	Observation Post.
O.A.C.	Ontario Agricultural College.
O.C.E.	Ontario College of Education.
Operation Overlord	Plan for invasion of Europe, June 6, 1944.
O.R.	Other rank.
Panzer Div.	German Armoured Division.
Perths	The Perth Regiment.
P.O.W.	Prisoner of War.
Pro. Station	Prophylactic Station.
Quad	Four-wheel gun-towing vehicle, also known as F.A.T.s.
Q.M.	Quartermaster.
Recce	Reconnaissance.
R.A.P.	Regimental Aid Post.
R.H.Q.	Regimental Headquarters.
R.A.	Royal Artillery.
R.C.A.F.	Royal Canadian Air Force.
R.C.A.S.C.	Royal Canadian Army Service Corps.
2/Lt.	Second Lieutenant, lowest officer rank in the army; entitled to wear one pip on each shoulder—hence "one pipper."
Sgt.	Sergeant.
S.A.	Small Arms.

S.P.	Self-propelled.
Shelrep	Shell report.
Sigmn.	Signalman.
Spam	Tinned pork product.
Spandau	German machine gun.
Tarp.	Tarpaulin.
TBSM	Troop Battery Sergeant Major.
Theatre Grid	A survey grid applicable to all units in a particular theatre of war.
3-tonner	Three-ton truck used mostly to transport ammunition and supplies.
Tp.	Troop, two to each of the three batteries in a field artillery regiment. Four guns to a troop.
25-pdr.	World War II gun—howitzer using a high explosive shell weighing twenty-five pounds.
22nd boys	Men of the Royal 22e Régiment.
Uncle Target	Target calling for fire of guns of a division.
V.A.D.	Voluntary Aid Detachment.
V-1	Robot bomb with a jet engine, also called Buzz Bomb.
V.C.	Victoria Cross.
W.L.A.	Women's Land Army.

INDEX

ABOUT THE AUTHOR

Alexander M. Ross was born in Embro, Ontario. He graduated from Queen's University, Kingston, in 1940. On July 10, 1942 he enlisted and eventually served in Italy and The Netherlands with the 17th Field Regiment, Royal Canadian Artillery. He was discharged on 20 June 1946 having attained the rank of Captain and been awarded the Military Cross.

After his return to Canada, he gained his M.A. from Queen's University and joined the staff of the Lakehead Technical Institute in Port Arthur, Ontario. In 1954 he moved to the Department of English at the Ontario Agricultural College. From 1965 to 1974 he served as Professor and Chairman of the Department of English Language and Literature at the University of Guelph. In 1987 the University conferred upon him the honorary rank of Professor Emeritus.

Professor Ross's publications include many articles in learned journals and four books: *The College on the Hill; William Henry Bartlett, Artist, Author, and Traveller; The Imprint of the Picturesque on Nineteenth-Century British Fiction;* and *Slow March to a Regiment.*